Fabulous
Québec

CAPTURE THE EXCITEMENT OF QUÉBEC!

Table of Contents

Attraction Classification

★	Interesting
★ ★	Worth a visit
★ ★ ★	Not to be missed

Parc National de la Gaspésie - *Inukshuk*
Jean-Pierre Huard, Sépaq
Dogsledding expedition *(page 1)*
ATR Charlevoix

Writing and Research
François Rémillard
Benoit Prieur

Editors
Claude Morneau
Daniel Desjardins

Artistic Director
André Duchesne

Production Manager
Isabelle Lalonde

Copy Editing
Jennifer McMorran
Elke Love

Computer Graphics
Marie-France Denis
Assistant
Christian Lapointe

Photography (Cover page)
Dale Wilson (Wonderfile)

Translation
Cindy Garayt
Danielle Gauthier

Illustrators
Vincent Desruisseaux
Myriam Gagné
Lorette Pierson
Marie-Annick Viatour

Image Research
Marc Rigole
Alain Legault
Geneviève Décarie-Landry

Additional Writing and Research:
Gabriel Audet, Alexandre Chouinard,
Pierre Daveluy, François Hénault,
Stéphane G. Marceau, Yves Ouellet,
Joël Pomerleau, Yves Séguin

We acknowledge the financial support of the Government of
Canada through the Book Publishing Industry Development
Program (BPIDP) for our publishing activities. We would also
like to thank the government of Québec for its SODEC
income tax program for book publication.

Offices

Canada: Ulysses Travel Guides, 4176 St. Denis Street, Montréal, Québec, H2W 2M5,
☎(514) 843-9447, fax: (514) 843-9448, info@ulysses.ca, www.ulyssesguides.com

Europe: Les Guides de Voyage Ulysse SARL, 127 rue Amelot, 75011 Paris, France,
☎(01 43 38 89 50, fax: 01 43 38 89 52, voyage@ulysse.ca, www.ulyssesguides.com

U.S.A.: Ulysses Travel Guides, 305 Madison Avenue, Suite 1166, New York, NY 10165,
info@ulysses.ca, www.ulyssesguides.com

Distributors

U.S.A.: Hunter Publishing, 130 Campus Drive, Edison, NJ 08818, ☎800-255-0343,
fax: (732) 417-1744 or 0482, comments@hunterpublishing.com,
www.hunterpublishing.com

Canada: Ulysses Travel Guides, 4176 St. Denis Street, Montréal, Québec, H2W 2M5,
☎(514) 843-9882, ext. 2232, fax: 514-843-9448, info@ulysses.ca, www.ulyssesguides.com

Great Britain and Ireland: Roundhouse Publishing, Millstone, Limers Lane, Northam, North
Devon, EX39 2RG, ☎1 202 66 54 32, fax: 1 202 66 62 19, roundhouse.group@ukgateway.net

Other countries: Ulysses Travel Guides, 4176 St. Denis Street, Montréal, Québec,
H2W 2M5, ☎ (514) 843-9882, ext. 2232, fax: 514-843-9448, info@ulysses.ca,
www.ulyssesguides.com

Canadian Cataloguing-in-Publication Data, page 6
© July 2004, Ulysses Travel Guides.
All rights reserved. Printed in Canada
ISBN 2-89464-716-6

Lac aux Américains
Parc National de la Gaspésie
Sépaq

Special Thanks

Ulysses Travel Guides would like to especially thank Isabelle Labarre and Marika Perron of Sépaq.

Sean Simard, National Archives of Canada; Nicole Gaulin, Tourisme Abitibi-Témiscamingue; Nancy Arpin, Office du Tourisme et des Congrès de Val-d'Or; Serge Guay and Annie St-Laurent, Musée de la Mer; Josée Roy, Musée François-Pilote; Danielle Longchamps, Tourisme Cantons-de-l'Est; Marie-Ève Lambert, Tourisme Centre-du-Québec; Colombe Bourque, Hôtel Sacacomie; Michel Trudel, Cité de l'Énergie; Hélène Bernard, Association Touristique Chaudière-Appalaches; Nancy Carrier, Seigneurie des Aulnaies; Diane Lemieux, Musée Maritime du Québec; Annick Léveillé, Domaine Joly-De Lotbinière; Monique Tremblay, Sucrerie Jean-Louis Massicotte et Filles; Benoît Renaud, Tourisme Charlevoix; Danny Bourdeau, Association Touristique Régionale de Duplessis; Marline Charbonneau, Déclic Communications; Madelyne Lechasseur, Association Touristique Régionale de Manicouagan; Isabelle Cummings, Tourisme Îles de la Madeleine; Audrey Rivest, Tourisme Lanaudière; Luce Ostiguy, Mont Saint-Sauveur International; Julie Pominville, Municipalité d'Oka; Pascale Tremblay, Tourisme Laurentides; Hélène Vezina, Tourisme Laval; Ragnhild Milewski, ONF/Cinémathèque; Julie Garin and Claire Vagogne, Société des Directeurs des Musées Montréalais; Linda-Anne D'Anjou, Musée des Beaux-Arts de Montréal; Sylvia Deschênes, Musée Stewart; Steve Fontaine, Centre Canadien d'Architecture; Valérie Lafleur, Musée Marguerite-Bourgeoys/Chapelle Notre-Dame-de-Bon-Secours; Nike Langevin and Stéphanie Poisson, McCord Museum; Albane Le Nay, Jardin Botanique and Insectarium de Montréal; Marie Julie Archambault, Musée d'Art Contemporain de Montréal; Marie-France Lapointe, Pointe-à-Callière, Musée d'Archéologie et d'Histoire de Montréal; Maurice Binette, Château Dufresne; Hélène Petit, Fondation du Patrimoine Religieux du Québec; Ginette Robert and Marie-Noëlle Richer, Archives Nationales du Québec; Nathalie-Myriam Léger, Tourisme Montérégie; Éric Turcotte, Commission de la Capitale Nationale du Québec; Suzanne Chalifour, La Citadelle de Québec; Francine Desbiens, Musée de la Civilisation de Québec; Ryan Fortner, Hôtel de Glace; Nancy Picard, Site Traditionnel Huron; Chantal Cleary, Société Touristique des Autochtones du Québec; Jean-François Labrecque, Québec en Images; Steve Donovan, Tourisme Baie-James; Robert Brown, Tourisme Outaouais; Lauraine Gagnon, Centre de Conservation de la Biodiversité Boréale (CCBB), Zoo Sauvage de Saint-Félicien; André Turgeon, Village Historique de Val-Jalbert; Johanne Lapointe, La Pulperie de Chicoutimi; Danielle Beauchemin and Jean Boisclair, Société de la Faune et des Parcs du Québec; Marie-Josée Gagnon, Comité de la Fête Nationale; Jean Dallaire, Assemblée Nationale; Christiane Beaudoin and Frédérick N. Étienne, Hydro-Québec; Carole Cloutier, National Library of Canada; Annie Tardif, Musée Maritime du Québec; Linda Mallette, Site Historique de l'Île-des-Moulins; Céline Perreault and Robert-David Church, Tourisme Montréal; Marie-Claude Parent, Musée Louis-Hémon; Sophie Vaillancourt, Office de Tourisme et Congrès de Beauce; Martin Guay, Parks Canada; Canada's National Capital Commission.

National Library of Canada cataloguing in publication

Main entry under title:

    Fabulous Québec
    Translation of: Fabuleux Québec.

    Includes index.
    ISBN 2-89464-716-6

    1. Québec (Province) - Pictorial works. 2. Québec (Province).
    FC2912.F3213 2004   917.14'0022'2   C2003-942085-X

Les régions touristiques du Québec
Québec's Tourist Regions

1. Îles de la Madeleine
2. Gaspésie
3. Bas-Saint-Laurent
4. Région de Québec/ Québec City Region
5. Charlevoix
6. Chaudière-Appalaches
7. Mauricie
8. Cantons-de-l'Est
9. Montérégie
10. Lanaudière
11. Laurentides/Laurentians
12. Montréal
13. Outaouais
14. Abitibi-Témiscamingue
15. Saguenay– Lac-Saint-Jean
16. Manicouagan
17. Duplessis
18. Nord-du-Québec
19. Laval
20. Centre-du-Québec

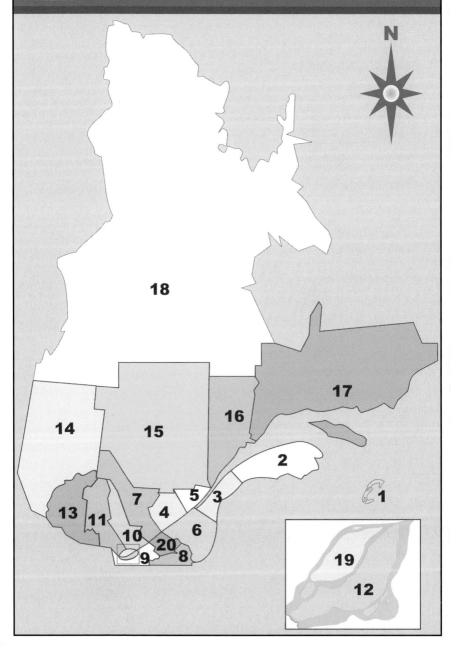

List of Maps

PORTRAIT

Old houses in Vieux-Québec

THE BORDERS OF QUÉBEC

Situated in the extreme northeast of North America, Québec is Canada's largest province. It covers a surface area of 1,550,000 km², roughly equivalent to the size of France, Germany and the Iberian peninsula put together. With the exception of certain southern regions, Québec is sparsely populated and is characterized by an expansive wilderness of lakes, rivers and forests.

The province forms a huge northern peninsula, with James Bay and Hudson Bay to the west, Hudson Strait and Ungava Bay to the north, and the Gulf of St. Lawrence to the south. Québec also has very long land borders that it shares with Ontario to the west and southwest, with New Brunswick and the state of Maine to the southeast, with the states of New York, Vermont and New Hampshire to the south and with Labrador, part of the province of Newfoundland and Labrador, to the northeast.

ROCKY TERRAIN

Québec's geography is dominated by the St. Lawrence River, the Appalachian Mountain range and the Canadian Shield, three of the most distinct geographical formations in North America. More than a 1000km long, the St. Lawrence is the largest river leading to the Atlantic Ocean on the continent. The river has its source at the Great Lakes and is also fed by a number of major waterways, such as the Ottawa, the Richelieu, the Saguenay and the Manicouagan. Traditionally the primary route into the continent, the St. Lawrence played a central part in Québec's development.

Even today, most of the province's population lives along the river, particularly in the Montréal region where nearly half Québec's population resides. To the south, near the U.S. border, the Appalachian mountains cross the St. Lawrence lowlands from southwestern Québec to the Gaspé peninsula. The hilly scenery of these regions is very similar to that of New England, although the mountains rarely exceed 1,000m in height. The remaining 80% of Québec's land mass is part of the Canadian Shield, a very old, heavily eroded mountain range extending over all of northern Québec.

FIRST SETTLERS

By the time European settlers arrived in the New World, a mosaic of indigenous peoples had already been living on the continent for thousands of years. The ancestors of these people were nomads who began to cross the Bering Strait from northern Asia toward the end of the ice age, more than 12,000 years ago, and slowly populated the continent. Over the following millennia, as the glaciers receded, some of these groups began to settle in the northernmost parts of the continent, including the peninsula now known as Québec. A variety of native peoples, belonging to three language groups (Algonquian, Iroquoian and Inuit), were thus sharing the territory when the Europeans first began to explore North America.

Aerial view of Baie des Onze Îles in La Mauricie National Park
Parks Canada / S. Paradis

ABORIGINAL SETTLEMENTS

Established societies with very diverse ways of life occupied this vast region. For example, native peoples occupying the valley of the St. Lawrence River lived primarily on fish, game, and produce they grew themselves, while communities farther north depended mostly on meat gathered during hunting expeditions. All, however, made ample use of the canoe as a means of travelling along the "paths that walk", and maintained very close trade relations with the neighbouring nations. These societies, well-adapted to the rigours and distinctive features of the territory, were quickly marginalized with the onset of European colonization at the beginning of the 16th century.

JACQUES CARTIER, CANADA'S DISCOVERER

During his first exploration of the mouth of the St. Lawrence and the shores of what is now Newfoundland, the French explorer Jacques Cartier came into contact with fishermen from various parts of Europe. In fact, these waters were first explored by the Vikings sometime around the year 900, and were being visited regularly by European cod fishermen and whalers. However, Jacques Cartier's three voyages, which began in 1534, did represent an important step forward, as they established the first official contact between whites and the peoples and territory of this part of North America. On these expeditions, the Breton navigator sailed far up the St. Lawrence to the villages of Stadacona (now Québec City) and Hochelaga (on the island of Montréal). However, as Cartier's mandate from the King of France had been to find gold or a passage to Asia, his discoveries were considered unimportant and uninteresting. For several decades after this "failure," the French crown forgot about this distant, inhospitable place.

SAMUEL DE CHAMPLAIN, FATHER OF NEW FRANCE

French interest in North America was rekindled when fur coats and hats became increasingly fashionable and therefore profitable in Europe. As the fur trade required a direct and constant link with local suppliers, a permanent presence in the New World was indispensable.

During the latter part of the 16th century, various unsuccessful attempts at setting up trading posts on the Atlantic coast and in the interior of the continent were made. Finally, in 1608, under the leadership of Samuel de Champlain, the first permanent outpost was set up. Champlain and his men chose a location at the foot of a large cliff overlooking a considerable narrowing of the St. Lawrence. The collection of fortified buildings they constructed was named the Abitation de Québec (*kebec* is an Algonquian word meaning "where the river narrows"). During that first harsh winter in Québec, 20 of the 28 men posted there died of scurvy or malnutrition before ships carrying fresh supplies arrived in the spring of 1609. When Samuel de Champlain died on Christmas Day, 1635, there were about 300 pioneers living in New France.

Portrait of Jacques Cartier

THE FUR TRADE

Between 1627 and 1663, the Compagnies des Cents Associés held a monopoly on the fur trade and ensured the slow growth of the colony. Meanwhile, French religious orders became more and more interested in New France. The Récollets arrived first, in 1615; they were replaced by the Jesuits, who began arriving in 1632.

Determined to convert the natives, the Jesuits settled deep in the interior of the continent, near the shores of Georgian Bay, where they founded the Sainte-Marie-des-Huron mission. The Huron people, it can be assumed, put up with the presence of the Jesuits to maintain the trading arrangements they had established with the French. The mission was nevertheless abandoned after five Jesuits were killed during the Huron-Iroquois war of 1648-1649. This war was part of an extensive offensive campaign launched by the powerful Iroquois Five Nations between 1645 and 1655 and intended to wipe out all rival nations. The Huron, Pétun, Neutrals and Erie nations, each at least 10,000 strong, were almost completely annihilated within the space of 10 years. The offensive also threatened the existence of the French colony.

A FRENCH PROVINCE

In 1660 and 1661, Iroquois warriors mounted strikes all over New France, destroying crops and bringing about a decline in the fur trade. Louis the XIV, the King of France, decided to take the situation in hand. In 1663, he dissolved the Compagnies des Cents Associés and took on the responsibility of administering the colony himself, officially declaring New France, with its 3,000 settlers (or *habitants*), a French province. Emigration to New France continued under the royal regime. Most people sent over were agricultural workers, though some also belonged to the military. In 1665, for example, the Carignan-Salières regiment was dispatched to the New World to fight the Iroquois. The Crown also took steps to encourage the natural growth of the population, which had theretofore been hindered by the lack of unmarried female immigrants. Between 1663 and 1673, 800 young women, known as the *filles du roi*, and each provided with a dowry, were sent to find husbands in the New World.

PEAK AND DECLINE OF NEW FRANCE

The territorial claims made by the French in North America increased rapidly during this era as a result of expeditions made by religious orders, coureurs des bois and explorers, to whom we owe the discovery of most of the North American continent. New France reached its peak at the beginning of the 18th century. At this time, it had a monopoly on the North American fur trade, control of the St. Lawrence and was beginning to develop Louisiana. New France was thus able to contain the expansion of the more populous British colonies located between the Atlantic and the Appalachians.

This changed following military defeat in Europe and the Treaty of Utrecht (1713) in which France relinquished control of Hudson Bay, Newfoundland and Acadia to the British. France thereby lost a large stake in the fur trade, as well as certain strategic military locations, all of which severely weakened its position in North America and marked the beginning of the end of New France.

The fur trade

ACADIAN DEPORTATION

Over the following years, the stakes continued to mount. In 1755, British colonel Charles Lawrence took what he viewed as a preventive measure and ordered the deportation of the Acadians, French-speaking settlers living in what is now Nova Scotia. At least 7,000 Acadians, who had been considered British citizens since 1713, were displaced as a result of this directive.

ENGLISH CONQUEST

The fight for control of the colony came to an end several years later. Though Montréal was last to fall in 1760, it was the infamous battle of the Plains of Abraham a year before, where Montcalm's and Wolfe's troops met, that sealed the fate of New France with the loss of Québec City. At the time of the British conquest, the population of the colony had risen to 60,000. Of this number, 8,967 lived in Québec City, and 5,733 lived in Montréal.

ENGLISH REGIME

With the Treaty of Paris in 1763, French Canada, holdings east of the Mississippi and what remained of Acadia were officially ceded to England. For former subjects of the French crown, the first years under British rule were difficult ones. Territorial divisions dictated by the Royal Proclamation of 1763 denied the colony control of the fur trade, the most dynamic sector of its economy.

In addition, the introduction of British civil law and the refusal to recognize the authority of the Pope put an end to both the seigneurial system and the Catholic hierarchy, the pillars on which French colonial society had been based. Finally, the Test Oath, required of anyone in a high-ranking administrative position, discriminated against French Canadians, since it denied the transubstantiation of the Eucharist and the authority of the Pope. A large segment of the French elite returned to France while English merchants gradually took control of most businesses.

UNDER BRITAIN'S RULE

England, however, soon agreed to do away with the Royal Proclamation. To better resist the trend towards independence in its 13 colonies to the south, it sought to secure its place in Canada by gaining the favour of the population. In 1774, the Québec Act replaced the Royal Proclamation, introducing policies much more appropriate to a French Catholic colony. Important powers were given to the Catholic Church, which were maintained until 1963.

Portrait of James Wolfe
National Archives of Canada / C-003916

THE LOYALISTS

The Canadian population remained French until the end of the American Revolution, when Canada experienced the arrival of a first big wave of Anglo-Saxon colonists. The new arrivals were Loyalists, Americans wishing to remain faithful to the British crown. Most moved to the Maritimes (formerly Acadia) and around Lake Ontario, but some also settled in regions inhabited strictly by francophones.

With the arrival of these new colonists, British authorities passed the Constitution Act of 1791, which divided Canada into two provinces. Upper Canada, situated west of the Ottawa River and mainly populated by anglophones, would be governed by British common law. Lower Canada, which was mostly francophone, would be governed according to the French tradition of civil law. In addition, the Act planted the seeds of a parliamentary system in Canada by creating a Legislative Assembly in each province.

CRISIS IN FRENCH CANADA

Meanwhile, Napoleon's "Continental System" (blockade) forced Britain to get its lumber from Canada. From an economic standpoint, this was good for the colony. The development of a new industry was especially timely, as the fur trade, the original reason for the existence of the colony, was in steady decline. In 1821, the take-over of the Montréal-based Northwest Company by the Hudson's Bay Company marked the end of Montréal as the centre of the North American fur trade. Meanwhile, rural Québec suffered through an agricultural crisis caused by the exhaustion of farmlands and rapid population growth resulting from high birth rates among French-Canadian families, whose diet consisted almost entirely of pea soup and buckwheat pancakes (*galettes*).

Artist's rendition of a Patriote

Henri Julien, The Montreal Star, 1887

THE PATRIOTES AND THE REBELLION OF 1837-1838

These economic difficulties and the struggle for power between francophones and anglophones in Lower Canada combined to spark the Patriotes Rebellion of 1837 and 1838. The period of political conflict that fuelled the rebellion was initiated by the 1834 publication of the 92 Résolutions, a scathing indictment of British colonial policy. The authors of the resolutions, a group of parliamentarians led by Louis-Joseph Papineau, decided to hold back from voting on the budget until Britain addressed their demands. Britain's response came in 1837 in the form of the 10 Resolutions, written by Lord Russell, which categorically refused any compromise with their opponents in Lower Canada.

In the fall of 1837, Montréal was the scene of violent clashes between the Fils de la Liberté (Sons of Liberty), made up of young French Canadians, and the Doric Club, comprised of

Loyalists. Further confrontations occurred in the Richelieu valley region and in the county of Deux-Montagnes, where small insurgent groups stood up to the British army before being crushed. The following year, in an attempt to rekindle the rebellion, a group of Patriotes met with the same fate in Napierville where they confronted 7,000 British troops. This time, however, colonial authorities sent a strong message to prospective rebels. In 1839, they hanged 12 Patriotes and deported many others.

LORD DURHAM'S REPORT

When hostilities first broke out, London had sent an emissary, Lord Durham, to study the problems in the colonies. Expecting to find a population rebelling against colonial authority, Durham found instead two peoples, one French and one British, in battle. The solution he later proposed in his report, known as the Durham Report, was radical. He suggested to authorities in Britain that gradual efforts should be made to assimilate French Canadians.

The Union Act, laid down by the British government in 1840, was largely based on the conclusions of the Durham Report. A new parliamentary system was introduced giving the two former colonies the same number of delegates, despite the fact that Lower Canada had a much larger population than Upper Canada. Financial responsibilities were also divided equally between the provinces, and English was made the sole official language. As armed insurrection had proven futile in the past, French Canada's political class sought to align itself with progressive anglophones in an attempt to resist these changes. Later, the struggle for responsible government became the central goal of this coalition.

THE AMERICAN DREAM

The agricultural crisis, furthermore, remained as severe as ever in Lower Canada. Intensified by the constant arrival of immigrants and by the high birth rate, the situation resulted in a massive emigration of French Canadians to the United States. Between 1840 and 1850, 40,000 French Canadians left the country to seek employment in the factories of New England. To counteract this exodus, the Catholic Church and the government launched an extensive campaign to colonize outlying regions, such as Lac Saint-Jean. The harsh life in these newly settled regions, where colonists worked as farmers in the summer and lumberjacks in the winter, is poignantly depicted in Louis Hémon's novel *Maria Chapdelaine*.

Nevertheless, the mass exodus from Québec did not stop until the beginning of the next century. It is estimated that about 750,000 French Canadians left the province between 1840 and 1930. From this point of view, the colonization campaign, which doubled the amount of farmland in Lower Canada, ended in failure. The swelling population of rural Québec was not effectively absorbed until several decades later with the start of industrialization.

FRENCH CANADIANS, PRACTISING CATHOLICS

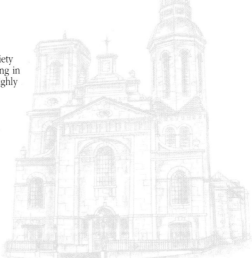

Despite rapid changes in Québec society (by 1921, half the population was living in urban centres), the church was still highly influential. With 85% of the overall population as members, including virtually all French Canadians, the Catholic Church was a major political force in the province. Because of the control it wielded over education, health care and social services, its authority was inescapable. The Catholic Church, moreover, did not hesitate to intervene in the political arena, often confronting politicians it considered to be too liberal.

CONFEDERATION OF 1867 AND THE PROVINCE OF QUÉBEC

Under Canadian Confederation, Lower Canada became the Province of Québec. Three other provinces, Nova Scotia, New Brunswick, and Ontario (formerly Upper Canada) joined the Confederation, which would eventually unite a vast territory stretching from the Atlantic to the Pacific Ocean. For French Canadians, this new political system reinforced their minority status, which began with the Union Act of 1840. The creation of two levels of government did, however, grant Québec jurisdiction over education, culture and civil law.

Confederation was slow to bring about positive economic change. The economy fluctuated for three decades before experiencing a real boom. The first years after Confederation did, however, see the development of local industry (thanks to the implementation of protective tariffs), the creation of a large, unified market and the development of the railway system across the territory. The industrial revolution that had begun in the mid-19th century picked up again in the 1880s. While Montréal remained the undisputed centre of this movement, it was also felt in many smaller towns.

START OF INDUSTRIALIZATION IN QUÉBEC

The lumber industry, which had been one of the mainsprings of the economy during the 19th century, began exporting more cut wood than raw lumber, giving rise to a processing industry. Montréal was also the hub of the expanding railroad, leading the city to specialize in the production of rolling stock. The leather goods, clothing and food industries also enjoyed significant growth in Québec. This period of growth was also marked by the emergence of the brand-new textile industry, which would remain for many years Québec's flagship industry. Benefitting from a huge pool of unskilled labour, the textile industries initially employed mostly women and children.

This wave of industrialization accelerated the pace of urbanization and created a large and poor working class clustered near the factories. Montréal's working-class neighbourhoods were terribly unhealthy. Infant mortality in these areas was twice that of wealthy neighbourhoods. Québec's cities were going through tremendous changes, and the situation in rural areas finally began to improve. Dairy production was gradually replacing subsistence farming, contributing to an improved standard of living among farmers.

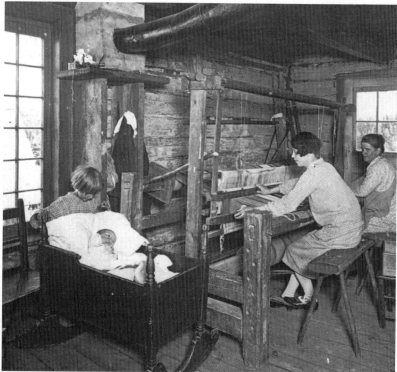

Woman weaving with her children close by

National Archives of Canada / PA-100441

James Bay spillway

HYDROELECTRICITY: ANCHOR OF A NEW INDUSTRIALIZATION

Central to the new era was the production of electric power. With its numerous powerful rivers, Québec became a major producer of hydroelectric power in a matter of years. The resulting availability of affordable energy attracted industries with large electricity needs. Aluminium smelters and chemical plants were constructed in the vicinity of hydroelectric power stations.

The mining industry also began to enjoy modest growth during this period with the development of asbestos mines in the Eastern Townships and copper, gold, zinc and silver mines in Abitibi. Above all, Québec's pulp and paper industry found huge markets in the United States, due to the depletion of U.S. forests and the rise of the popular press. To promote the development of processing industries in Québec, the exportation of logs was forbidden by the provincial government in 1910.

WORLD WAR I

When World War I began, the Canadian government gave its full support to Britain without hesitation. A significant number of French Canadians voluntarily enrolled in the army, although the percentage of volunteers per capita was far lower than that in other provinces. This lack of enthusiasm can doubtless be attributed both to Québec's long severed ties with France and, more importantly, to francophones' somewhat ambivalent feelings toward Britain. Canada soon set a goal of recruiting 500,000 men. Since there were not enough volunteers, the government voted in 1917 to introduce conscription.

Reaction to this in Québec was violent and marked by fights, bombings and riots. In the end, conscription failed to appreciably increase the number of French Canadian recruits. Instead, it simply underlined once again the ongoing friction between English and French Canada.

THE GREAT DEPRESSION

Between 1929 and 1945, two international-scale events, the Depression and World War II, greatly disrupted the country's political, economic and social progress. The Great Depression of the 1930s, originally viewed as a cyclical, temporary crisis, lengthened into a decade-long nightmare and put an end to Québec's rapid economic expansion. With Canada strongly dependent on foreign markets, the country as a whole was hard hit by the international stock market crash.

Québec was unevenly affected. With its economy based to a large extent on exports, Montréal, along with towns dependent on the development of natural resources, took the hardest blows. The textile and food industries, which sold to the Canadian market, held up better during the first years of the Depression, before foundering as well. The trend towards urbanization slowed as people began to view the countryside as a refuge where they could grow their own food. Poverty became more and more widespread, and unemployment levels reached 27% in 1933.

SOLUTIONS TO THE ECONOMIC CRISIS

Governments were at a loss in the face of this crisis, which they had expected to be short-lived. The Québec government started by introducing massive public works projects to provide jobs for the unemployed. As this proved insufficient, more direct help was gradually given. Very timidly put forward at first, since unemployment had always been considered a personal problem, these measures later helped many Quebecers.

The federal government was also compelled to question the merits of economic liberalism and to redefine the role of the state. Part of this trend included establishing the Bank of Canada in 1935, which permitted greater control over the monetary and financial system. However, it was not until the ensuing war years that a full-scale welfare state was created. In the meantime, the crisis led to the proliferation of political ideologies in Québec. The most popular of these, traditional nationalism, put great emphasis on values such as rural life, family, religion and language.

WORLD WAR II

World War II began in 1939, and Canada became officially involved on September 10th of that year. The Canadian economy received a much needed boost as industry set out to modernize the country's military equipment and to meet the requirements of the Allies. Canada's close ties to Great Britain and the United States gave it an important diplomatic role, as indicated by the conferences held in Québec in 1943 and 1944.

Early in the war, however, the problem of conscription surfaced again. While the federal government wanted to avoid the issue, mounting pressure from the country's anglophones forced a plebiscite on the issue. The results once again showed the division between francophones and anglophones: 80% of English Canadians voted in favour of conscription, while the same percentage of French Canadians were opposed to the idea. Mixed feelings toward Britain and France left French Canadians very reluctant to become involved in the fighting. However, they were forced to follow the will of the majority. In the end, 600,000 Canadians were recruited, 42,000 of whom died in action.

POSITIVE EFFECTS OF THE WAR

Québec was profoundly changed by the war. Its economy became much stronger and more diversified than before. As far as relations between Ottawa and Québec City were concerned, the federal government's massive intervention during the war marked the beginning of its increased role in the economy and of the relative marginalization of provincial governments.

In addition, the contact thousands of Quebecers had with European life and the jobs women held in the factories modified people's

Training of a female parachutist, member of the airborne forces during World War II
National Archives of Canada / PA-128903

expectations. The winds of change were blowing, but were to come up against a serious obstacle: Premier Maurice Duplessis and his political allies.

1945-1960: THE DUPLESSIS ERA

The end of World War II signalled the start of a period of considerable economic growth, during which consumer demands repressed by the economic crisis and wartime rationing could finally be satisfied. Despite a few fluctuations, the economy performed spectacularly until 1957. However, this prosperity affected Québec's various social and ethnic groups unequally. Many workers, particularly non-unionized ones, continued to receive relatively

Maurice L. Duplessis

National Archives of Canada / C-086343

low wages. Furthermore, the anglophone minority in Québec still enjoyed a far superior standard of living to that of the francophone majority. A francophone employee with the same skills and experience as an anglophone employee would routinely be paid less. With an economy largely controlled by English Canadians and Americans, French Canadians were held back.

Be that as it may, the economic growth encouraged a stable political environment, such that the leader of the Union Nationale Party, Maurice Duplessis, remained in power as Premier of Québec from 1944 until he died in 1959. Duplessis's influence characterized this era, often referred to as *la grande noirceur*, or the great darkness.

THE DUPLESSIS IDEOLOGY

The Duplessis ideology was based on a sometimes paradoxical amalgam of traditional nationalism, conservatism and unbridled capitalism. He professed a respect for rural life, religion and authority, while at the same time providing major foreign business interests with highly favourable opportunities to exploit Québec's natural resources. In his mind, a cheap work force was one of those resources and it had to be preserved. To this end, he fought fiercely against unionization, not hesitating to use intimidation tactics when he felt it was necessary. These years were marked by many strikes but it was the asbestos strike of 1949 that most influenced the collective conscience.

While Maurice Duplessis was the dominant personality of this period, his rule could only have been sustained through the tacit collaboration of much of the traditional and business elite, both francophone and anglophone. The Catholic Church, seemingly at the height of its glory during these years, felt its authority weakening, which prompted it to support the Duplessis government in full measure.

REFUS GLOBAL:
SEED OF THE QUIET REVOLUTION

Despite Duplessis's iron hand, opposing voices nonetheless emerged. The Liberal Party of Québec had difficulty getting organized, so opposition came mainly from outside the parliamentary structure. Artists and writers made their anger known by publishing the *Refus Global*, a bitter attack on the repressive atmosphere in Québec. The most organized opposition came from union leaders, journalists and the intellectual community.

All these groups wanted modernization for Québec and endorsed the same neo-liberalist economic credo favouring a strong welfare system. However, from quite early on, two different camps developed among these reformists. Certain individuals, such as Gérard Pelletier and Pierre Trudeau, believed modernization would result from a strong federal government, while neo-nationalists like André Laurendeau wanted change through a more powerful provincial government. These two groups, which quickly overshadowed traditionalism during the Quiet Revolution, would remain at odds with each other throughout modern Québec history.

A QUIET REVOLUTION

In 1960, the Liberal Party under Jean Lesage was elected on a platform of change and stayed in power until 1966. This period, referred to as the Révolution Tranquille, or Quiet Revolution, was indeed marked by a veritable race for modernism.

Over the course of just a few years, Québec caught up to the modern world. Control of education, health care and social services meant the provincial government played a bigger role in society. The church, thus stripped of its main spheres of influence, lost its authority and eventually its following, as dissatisfied Québec Catholics moved away from the church. State control of the production of hydroelectricity increased the provincial government's interests in the economy. Powerful economic resources thus permitted the government to establish itself, and French Canadians in general, in the business world. The great vitality brought to Québec society during the Quiet Revolution was symbolized by two events of international scope that took place in Montréal: Expo '67 and the 1976 Olympics.

THE FRONT DE LIBÉRATION DU QUÉBEC: FLQ

The lively nature of Québec society in the 1960s engendered a number of new ideological movements, particularly on the left. The extreme was the Front de Libération du Québec (FLQ), a small group of radicals who wanted to "decolonize" Québec and launched a series of terrorist strikes in Montréal. In October 1970, the FLQ abducted James Cross, a British diplomat, and Jean Laporte, a Québec cabinet minister. The Canadian Prime Minister at the time, Pierre Elliot Trudeau, fearing a political uprising, called for the War Measures Act to be enforced. The Canadian army took to the streets of Montréal, thousands of searches were carried out and hundreds of innocent people temporarily imprisoned. Shortly afterward, Pierre Laporte was found dead.

The crisis finally ended when James Cross' kidnappers agreed to let him go in exchange for their safe conduct to Cuba. During this entire crisis, and long afterwards, Trudeau was severely criticized for invoking the War Measures Act. Some accused him of having done so mainly to quash the growing Québec independence movement.

Pierre Elliott Trudeau
ID #21035,
National Archives of Canada PA-180808

THE RISE OF QUÉBEC NATIONALISM

The most significant political phenomenon in Québec between 1960 and 1980 was the rapid rise of moderate nationalism. Breaking with the traditionalism of the past, this new vision of nationalism championed a strong, open and modern Québec with increased powers for the provincial government, and, ultimately, political independence for the province.

The nationalist forces rallied around René Lévesque, founder of the Mouvement Souveraineté-Association and then, in 1968, the Parti Québécois. After two elections, which saw only a handful of its representatives elected to Parliament, a stunning 1976 victory brought the Parti Québécois to power. With a mandate to negotiate sovereignty for Québec, the party called a referendum in 1980.

THE REFERENDUM OF 1980

From the beginning, the referendum campaign revived the division

René Lévesque

Collection Assemblée Nationale

between Québec sovereignists and federalists. The struggle was intense and mobilized the entire population right up until the vote. Finally, after a campaign based on promises of a new style of federalism, the "No" (No to Sovereignty Association) side won out with 60% of the vote.

Despite this loss, sovereignists were consoled by how far their cause had come in only a few years. From a marginal trend in the 1960s, nationalism quickly proved itself to be a major political movement. The night of the defeat, Parti Québécois leader René Lévesque, charisma intact, vowed to his supporters that victory would be theirs "next time".

DEPRESSION AND RECESSION

The independence movement and desire for self-determination amongst Quebecers engendered by the Quiet Revolution suffered a great setback with the loss of the referendum on sovereignty. For many, the 1980s began with a post-referendum depression, accentuated by a period of economic crisis in Canada unmatched since the 1930s. As the economy improved slightly over time, the unemployment rate remained very high and government spending resulted in a massive deficit. Like many other Western governments, Québec had to reassess the policies of the past, though some feared that the new direction chosen would sacrifice the achievements of the Quiet Revolution.

The 1980s and early 1990s were a time of streamlining and one that saw the creation of global markets and the consolidation of large economic blocks. Canada and the United States signed the Free Trade Agreement in 1989. The 1994 North American Free Trade Agreement (NAFTA) brought Mexico into this market, creating the largest tariff-free market in the world.

A NEW RISE IN NATIONALIST PASSION

From a political standpoint, the question of Québec's political status surfaced again. In the early 1990s, the sovereignist movement regained surprising momentum, spurred along by Quebecers' resentment at the failure in June 1990 of the Meech Lake Accord, an agreement aimed at reintegrating Québec into the "constitutional family" by giving it special status. In an attempt to resolve this impasse, the governing bodies involved called for a Canada-wide referendum on a new constitutional offer, held on October 26, 1992. The offer was flatly rejected everywhere in Canada, but for differing reasons.

The federal election of October 25, 1993, saw the sovereignist Bloc Québécois win two-thirds of the ridings in Québec and form the official opposition in the Canadian Parliament. The next year, the Parti Québecois was elected in Québec; holding a referendum on the sovereignty of Québec was high on its to-do list.

THE REFERENDUM OF 1995

Less than one year after its election, the Parti Québecois, launched a referendum campaign, as promised, for the sovereignty of Québec. As with the first referendum, 15 years earlier in 1980, the Québec population was very divided on the issue. This time, however, the results were unbelievably close. The suspense lasted right until the last ballot was counted on referendum night, October 30, 1995. The results told of a population divided: 49.4% of Quebecers voted "yes" to Québec sovereignty and 50.6% voted "no".

Saint-Jean-Baptiste Day
Comité de la Fête Nationale

The profound question of Québec's political status thus remained unresolved following this referendum, which in effect only served to underline the division that exists within the population. Seeing their goal within their reach, the sovereignists did not hesitate to promise that another referendum would be held in the near future. Since then, tensions have eased somewhat, but the situation remains unresolved, and no one can say how the next round will play out...

Saint-Jean-Baptiste Day celebrations
Comité de la Fête Nationale

ABITIBI-TÉMISCAMINGUE

The Lac Lahaie suspension bridge in Parc National d'Aiguebelle

Abitibi-Témiscamingue

Home to 100,000 lakes

and 150,000 people, the region of Abitibi-Témiscamingue can unquestionably be considered Québec's last frontier, excluding Northern Québec and James Bay. Although the fertile land bordering Lac Témiscamingue and the Ottawa River was occupied by European colonists as early as the 19th century, colonization of the greater part of the region did not begin until the early 20th century, with the arrival of women and men determined to live off the land despite the poorness of the soil.

After hardscrabble years of clearing and meagre crops, the discovery of gold deposits in the 1920s engendered a second wave of migration akin to a veritable gold rush. The nascent gold-mining boom, as well as that of copper and silver, in what is known as the Cadillac Fault, caused towns to mushroom here virtually overnight. In fact, the region still retains a boomtown atmosphere.

When Abitibi was still in its infancy, a wave of colonists descended upon it in the hopes of finding the riches promised by the Catholic Church. Reality proved altogether different, however. Indeed, they were confronted with virgin territory that was for the most part inaccessible as roads had not even been cleared. But through hard labour and by the sweat of their brow, these settlers managed to carve out a piece of the country all their own. Nowadays, the region allows people to relive the glory days of the gold rush, but mostly to enjoy its wide-open spaces, vast forests and countless lakes.

Philippe Renault

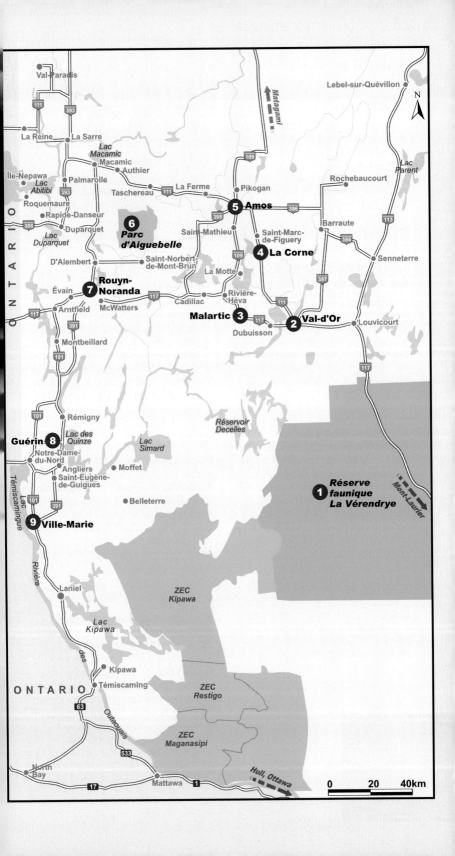

ABITIBI ★

The rolling countryside of Abitibi has countless lakes and rivers and is blanketed by extensive forests, making it ideal for hunting and fishing. The Abitibi-Témiscamingue region is crossed by a watershed between the waters of the St. Lawrence valley and those of James Bay. The Algonquin word "Abitibi" actually means "watershed."

Camping in Abitibi-Témiscamingue   Benoît Chalifour, Sépaq

1. Réserve Faunique La Vérendrye ★★

At 13,615km², this wildlife reserve is the second-largest natural area in Québec, after the Lacs Albanel-Mistassini-et-Waconichi reserve (16,400km²). Over the years, it has become a paradise for outdoors enthusiasts of all kinds.

2. Val-d'Or

The **Village Minier de Bourlamaque ★** was established in the spring of 1935 to accommodate the miners and their families. This gold-rush town has been preserved down to the smallest detail, first by the Lamaque company, which built it, and then by the town of Val-d'Or, which has had control of the town since 1965.

At **La Cité de l'Or ★★**, you head 80m underground into an old mine and learn about various gold-mining techniques. The tour offers a chance to see the incredible working conditions of the miners.

3. Malartic

The **Musée Minéralogique de Malartic ★** was founded by a group of miners who wanted to share their experiences with the public. Today, it is firmly planted in the 21st century, with very educational exhibits. The process that led to the creation of the Earth, and the uses of its minerals in our everyday lives, are dealt with.

4. La Corne

In La Corne, located just south of Saint-Marc-de-Figuery, is an interesting attraction: the **Dispensaire de la Garde ★★**. The dispensary was once owned and operated by a colony nurse, one of many worked as midwives and veterinarians in the territory's most remote regions at the height of colonization.

5. Amos

The **Cathédrale Sainte-Thérèse-d'Avila ★** promoted to the rank of cathedral in 1939, was built in 1923 from a design by Montréal architect Aristide Beaugrand-Champagne. Its unusual circular structure, large dome and Roman Byzantine appearance are reminiscent of the Church of St. Michael's and St. Anthony's in Montréal, designed by the same architect. The interior is decorated with Italian marble, beautiful mosaics and French stained-glass windows.

The Cité de l'Or
Collection Cité de l'Or

WINTER WONDERLAND…

During winter, Abitibi-Témiscamingue is a veritable snowmobilers paradise. More than 3,500 kilometres of snowmobile trails crisscross the region. Lots of snow, ideal temperatures, cold but not damp, and a warm welcome from the locals all make for terrific northern adventures for lovers of the great outdoors.

A pair of snowshoers in Abitibi-Témiscamingue

Jean-Pierre Huard, Sépaq

Moose   Phillipe Renault

The **Refuge Pageau** ★ ★ takes in wounded animals, treats their injuries, then sets them free again. Unfortunately, not all these animals can safely return to the wilderness, so they stay on the reserve, to the delight of visitors. In autumn, you can take in the magnificent spectacle of the migratory birds that stop here on their way south.

6. Parc National d'Aiguebelle ★ ★

Parc National d'Aiguebelle is a provincial park covering 267km². In addition to many lakes and rivers, the park has the region's highest hills. Several outdoor activities are possible, including canoeing, fishing, cycling (10km) and hiking (60km) during the summer, and cross-country skiing (35km) and snowshoeing (40km²) during the winter.

7. Rouyn-Noranda

Visitors can tour the **Noranda Horne Smelter** ★ and its facilities, opened in 1927 and still going strong. It ranks among the world's biggest producers of copper and precious metals.

TÉMISCAMINGUE ★

Beautiful Lac Témiscamingue, the namesake of the entire region, feeds the Ottawa River.

Témiscamingue, which means "place of deep waters," was once the heart of Algonquin territory.

8. Guérin

The **Musée de Guérin** ★ features an interesting collection of religious artifacts and farm implements on exhibit in several restored heritage buildings showcasing local history. Among these are a farmhouse and colonial church.

9. Ville-Marie

The **Fort-Témiscamingue-Duhamel National Historic Site** ★ ★ is located 8km south of Ville-Marie. It commemorates the important role the fur trade played in the Canadian economy. From the North West Company and the French regime to the Hudson's Bay Company, Fort-Témiscamingue was a meeting point for different cultures and religions—that is to say, between Westerners and First Nations peoples.

Parc National d'Aiguebelle
Jean-Pierre Huard, Sépaq

BAS-SAINT-LAURENT

Philippe Renault

Bas-Saint-Laurent farmland

Bas-Saint-Laurent

Fertile agricultural lands

next to the St. Lawrence River and forestry development areas covering gently rolling hills sparkling with lakes and streams make up the Bas-Saint-Laurent region. It extends east along the river from the little town of La Pocatière to the village of Sainte-Luce and south to the borders of the United States and New Brunswick.

A permanent European presence in the Bas-Saint-Laurent region began with the founding of New France and continued in stages that corresponded to the development of different economic activities. Before the end of the 17th century, colonists attracted by the fur trade founded trading posts at Rivière-du-Loup, Bic, Cabano and Notre-Dame-du-Lac. Much of the fertile land along the St. Lawrence River Valley was cleared and cultivated at the beginning of the following century. The layout of farms in the region still reflects the seigneurial system originally used to divide land among peasant farmers. Inland areas, used for agriculture and forestry, were first colonized around 1850. There was a final wave of settlers in the 1930s during the Depression, when unemployed city dwellers took refuge in the country. The various periods of colonization are reflected in the area's rich architectural heritage.

This region lies at the eastern edge of those lands in the St. Lawrence Valley that were cleared and cultivated under the French regime. As elsewhere in New France, the inhabited areas formed a narrow band alongside the river. In the 10th century, the Bas-Saint-Laurent region became one of the favourite vacation areas for rich Montrealers, who built luxurious Victorian residences here.

Patrick Escudero

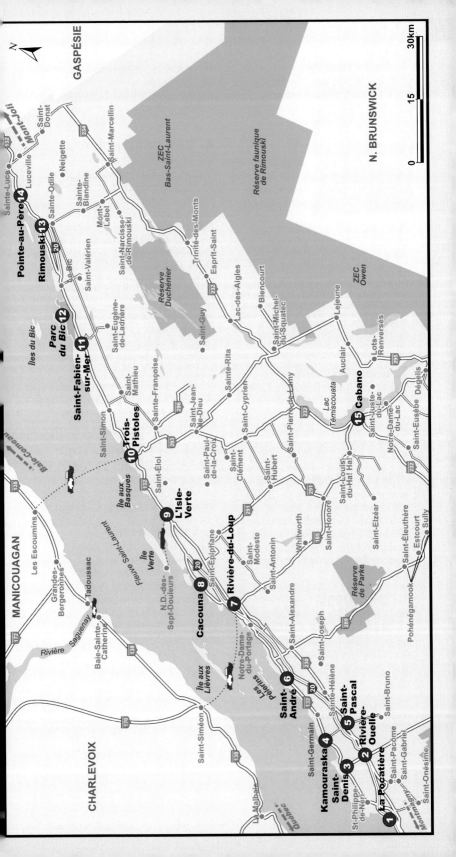

1. La Pocatière

Josée Roy

The **Musée François-Pilote** ★ is named after the founder of the École d'Agriculture de Sainte-Anne-de-La-Pocatière (agricultural school). Set up in the former convent of the nuns of Sainte-Famille, the museum showcases various collections that offer an overview of rural life in Quebec at the turn of the 20th century (doctor's office, middle-class home, farming implements, First Nations artifacts, maple-sugar-making equipment, etc.).

2. Rivière-Ouelle

The **Église Notre-Dame-de-Liesse** and its **presbytery** ★. Rebuilt in 1877 over the ruins of another place of worship built in 1792, Rivière-Ouelle's church was designed by architect David Ouellet, a native of La Pocatière. The structure harbours a few treasures, including a high altar imported from France (1716) and seven paintings by Louis Dulongpré. The neighbouring presbytery, built in 1881, is a fine example of the Second Empire style, characterized by a high mansard roof.

3. Saint-Denis

Jean-Charles Chapais extended the old **Maison Chapais** ★ in 1866 in order to give it equal standing with his prestigious political career.

The structure was thus heightened and the facade adorned with porches and twisting stairways, making it worthy of one of the Fathers of Confederation.

4. Kamouraska ★★

On January 31, 1839, the young Seigneur of Kamouraska, Achille Taché, was murdered by a former friend, Doctor Holmes. The Seigneur's wife had plotted with Holmes, her lover, to do in her husband and flee to distant lands. The incident inspired Anne Hébert's novel *Kamouraska*, which was made into a film by prominent Québec director Claude Jutra.

The novel, and later the film, brought a level of fame to the village. Kamouraska, an Algonquin word meaning "bulrushes by the water," earned a place in the colourful history of rural Québec. For many years, the village was the eastern-most trading post on the Côte-du-Sud. Kamouraska stands on several ranges of rocky hillocks that provide a striking contrast to the adjacent coastal plain. The unusual rugged terrain is a remnant of ancient mountains long worn down by glaciers and typical of the area.

5. Saint-Pascal ★

The small town of Saint-Pascal experienced prosperity in the 19th century thanks to the powerful currents of the Rivière Perles, which led entrepreneurs to build flour, saw and textile mills on its banks. Also to be seen here are manor houses and a church built in 1845.

THE SANDBANKS OF KAMOURASKA

In Saint-André de Kamouraska, major sandbanks—parts of the shore exposed at low tide—filter the river water and are thus home to many species of birds as well as several invertebrates. The Halte Écologique des Battures de Kamouraska has in fact opened an interpretive site here, complete with walking trails, picnic areas and campsites, where visitors can view salterns as well as the local flora and fauna. Moreover, lookouts provide unimpeded views of the St. Lawrence River, the Charlevoix mountains and glorious sunsets.

6. Saint-André ★

The countryside around Saint-André is a dramatic mix of steep hills plunging straight into the river and expansive fields. In autumn, the tidal flats are typically lined with tall wooden fences strung with eel nets. The nearby rocky slopes of the Îles Pèlerins provide a striking backdrop. The islands are home to thousands of birds (including cormorants and black guillemots) and a penguin colony.

The **Église Saint-André ★★**, built between 1805 and 1811, is one of the oldest churches in the region. Its Récollet design, characterized by an absence of side chapels, a narrowing of the nave around the chancels and a flat caveat, differs from the Latin-cross design usually found in Québec churches. The gracious profile of the church topped by a tall steeple with double openings is an elegant example of traditional Québec architecture.

The **Maison de la Prune ★** offers tours of the plum orchard, the traditional processing workshop as well as the old general store where you can purchase the delicious jellies, jams and syrups made on site from orchard produce.

The **Halte Écologique des Battures du Kamouraska ★** explains the importance of the wetlands, or *battures*, along the river's edge in Kamouraska. Shaped by the saltwater tides for centuries, the wetlands have been used as fishing grounds for eel, as pastures and for the construction of dykes.

Cormorant

ÎLE AUX BASQUES

The Société Provancher d'Histoire Naturelle du Canada, whose motto is "*J'aime, j'instruis, je protège*" (I Love, Educate and Protect), has taken Île aux Basques under its wing. Nature-lovers are sure to appreciate this island, as will archaeology buffs, since it harbours the former base camp of Basque whalers who came to hunt their prey in the St. Lawrence River every year between 1508 and 1640. Several ovens, which the Basques used to extract oil from whale blubber—whale oil being the primary source of artificial lighting at the time—are in fact still visible on the riverbank.

Moreover, archaeologists claim that Île aux Basques was the site of the first encounter between Europeans and First Nations peoples. On the St. Lawrence's south shore, a stone's throw away from the island, lies the city of Trois-Pistoles and its **Parc de l'Aventure Basque en Amérique**, an essential historical complement to a tour of Île aux Basques.

View of the river and Île aux Basques

7. Rivière-du-Loup ★

Rivière-du-Loup and its inhabitants seem almost to drift aimlessly on a wild sea, thanks to the town's topography of evenly dispersed rolling hills and the constant ups and downs of life here. Set on either side of the river for which it is named, Rivière-du-Loup has become one of the most important towns in the Bas-Saint-Laurent region. Its strategic location made it a marine communications centre for the Atlantic Ocean, the St. Lawrence River, Lac Témiscouata and the St. John River in New Brunswick. Later, it was an important railway centre, when the town was the eastern terminus of the Canadian train network.

The **Musée du Bas-Saint-Laurent** ★ displays objects characteristic of the region, and holds contemporary art exhibits (including works by Riopelle, Lemieux, Tousignant, Gauvreau, etc.).

8. Saint-Georges-de-Cacouna ★

Cacouna is an Algonquin word meaning "land of the porcupine." The Victorian mansions scattered throughout the village are reminders of a golden age of vacationing in Québec, when Saint-Georges-de-Cacouna was a favourite summer resort among the Montréal elite.

9. L'Isle-Verte ★

The village of L'Isle-Verte was once an important centre of activity in the Bas-Saint-Laurent region; several buildings remain from this period. Just off shore lies Île Verte, the island named by the explorer Jacques Cartier who, upon spotting the lush island, exclaimed, "*Quelle île verte!*", literally "What a green island!".

Visitors to **Île Verte** ★ ★, the island, have the opportunity to watch sturgeon and herring being salted in little smokehouses, taste excellent local lamb, watch beluga and blue whales and photograph the waterfowl, black ducks and herons. The **lighthouse**, located on the eastern tip of the island, is the oldest on the St. Lawrence (built in 1806).

10. Trois-Pistoles

When the colossal **Église Notre-Dame-des-Neiges** ★ ★ was built in 1887, the citizens of Trois-Pistoles believed their church would soon be named the cathedral of the diocese. This explains the size and splendour of the building, topped by three silver steeples. The honour eventually fell to the Rimouski church, the masterpiece of architect David Ouellet, to the great dismay of the congregation of Notre-Dame-des-Neiges.

The Société Provancher offers excursions to **Île aux Basques** ★ ★, which it safeguards as a migratory bird sanctuary. Birdwatchers will certainly enjoy a trip here. The island is also of historical interest. A few years ago, facilities used by Basque fishers were discovered. They came here on whaling expeditions during the 15th century.

The beach at Trois-Pistoles — Patrick Escudero

II. Saint-Fabien-sur-Mer ★★

In Saint-Fabien-sur-Mer, a line of cottages lies wedged between the beach and a 200-m-high cliff. Pic Champlain (346m) is as definitive Saint-Fabien-sur-Mer as the Rockies are of Alberta.

12. Le Bic ★★

Parc National du Bic, a provincial park between Saint-Fabien-sur-Mer and Le Bic, covers 33km² and features a jumble of coves, jutting shoreline, promontories, hills, escarpments and marshes, as well as deep bays teeming with a wide variety of plant and animal life. The park is a good place for hiking, cross-country skiing and mountain biking, among other activities, and also has an information centre.

Parc National du Bic
Jean-Pierre Huard, Sépaq

13. Rimouski ★

At the end of the 17th century, a French merchant named René Lepage, originally from Auxerre, France, undertook the monumental task of clearing the seigneury at Rimouski, a Micmac word meaning house of the dog. The land thus became the easternmost area on the Gulf of St. Lawrence to be colonized under the French regime. Today, Rimouski is considered the administrative capital of eastern Québec, and prides itself on being at the cutting edge of the arts.

The **Musée Régional de Rimouski** ★ focuses on art and ethnology and is housed in the former Église Saint-Germain, built between 1823 and 1827. The simple church, with its central bell tower, is reminiscent of churches built under the French regime.

The **Canyon des Portes de l'Enfer** ★★ is a fascinating natural spectacle, especially in winter. Literally the "gates of hell," this canyon starts at the 18m-high Grand Saut falls, and stretches nearly 5km on either side of the Rivière Rimouski, with cliffs reaching as high as 90m in places. Guided boat tours are conducted in the canyon.

14. Pointe-au-Père

Musée de la Mer and the **Pointe-au-Père Lighthouse National Historic Site** ★★. It was off the shores of Pointe-au-Père that the *Empress of Ireland* sank in 1914, claiming the lives of 1,012 people. The Musée de la Mer houses a fascinating collection of objects recovered from the wreck and provides a detailed account of the tragedy. The nearby lighthouse, which is open to the public, marks the exact spot where the river officially becomes the Gulf of St. Lawrence.

15. Cabano ★

Only part of the 19th-century town, known as Fraser Village, survives, the remainder having been destroyed by a terrible fire in 1950. However, the town boasts a beautiful setting by the shores of Lac Témiscouata, surrounded by mountains and rivers.

Fort Ingall ★★, which bears the name of the lieutenant under whose command it once was, is one of several such military posts built as a deterrent by the British in the 17th century. It never saw war, though, and was gradually abandoned following the peace settlement established by the Webster-Ashburton Treaty of 1842, after which it sank into oblivion. It wasn't until 1973 that six of its 11 buildings were reconstructed from archaeological remains.

Musée de la Mer and the Pointe-au-Père Lighthouse National Historic Site
Musée de la Mer Collection

CANTONS-DE-L'EST

The abbey at Saint-Benoît-du-Lac

Cantons-de-l'Est
Mountainous countryside

The steeple of the Église Sainte-Catherine-de-Hatley   Sylvain Majeau

and a rich architectural heritage give the Cantons de l'Est, often referred to in English as the Eastern Townships, a distinctive character reminiscent in many ways of New England. This beautiful region in the southernmost part of Québec lies in the Appalachian foothills.

As may be gathered from many place names, such as Massawippi and Coaticook, this vast region was originally explored and inhabited by the Abenaki First Nation. Later, when New France came under British control and the United States declared its independence, many American colonists still loyal to the British monarchy (known as Loyalists) settled in the Eastern Townships. Many towns and villages are graced with majestic Anglican churches surrounded by beautiful 19th-century Victorian or vernacular American-style homes.

The Townships are still home to a handful of prestigious English institutions. Today, the region competes with the Laurentians, to the northwest, as Montrealers' preferred choice for cottage country.

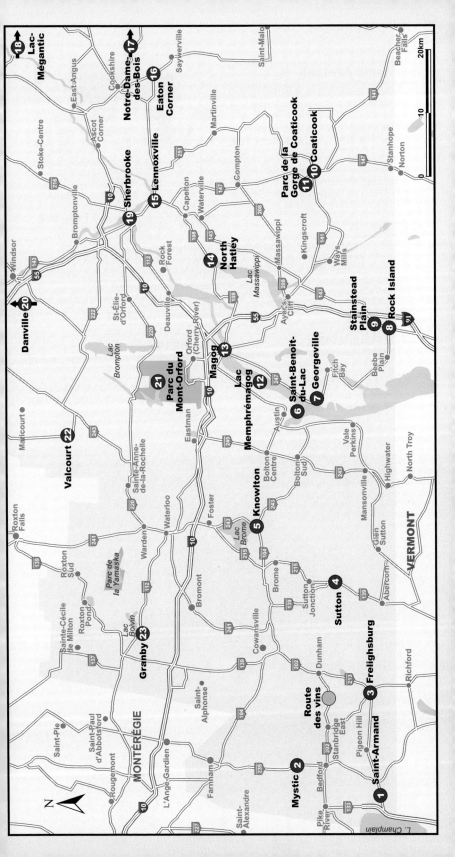

I. Saint-Armand ★

This village was once a major railway junction, as evidenced by its train station, now the **town hall**. This Neo-Renaissance-style brick building was erected in 1865, making it one of the oldest railway stations in the country. Moreover, the **covered bridge (1845) spanning the Groat river** is one of the first such bridges built in Canada.

Holstein cow

2. Mystic ★

Mystic is like a little piece of New England in Québec. Its population is still mainly anglophone. Blink, and the village is gone: its central focus is the dodecagonal (12-sided) Walbridge Barn (1885).

3. Frelighsburg ★

Eastern Townships' architecture differs from that of the rest of Québec, due to its Anglo-American origins, which account for the frequent use of red brick and white clapboard and the predominance of sash windows.

Frelighsburg's Anglican Church ★ is very well situated atop a hill overlooking the village. Both its oblong structure and its steeple, which is at the side of the nave and marks the main entrance, are uncommon architectural features in the Eastern Townships.

4. Sutton ★

Sutton, which is located at the base of the mountain of the same name, is one of the major winter resorts in the Eastern Townships. The area also has several well-designed golf courses.

A snowboarder on Mont Sutton

Ski Sutton

SLAVE CEMETERY

The value of the historic site of the black-slave cemetery of Saint-Armand, in the Eastern Townships, has finally been recognized by the Québec government, which presented the municipality with a commemorative plaque in 2003. Known as "Nigger Rock," the local landmark dates from end of the 18th century.

This sordid story begins in 1783, with the arrival of a certain Phillip Luke, a Loyalist from the Lake Champlain area who inherited six slaves from his mother. On the land owned by the Lukes, who were potash producers—the production of which relied on a large workforce, hence the exploitation of slaves—lies a family cemetery with tombstone inscriptions and, a few-dozen metres away, at the foot of an outcropping of slate known as "Nigger Rock," a plot where black slaves were buried between 1794 and 1833. It was said, not so long ago, that two signs could be found on the Luke's land—Luke Cemetery and Negro Cemetery—pointing in opposite directions.

The historic site of Nigger Rock still harbours its secrets, as do the old documents. However, though the site is on private land and off limits to the public, the foundations of what were likely cabins inhabited by black slaves can still be seen here. The village of Saint-Armand, for its part, harbours the ruins of a building dating back to 1831 that served as a chapel for the black community.

5. Knowlton ★★

When the Townships are compared to New England, Knowlton is often given as an example. Quaint shops and restaurants welcome visitors strolling through this well-to-do little village.

Lac Brome ★ is popular among windsurfers, who can use a parking lot and a little beach on the side of the road near Knowlton.

The **Brome County Museum** ★ occupies five Loyalist buildings and traces the lives and history of the region's inhabitants. In addition to the usual furniture and photographs, visitors can see a reconstructed general store, a 19th-century court of justice and, what's more unusual, a collection of military equipment, including a World War I airplane.

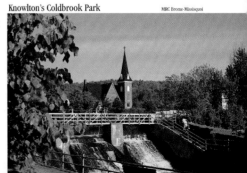

Knowlton's Coldbrook Park

MRC Brome-Missisquoi

THE WINE ROUTE

European visitors might consider it quite presumptuous to call the road between Dunham and Stanbridge East (Rte. 202 W.) the "Wine Route," (indicated by blue road signs from Autoroute 10) but the concentration of vineyards in this region is unique in the province, and Québec's attempts at wine-making have been so surprisingly successful that people have been swept away by their own enthusiasm.

There are no châteaux or distinguished old counts here, only growers who sometimes have to go as far as renting helicopters to save their vines from freezing. The rotor blades cause the air to circulate, preventing frost from forming on the ground during crucial periods in May. The region is, however, blessed with a microclimate and soil favourable for grape growing (slate). Most of the local wines are sold only at the vineyards where they are produced.

The abbey of Saint-Benoît-du-Lac in winter

Sylvain Majeau

6. Saint-Benoît-du-Lac ★★

This municipality consists solely of the estate of the **Abbaye de Saint-Benoît-du-Lac ★**, an abbey founded in 1913 by Benedictine monks who were driven away from the Abbaye de Saint-Wandrille-de-Fontenelle in Normandy. Aside from the monastery, there are guest quarters, an abbey chapel and farm buildings. However, only the chapel and a few corridors are open to the public.

Georgeville   Peter Quine

7. Georgeville ★

Most of director Denys Arcand's *The Decline of the American Empire* was shot in the heart of this area's rolling countryside, synonymous with relaxing vacations. For a long time now, the little village of Georgeville has been a favourite resort area among English-speaking families. The Molsons, for example, own an island in the vicinity.

The **Musée Colby-Curtis ★**, located in a house complete with all of its original furnishings, provides an excellent indication of how the local bourgeoisie lived during the second half of the 19th century. The residence, which has a grey granite facade, was built in 1859 for a lawyer named James Carroll Colby, who called it *Carrollcroft*.

8. Rock Island ★

Straddling the Canadian-US border, Rock Island is one of the strangest villages in the province. Walking down its streets, visitors will find themselves in the United States in certain spots and in Canada in others. Notices written in French give way suddenly to signs in English.

The **Haskell Free Library and Opera House ★** is both a library and a theatre. Straddling the Canadian-American border, it was built as a symbol of the friendship between the two nations.

The Musée Colby Curtis   Brian Merett, Société Hist. de Stanstead

9. Stanstead Plain ★

Some of the most beautiful houses in the Eastern Townships are located in this prosperous community. The distilleries of the 1820s, and later, the granite quarries, enabled a number of the area's inhabitants to amass large fortunes in the 19th century.

10. Coaticook

Located in the heart of Coaticook's residential area, the **Musée Beaulne ★** occupies a large wooden mansion built in 1912 for the Norton family. Some of its rooms have been kept in the style typical of bourgeois homes at the dawn of the 20th century, while others contain textile and costume displays.

II. Parc de la Gorge de Coaticook ★

Parc de la Gorge de Coaticook protects the part of the impressive 50m gorge created by the Rivière Coaticook. Trails wind across the entire area, enabling visitors to see the gorge from different angles. Cross the suspension bridge over the gorge, if you dare!

Suspension bridge over Coaticook Gorge   Paul Laramée

12. Lac Memphrémagog ★★

Lac Memphrémagog, which is 44.5km long and only 1 to 2 km wide, will remind some visitors of a Scottish loch. It even has its own equivalent of the Loch Ness monster, named "Memphre," sightings of which go back to 1798!

13. Magog ★

Equipped with more facilities than any other town between Granby and Sherbrooke, Magog has a lot to offer sports enthusiasts. It is extremely well situated on the northern shore of Lac Memphrémagog. The town's cultural scene is also worth noting. Visitors can go to the theatre or the music complex, set in the natural mountain surroundings.

14. North Hatley ★★

Attracted by North Hatley's enchanting countryside, wealthy American vacationers built luxurious villas here between 1890 and 1930. Most of these still line the northern part of Lac Massawippi, which, like Lac Memphrémagog, resembles a Scottish loch.

Hovey Manor ★, a large villa built in 1900, was modelled on Mount Vernon, George Washington's home in Virginia. It used to be the summer residence of an American named Henry Atkinson, who entertained American artists and politicians here every summer.

15. Lennoxville ★

This little town, the population of which is still mainly English-speaking, is home to two prestigious English-language educational institutions: Bishop's University and Bishop's College.

Bishop's University ★, one of three English-language universities in Québec, offers 1,300 students from all over Canada a personalized education in an enchanting setting. It was founded in 1843, through the efforts of a minister named Lucius Doolittle.

Bishop's University, Lennoxville
Stéphane Lemire

The Mont Mégantic ASTROlab

Jean-Pierre Huard, Sépaq

16. Eaton Corner ★

Eaton, or Eaton Corner, derives its name from its location, at the junction of two roads—namely the road to Sherbrooke, and the one that runs from the United States—that played a major role in the region's colonization.

The **Compton County Historical Museum Society** ★ now occupies the old congregationalist church, built in 1841. This beautiful neoclassical wooden building houses Loyalist furniture as well as documents and photographs that recount the lives of the first colonists to settle east of Sherbrooke.

17. Notre-Dame-des-Bois

The **ASTROlab du Parc National du Mont-Mégantic ★ ★** is an interpretive centre focusing on astronomy. The various rooms and multimedia show at the interactive museum use the latest technology to reveal the beginnings of astronomy.

A vast expanse of crystal-clear water, **Lac Mégantic ★ ★** is teeming with all sorts of fish, especially trout, and attracts a good many vacationers eager to go fishing or simply enjoy the local beaches.

18. Lac-Mégantic ★

The town of Lac-Mégantic was founded in 1885 by Scottish settlers from the Hebrides. Unable to make enough money from the relatively poor soil, the residents soon turned to forestry. The town is beautifully located on the shores of Lac Mégantic.

In the **Église Sainte-Agnès ★**, erected in 1913, visitors will discover a beautiful stained-glass window designed in 1849 for the Catholic Church of the Immaculate Conception in Mayfair, London.

Downtown Sherbrooke   Stéphane Lemire

19. Sherbrooke ★★

Sherbrooke, the Eastern Townships' main urban area, is nicknamed the Queen of the Eastern Townships. It spreads over a series of hills on both sides of the Rivière Saint-François, accentuating its disorderly appearance. An industrial city, it nevertheless has a number of interesting buildings, the majority of which are located on the west bank.

The **Hôtel de Ville ★**, or city hall, occupies the former Courthouse (the city's third). It is a granite building dating from 1904 that was designed by Elzéar Charest, head architect of the Department of Public Works. It is an example of Quebecers' continuing fondness for the enduring spirit of Second Empire architecture.

An important financial institution in the 19th century, now merged with the CIBC, the former **Eastern Townships Bank ★★** was established by the region's upper class, who were unable to obtain financing for local projects from the banks in Montréal. Following a donation from the Canadian Imperial Bank of Commerce (CIBC) and major renovations, the building now houses the **Musée des Beaux-Arts de Sherbrooke**.

Parc National du Mont-Orford   Jean-Pierre Huard, Sépaq

Some of the loveliest houses in Sherbrooke are located on **Parc Mitchell ★★**, which is adorned with a fountain by sculptor George Hill (1921).

Facing straight down the centre of Rue Court, the former **Palais de Justice ★**, Sherbrooke's second courthouse, was converted into a drill hall for the city's Hussards regiment at the end of the 19th century.

The Musée J. Armand Bombardier   Valcourt

The Séminaire Saint-Charles, built in 1898, now houses the **Musée de la Nature et des Sciences de Sherbrooke ★**. Formerly a museum established by priests at the Séminaire de Sherbrooke, this brand new museum now focuses on the natural sciences and is primarily aimed at young people.

Sherbrooke's former textile industry started up in the second half of the 19th century, and was very profitable, as it was in many New England towns. The **Filature Paton ★** once was the most important textile mill in the Eastern Townships. Today, the mill is not only a model of how an area's industrial heritage may be preserved and such spaces transformed, but also provides a new focus for downtown Sherbrooke.

Tigers at the Granby Zoo   Granby Zoo

20. Danville ★

This attractive, shady village has preserved a number of noteworthy Victorian and Edwardian residences, which bear witness to a time when wealthy Montréal families summered in Danville.

21. Parc National du Mont-Orford ★★

Parc National du Mont-Orford, a provincial park, covers some 58km² and includes—in addition to the mountain—the area around Lac Stukely and Lac Fraser. During the summer, visitors can enjoy the beach, the magnificent golf course, back-country campsites, and some 80km of hiking trails (the most beautiful path leads to Mont Chauve).

22. Valcourt

The **Musée J.-Armand-Bombardier ★** traces the development of the snowmobile, and explains how Bombardier's invention was marketed all over the world. Different prototypes are displayed, along with a few examples of various snowmobiles produced since 1960.

23. Granby

Visitors to the **Granby Zoo ★★** can see some 250 animal species, mainly from North America and Africa. This is an old-style zoo, so most of the animals are in cages and there are few areas where they can roam freely. It is nevertheless an interesting place to visit, particularly for young children.

The Mont Mégantic ASTROlab
(next page)
M. Pitre, Sépaq

CHARLEVOIX

Parc des Hautes-Gorges-de-la-Rivière-Malbaie

Charlevoix

Artists have been captivated

by the beauty of the Charlevoix region for years. From the town of Saint-Joachim to the mouth of the Rivière Saguenay, dramatic mountainous countryside contrasts sharply with the expansive open water of the St. Lawrence. A scattering of charming villages and towns dot the coastline, dwarfed by mountains that recede into the salt water of the river and steep-sided valleys. Away from the river, Charlevoix is a wild, rugged region where Boreal forest sometimes gives way to tundra.

The old houses and churches found throughout the region are vestiges of Charlevoix's history as a French colony. In addition, the division of farmland in the area still reflects the seigneurial system of land grants used under the French regime. The rich architectural heritage and exceptional geography are complemented by a dazzling variety of flora and fauna. The Charlevoix region was declared a UNESCO World Biosphere Reserve in 1988 and it is home to many fascinating animal and plant species.

A number of whale species feed at the mouth of the Rivière Saguenay during the summer. In the spring and fall, hundreds of thousands of snow geese make migratory stops in the region, creating a remarkable sight near Cap-Tourmente, farther west. Deep in the hinterland, the territory has all the properties of tundra, a remarkable occurrence at this latitude. This area is home to a variety of animal species such as caribou and the large Arctic wolf. Charlevoix also has many types of plants not found in other parts of eastern Canada.

Jean-François Bergeron

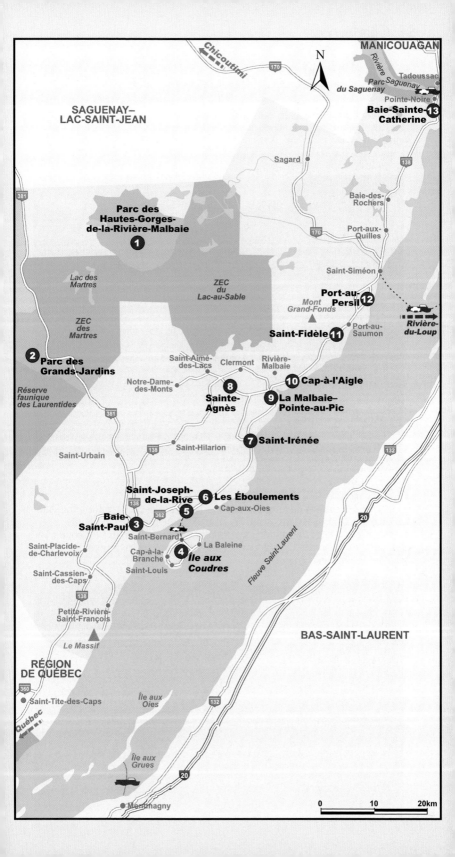

1. Parc National des Hautes-Gorges-de-la-Rivière-Malbaie ★★

Over 800 million years ago, a crack in the earth's crust formed the magnificent gorges after which the park is named; later, the terrain was shaped by glaciers. The Parc National des Hautes-Gorges-de-la-Rivière-Malbaie, a provincial park, which covers over 225km², was created to protect the area from commercial exploitation. Riverboat cruises are available. A trip down the river is the best way to truly appreciate the park.

Parc National des Hautes-Gorges-de-la-Rivière-Malbaie   Sépaq

2. Parc National des Grands-Jardins ★★

Located at the eastern edge of the Réserve Faunique des Laurentides, the Parc National des Grands-Jardins, a provincial park, is rich in flora and fauna characteristic of taiga and tundra, a very unusual occurrence this far south. The park's Mont du Lac des Cygnes (swan lake mountain) trail is among the most beautiful in Québec.

Jean Sylvain, Sépaq

Parc National des Grands-Jardins

Winter scene
Jean-François Bergeron

3. Baie-Saint-Paul ★★

A bend in the road reveals Baie-Saint-Paul in all its charm, and a slope leads to the heart of the village, which has maintained a quaint small-town atmosphere. Set out on foot along the pleasant Rue Saint-Jean-Baptiste, Rue Saint-Joseph, and Rue Sainte-Anne, where small wooden houses with mansard roofs now house boutiques and cafés. For over a century, Baie-Saint-Paul has attracted North American landscape artists, inspired by the mountains and a quality of light particular to Charlevoix.

Baie-Saint-Paul

François Rivard

A selection of paintings by Charlevoix artists is displayed in the **Centre d'Art de Baie-Saint-Paul ★**, designed in a modern-style in 1967 by architect Jacques DeBlois. A painting and sculpture symposium, where works by young artists are displayed, is held by the centre every August.

The **Centre d'Exposition de Baie-Saint-Paul ★★** is a museum and gallery, completed in 1992 according to blueprints by architect Pierre Thibault. It houses travelling exhibits from around the world, as well as the René Richard gallery, where several paintings by this Swiss-born artist are on display.

Since the death of painter René Richard in 1983, the **Maison René-Richard ★** and surrounding property have been open to the public. A tour of the grounds provides a fascinating glimpse into the Charlevoix of the 1940s, when artists and collectors from New York and Chicago congregated here during the summer.

The **Centre d'Histoire Naturelle de Charlevoix ★★★** explores all the natural wonders of the Charlevoix region. Audiovisual presentations, including a slide show thus cover topics like the geological and human history of the area as well as its flora, fauna and climate.

Snow goose

Maple leaf

Artic wolf

The **Laiterie Charlevoix ★**, founded in 1948, still makes its cheddar cheese the old-fashioned way—by hand. It is also home to the Économusée du Fromage.

Charlevoix countryside

François Rivard

AGE-OLD MOUNTAINS

The Charlevoix region boasts the oldest mountains in the world. This 6,000km² territory lies at the heart of the Canadian Shield, through which the Laurentian mountain range surges until it meets the salt waters of the St. Lawrence River. Île aux Coudres, on the other hand, consists of an ancient little riverside Laurentian mountain that was swallowed up by the 1663 earthquake, only to reappear as a small, reef-bordered island.

Mont des Éboulements sprang from the earth 350 million years ago, as a result of the impact of a meteorite that crashed to earth and shaped the region geographically. The passage of 3km- to 5km-thick glaciers, the encroachment of the Champlain Sea up to 180m above sea level and the earthquakes that regularly sweep through the region have also played a part in shaping the rugged landscape.

Île aux Coudres   Jean-François Bergeron

4. Île aux Coudres ★

The island was so named by Jacques Cartier in 1535 owing to its abundance of hazel trees (*coudriers*, in French). Over the years, the population of the island's two villages (L'Île-aux-Coudres and La Baleine) has acquired a certain independence due to its isolation, allowing it to keep alive certain old traditions long since lost in other regions of Quebec.

The **Musée Les Voitures d'Eau** ★ presents exhibits dealing with the history, construction and navigation of the small craft once built in the region. The museum was founded in 1973 by Captain Éloi Perron, who recovered the wreck of the schooner Mont-Saint-Louis, now on display.

Along with a forge and milling house, the mills known as the **Moulins Desgagné ★ ★**, or **Moulins de l'Île-aux-Coudres** were restored by the Québec government, which has also established on-site information centres. The machinery necessary for operation is still in perfect condition, and is now back at work grinding wheat and buckwheat into flour.

5. Saint-Joseph-de-la-Rive ★

The rhythm of life in this village on the St. Lawrence followed the rhythm of the river for many generations, as the boats beached along the shore eloquently testify.

The dimensions and white-painted wooden exterior of the **Église Catholique Saint-Joseph** ★ are reminiscent of the Anglican churches found in Québec's Eastern Townships region. Its singular interior is decorated with various objects from the sea.

The **Papeterie Saint-Gilles** ★ is a traditional paper-making workshop founded in 1966 by priest and poet Félix-Antoine Savard (1896-1982, author of *Menaud Maître-Draveur*) with the help of Mark Donohue, a member of a famous Canadian pulp and paper dynasty.

The **Musée Maritime de Charlevoix ★ ★**, located in a shipyard, recaptures the golden era of the schooner. Visitors are welcome to climb aboard the boats on the premises. It also houses the Économusée de la Goélette.

The Musée Maritime de Charlevoix
François Rivard

CHARLEVOIX EARTHQUAKES

Charlevoix's last major earthquake occurred in 1925 and reached 7.0 on the Richter Scale. Although there were no casualties, much damage was reported. Several chimneys crumbled, as did the steeple of the Église St-André and part of the Gare du Palais, in Québec City.

Another quake of even greater magnitude took place in 1663 and is mentioned in historical texts. On November 25, 1988, the earth shook near Chicoutimi, in the Saguenay. Tremors registering 6.0 on the Richter Scale at the epicentre once again literally shook Charlevoix to its foundations.

6. Les Éboulements ★

In 1663, a violent earthquake in the region caused a gigantic landslide; it is said that half a small mountain sank into the river. The village of Les Éboulements is named after the event (*éboulements* means landslide in English).

The **Manoir Sales-Laterrière (Camp le Manoir)** and its **communal mill** ★ ★. The communal mill was built in 1790 at the top of 30m-high falls, giving it a picturesque aspect from which painters and other romantics draw inspiration. Guided tours of the mill, the machinery of which is still in place, are offered in summer. The manor itself, wood-panelled and adorned with red shutters (circa 1810), is off-limits to the public, as it now serves as a school for the brothers of Sacré-Coeur. However, it can be seen from the pleasant interpretive trail laid out on the seigneurial estate, east of the mill.

Les Éboulements — Jean-François Bergeron

The communal mill of the Manoir Sales-Laterrière — François Rivard

Saint-Irénée   Anne Gardon

7. Saint-Irénée ★

Saint-Irénée, or Saint-Irénée-les-Bains, as it was known during the Belle Époque, is the gateway to the part of Charlevoix usually considered the oldest vacation spot in North America.

The **Domaine Forget** ★ was home to Sir Rodolphe Forget (1861-1919), a prominent French Canadian businessman in the early 20th century. The Salle Françoys-Bernier, at the Domaine Forget, can accommodate 600 music lovers, who are sure to be delighted with its wonderful acoustics.

8. Sainte-Agnès

The **Église Sainte-Agnès** ★ is a fine example of 19th-century colonial-era wooden churches, built in remote villages far inland. Thomas Baillairgé drew up the plans for the modest place of worship, based on French regime architecture, in 1839.

9. La Malbaie-Pointe-au-Pic ★

On his way to Québec City in 1608, Samuel de Champlain anchored in a Charlevoix bay for the night. To his surprise, he awoke the next morning to find his fleet resting on land and not in water. Champlain learned that day what many navigators would come to learn as well: the water recedes a great distance in this region and will trap any boat not moored in sufficiently deep water. In exasperation, he exclaimed "Ah! La malle baye!" (Old French, which translates roughly to "Oh what a bad bay!").

The **Manoir Richelieu** ★ ★, the only grand hotel in Charlevoix to survive, was built of wood in 1899. Many famous people have stayed at the hotel, from Charlie Chaplin to the King of Siam and the Vanderbilts of New York City.

The Salle Françoys-Bernier at the Domaine Forget   François Rivard

The Manoir Richelieu
Fairmont Le Manoir Richelieu

THE GREAT WHITE FLEET

Plying the waters from Québec City or Montréal, they were known as the *Saguenay*, *Magnet*, *Québec*, *Union*, *St. Lawrence*, *Canada* and *Richelieu*. They sailed for The Richelieu and Ontario Navigation Companies or for Canada Steamship Lines and offered excursions all the way to the furthermost part of the Saguenay Fjord.

This was the "Great White Fleet," passenger ships always greeted with much fanfare upon their arrival in Pointe-au-Pic or Cap-à-l'Aigle. People rushed up to help the ship dock and to watch the well-heeled ladies and gents disembarking from these luxurious, floating palaces. Paddlewheel steamboats and small liners specially designed for the St. Lawrence River paraded off the coast of Charlevoix from 1830 to 1965.

10. Cap-à-l'Aigle

From Boulevard de Comporté in La Malbaie, visitors can catch a glimpse of a stately stone house sitting high on the Cap-à-l'Aigle escarpment. The building is the old manor house of the Malcolm Fraser seigneurs, a property also known as Mount Murray. It is matched to the east of Rivière Malbaie by the John Nairne seigneury, established west of the waterway and simply named Murray Bay in honour of James Murray, British Governor at the time. Cap-à-l'Aigle forms the heart of the Mount Murray seigneury and its tourism industry dates back to the 18th century.

The **Manoir Fraser** ★ was built for the son of Malcolm Fraser in 1827, according to plans by architect Jean-Baptiste Duléger. Damaged during a fire in 1975, the manor was restored by the Cabot family, which has held the title to the Cap-à-l'Aigle seigneury since 1902.

11. Saint-Fidèle

East of Cap-à-l'Aigle, the mountains huddle even closer together against the sea, providing few openings inland.

Port-au-Persil's Anglican chapel

Patrick Escudero

The **Centre Écologique de Port-au-Saumon** ★ is a nature-study centre devoted to environmental protection that seeks to educate the public about various ecology-related subjects. The ecological centre also organizes educational activities dealing with the natural and environmental sciences within the framework of the Festival des Sciences de la Nature, and hosts a children's summer camp.

12. Port-au-Persil ★

This small but charming harbour town is set apart by its waterfall, Anglican chapel and winding road that leads through the beautiful mountain landscapes.

13. Baie-Sainte-Catherine ★

A tiny village on the north shore of the St. Lawrence, Baie-Saint-Catherine borders a bay on the Saguenay estuary and has a picturesque sandy beach.

CHAUDIÈRE-APPALACHES

The nave of Église Saint-Jean-Baptiste, Saint-Jean-Port-Joli

Chaudière-Appalaches

Charming villages,

each with very distinct geographic features, make up the Chaudière-Appalaches region. Located opposite Québec City, on the south shore of the St. Lawrence River, it stretches across a vast fertile plain before slowly climbing into the foothills of the Appalachian Mountains, all the way to the U.S. border. The Rivière Chaudière, which originates in Lac Mégantic, runs through the centre of this region, then flows into the St. Lawrence, across from Québec City.

A pretty, pastoral landscape unfolds along the river between Leclercville and Saint-Roch-des-Aulnaies, an area occupied very early on by the French.

Farther south, the picturesque Beauce region extends along the banks of the Rivière Chaudière. The river rises dramatically in the spring, flooding some of the villages along its banks almost every year, lending muddied local inhabitants the nickname "jarrets noirs," which translates somewhat inelegantly as "black hamstrings." The discovery of gold nuggets in the river bed attracted prospectors to the area in the 19th century. Farms have prospered in the rolling green hills of the Beauce for hundreds of years. Church steeples announce the presence of little villages, scattered evenly across the local countryside. Its local inhabitants, the "Beaucerons," are known for their sense of tradition and hospitality. The "asbestos" region, located a little farther west of the Rivière Chaudière, around Thetford Mines, has a fairly varied landscape, punctuated with impressive open-cut mines.

Louise Tanguay

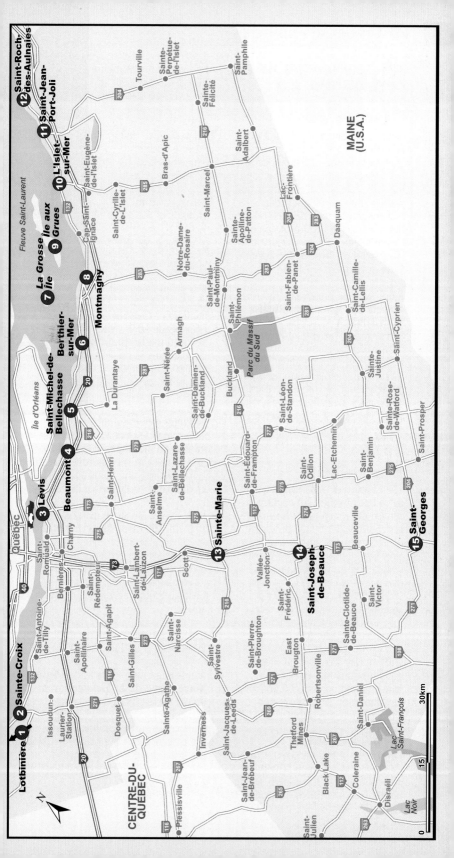

THE SEIGNEURIES OF THE CÔTE-DU-SUD ★★

I. Lotbinière ★

Granted to René-Louis Chartier de Lotbinière in 1672, the seigneury of Lotbinière is one of the few estates to have always remained in the hands of the same family. Because he had a seat on the Conseil Souverain (sovereign council), the first seigneur did not actually live on the premises. Nevertheless, he saw to it that the land and the village of Lotbinière were developed.

Along with its presbytery and former convent, the monumental **Église Saint-Louis ★★**, set parallel to the St. Lawrence, provides a lovely setting from which to enjoy a view of the river. The present building is the fourth Catholic church to be built in the seigneury of Lotbinière. Designed by François Baillairgé, it was begun in 1818. The spires, as well as the crown of the facade, are the result of modifications made in 1888.

2. Sainte-Croix

The Chartier de Lotbinière lineage dates back to the 11th century. In the service of French kings for many generations, the family preserved its contacts with the motherland even after it established itself in Canada, despite the British conquest and the distance between the two lands. In 1828, Julie-Christine Chartier de Lotbinière married Pierre-Gustave Joly, a rich Huguenot merchant from Montréal. In 1840, Joly purchased a part of the Sainte-Croix land from the Québec City Ursulines in order to build a seigneurial manor there, which would come to be known as the Manoir de la Pointe Platon, or the Domaine Joly-De Lotbinière.

The **Domaine Joly-De Lotbinière ★★** is part of the Jardins de Québec association. The main attraction here is the superb setting on the banks of the St. Lawrence. It is especially worthwhile to take the footpaths to the beach in order to gaze out at the river, the slate cliffs and the opposite shore, where the Église Sainte-Famille de Cap Santé is visible. Numerous rare centuries-old trees, floral plantings and an aviary adorn the grounds of the estate.

3. Lévis ★★

Originally known as Ville d'Aubigny, Lévis was given its present name in 1861, in memory of Chevalier François de Lévis, who defeated the British in the Battle of Sainte-Foy in 1760. The upper part of the city, consisting mostly of administrative buildings, offers some interesting views of Vieux-Québec, located on the opposite side of the river, while the very narrow lower part welcomes the trains and the ferry linking Lévis to the provincial capital.

Built during the stock market crash of 1929, the **Terrasse de Lévis ★★** offers spectacular views of downtown Lévis and Québec City. From here, you can take in Vieux-Québec's Place Royale, located along the river, and the Château Frontenac and Haute-Ville above.

In 1851, a parish priest named Joseph Déziel proposed building a large Catholic church to serve the flourishing town. Plans for the **Église Notre-Dame-de-la-Victoire ★** were drawn up by Thomas Baillairgé, the architect of so many churches in the Québec City area. On the grounds of the church, there is a plaque marking the exact location of the English cannons that bombarded Québec City in 1759.

The Domaine Joly-De Lotbinière

Louise Tanguay

4. Beaumont ★

The Côte-du-Sud corresponds to the south coast of the St. Lawrence estuary and technically begins at Beaumont. With its silver-roofed churches, Corpus Christi processional chapels and manors set in a landscape that seems larger than life, this is true French Canadian country. The seigneury of Beaumont (1672) is a fine example of the regional heritage.

The beautiful little **Église Saint-Étienne ★ ★**, built in 1733, is one of the oldest churches still standing in Québec. It looks straight down the axis of the main road, which then curves inland, forming a small triangular plaza in front of the church square. This formation is typical of classical 18th century French town planning.

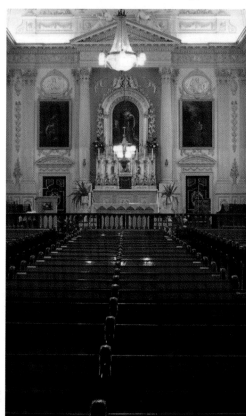

The nave of Église Saint-Louis, Lotbinière
Fondation du Patrimoine Religieux du Québec

ALPHONSE DESJARDINS

Alphonse Desjardins was born in Lévis in 1854, where 46 years later he founded the Caisse Populaire de Lévis, the first of a series in the important movement towards credit unions, that has grown into the present-day Caisses Populaires Desjardins.

The injustice of the loan system of the day prompted Desjardins to create a savings organization that would meet the needs of small-scale investors. Credit unions already existed in Europe; by adapting their methods to the Québec situation, Desjardins realized his idea of a cooperative system in which community solidarity could benefit all of its members.

In 1909, 22 Caisses were active across the province; the 100th was inaugurated in 1912. Each credit union functioned independently under Desjardins's guidance. At the end of his life, Alphonse Desjardins was as involved as ever in the activities of the Caisses Populaires. He who had so much faith in the human spirit of cooperation left behind a popular movement that today has close to five million members in 1,200 Caisses across Québec.

5. Saint-Michel-de-Bellechasse ★
The shaded streets of Saint-Michel are lined with lovely white-painted wooden houses, some of which feature architecture of foreign influence, both British and American. Saint-Michel-de-Bellechasse was completely laid to waste in 1759, when the British army, advancing toward Québec City, successively torched and pillaged the villages of the Côte-du-Sud.

6. Berthier-sur-Mer ★
This village is aptly named (Berthier by the Sea) because on arriving here from the west, visitors catch their first whiff of sea air. Here, Île d'Orléans has faded into the background, and the river, with its blue waves, starts to look like the ocean. On a clear day, typical sights include the mountains of Charlevoix, just opposite, and the fully equipped sailing harbour of this small summer resort founded back in the seigneurial era.

7. Grosse Île

An excursion to **Grosse Île and the Irish Memorial National Historic Site** ★★ is to step back into the sad history of North American immigration. Fleeing epidemics and famine, Irish emigrants to Canada were particularly numerous from the 1830s to the 1850s. In order to limit the spread of cholera and typhus in the New World, authorities required transatlantic passengers to undergo a quarantine before allowing them to disembark at the port of Québec City. Grosse Île was the logical location for this isolation camp, far enough from the mainland to sequester its residents effectively, but close enough to be convenient.

8. Montmagny

The **Centre Éducatif des Migrations** ★ is located on the Pointe-aux-Oies campsite. This information centre on bird migrations deals with the *sauvagine*, or snow goose; it also has a theatre presenting films on migrating birds among other subjects, exhibits, conferences and shows.

9. Île aux Grues ★★

Îles aux Grues is the only island of the Isle-aux-Grues archipelago that is inhabited year round. It is an excellent spot for watching snow geese in the spring, for hunting in autumn, and for walking in summer.

I0. L'Islet-sur-Mer ★

As its name ("Islet by the Sea") suggests, this village's activities centre on the sea. Since the 18th century, local residents have been handing down the occupations of sailor and captain on the St. Lawrence from father to son. Some have even become highly skilled captains and explorers on distant seas.

With artifacts related to fishing, ship models, an interpretive centre and

Grosse Île and the Irish Memorial National Historic Site
Parcs Canada / E. Kedl

The Musée Maritime du Québec   L'Islet

two actual ships, the **Musée Maritime du Québec** ★★ recounts the maritime history of the St. Lawrence from the 17th century to the present day. The institution, founded by the Association des Marins du Saint-Laurent, occupies the former Couvent de l'Islet-sur-Mer (1877) and bears the name of one of the village's most illustrious citizens, Captain J. E. Bernier (1852-1934). Bernier was one of the first individuals to explore the Arctic, thus securing Canadian sovereignty in the Far North.

JOSEPH-ELZÉAR BERNIER

Joseph-Elzéar Bernier, one of Québec's most famous sailors, was born in 1852 into a long line of captains, in the lovely village of L'Islet-sur-Mer. In 1869, at the age of 17, Joseph-Elzéar was named captain of a ship called the *Saint-Joseph*, previously piloted by his father, making him the youngest captain in the world. During the years that followed, he navigated all of the oceans and seas on Earth, setting speed records along the way.

Joseph-Elzéar Bernier

National Archives of Canada / PA-100441

In 1904 he made the first of his exploratory voyages to the Arctic Ocean, financed by the Canadian government. A plaque on the Melville Peninsula in the Northwest Territories commemorates his crowning achievement, the appropriation of this Arctic territory in the name of the government of Canada. Bernier then returned to commercial navigation in the Arctic and on the St. Lawrence River. Until his death, at the age of 82, he maintained a close relationship with the sea.

II. Saint-Jean-Port-Joli ★

Saint-Jean-Port-Joli has become synonymous with handicrafts, specifically wood carving. The origins of this tradition go back to the Bourgault family, which made its living carving wood in the early 20th century. The village is also known for its church, and for Philippe Aubert de Gaspé's novel *Les Anciens Canadiens* (*Canadians of Old*), written at the seigneurial manor.

The charming **Église Saint-Jean-Baptiste ★ ★**, built between 1779 and 1781, is recognizable by its bright red roof topped by two steeples, placed in a way altogether uncommon in Québec architecture: one at the front, the other at the back where the apse begins. The church has a remarkable interior made of carved, gilded wood.

12. Saint-Roch-des-Aulnaies ★★

Saint-Roch-des-Aulnaies, a lovely village on the shores of the St. Lawrence River, is actually two collections of homes. The one that includes the church is called Saint-Roch-des-Aulnaies, while the second, close to the manor house, is known as the village of Aulnaies. The area is so– named because of the abundance of alder trees along the Rivière Ferrée, which powers the seigneurial mill.

The **Seigneurie des Aulnaies ★★**. The Dionne estate was transformed into a wonderful interpretive centre on the seigneurial system. Visitors enter first through the miller's former residence, now a boutique and café. Cookies and muffins made from flour milled on site are served. The stone mill was constructed in 1842, and replaced an older pre-exiting mill.

LA BEAUCE ★

13. Sainte-Marie

The **Église Sainte-Marie ★**. Sainte-Marie's town centre lies right on the Chaudière river, periodically putting it at the mercy of strong spring floods that inundate homes and businesses year in, year out. At a slight angle from Rue Notre-Dame is this stately Gothic Revival-style Catholic church designed by Charles Baillargé in 1856.

14. Saint-Joseph-de-Beauce ★

Saint-Joseph is renowned for its extremely well-preserved group of religious buildings erected at the end of the 19th century on a hillock a good distance from the river, safe from floods.

The **Musée Marius-Barbeau ★** focuses on the history of the Beauce region and explains the different stages of development in the Vallée de la Chaudière, from the first seigneuries, through the 19th-century

The Seigneurie des Aulnaies   Émilius Papus

gold rush, to the building of major communication routes. The arts and popular traditions studied by Beauceron ethnologist and folklorist Marius Barbeau are also prominently displayed.

15. Saint-Georges

Divided into Saint-Georges-Ouest and Saint-Georges-Est, on either side of the Rivière Chaudière, this industrial capital of the Beauce region is reminiscent of a New England manufacturing town. Today, Saint-Georges is a sprawling city. Though the outskirts are somewhat grim, there are a few treasures nestled in the centre of town.

The **Église Saint-Georges ★★** stands on a promontory overlooking the Rivière Chaudière. Begun in 1900, it is unquestionably Québec City architect David Ouellet's masterpiece. The art of the Belle Époque is beautifully represented here by the central steeple towering 75m and the magnificent three-level interior, which has been lavishly sculpted and gilded.

Raccoon
(next page)
Société Touristique des Autochtones du Québec (STAQ), Michel G. Maillard

CÔTE-NORD

Fred Klus, Sépaq

Rorquals in Parc National du Saguenay

Manicouagan

Bordering the St. Lawrence

The St. Lawrence, as vast as the sea   Gilles Lapointe

River for some 300km, the Manicouagan region extends north into the Laurentian plateau to include the Monts Groulx and the Réservoir Manicouagan, and along with the Duplessis region forms what is called the Côte-Nord or north shore.

Covered by thick boreal forest, Manicouagan also has an extensive river system that powers the eight generating stations of the Manic-Outardes hydroelectric complex. One of the region's main attractions is the Saguenay– St. Lawrence Marine Park, where a variety of whale species can be spotted during the summer months.

Historically, the Côte-Nord was an area common to Inuit and various other Aboriginal peoples, mainly because of its huge river system and sea-mammal-hunting potential. Before the "discovery" of Canada by Jacques Cartier in 1534, the region was visited by Basque and Breton fishers hunting for highly valued whale blubber that was melted down on the shore in large ovens. The blubber was later used to make candles and ointments.

J.F. Bergeron, Sépaq

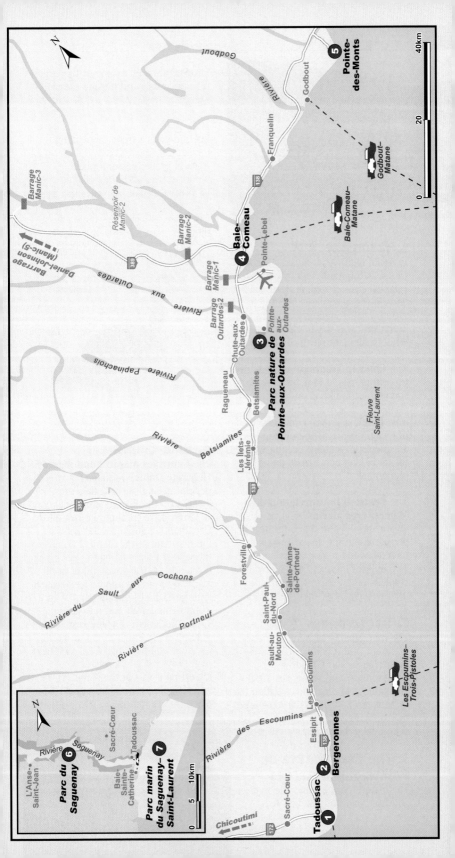

The Hôtel Tadoussac

Municipalité de Tadoussac

1. Tadoussac ★★

In 1600, eight years before Québec City was founded, Tadoussac was established as a trading post; it was chosen for its strategic location at the mouth of the Saguenay river. In fact, Tadoussac was the first permanent white settlement north of Mexico.

The **Chauvin Trading Post** ★ is open to visitors; take a look around this squared-log building and try to imagine a time when this was the only building on the continent lived in by Europeans. The building houses an interesting exhibit dealing with the fur trade between France and the Montagnais.

The **Centre d'Interprétation des Mammifères Marins** ★ is an information centre that educates people about the sea mammals that migrate to the region every summer. The bulk of the exhibit deals with whales and attempts to take some of the mystery out of their behaviour.

2. Bergeronnes ★

The municipality of Bergeronnes is made up of the hamlets of Petites-Bergeronnes and Grandes-Bergeronnes, and is the site of an archaeological dig. Knives dating back to between 200 and 1100 AD—used by Aboriginals to cut seal and whale skins—have been uncovered here.

3. The Parc Nature de Pointe-aux-Outardes ★

This nature park follows the river and has beautiful beaches. It is

known primarily as one of the largest bird migration and nesting sites in Québec.

More than 200 species of birds have been identified here. Depending on the season, snow geese, ducks, Canada geese, passeriformes, woodpeckers and birds of prey can be observed. The saltwater marsh is one of the most remarkable in the St. Lawrence estuary. This huge natural filtration plant of sorts attracts seabirds, fish, insects and small mammals.

Canada goose

4. Baie-Comeau

The **Centrales Manic 2 and Manic 5 (Barrage Daniel-Johnson)** ★★★ generating stations and dam are located on the Rivière Manicouagan. A 30min drive through the beautiful Canadian Shield landscape leads to the first dam in the Manic 2 complex, the largest hollow-joint gravity dam in the world. A 3hr drive farther north leads to the more impressive Manic 5 and the Daniel-Johnson dam. With a 214m central arch and measuring 1,314m in length, it is the largest multiple-arch structure in the world. As the accompanying poem (see next page) says, "if you knew how lonesome it was at the Manic, you would write to me more often", this place is very remote.

Manic-5 at night

ATR Manicouagan

DANIEL JOHNSON DAM: MANIC V

Si tu savais comme on s'ennuie
À la Manic
Tu m'écrirais bien plus souvent
À la Manicouagan

Extract from "*La Manic*" 1966
Georges Dor

Daniel-Johnson Dam   ATR Manicouagan

Harnessing the Rivière
Manicouagan, Manic V, along with the Daniel Johnson Dam, located
200km from Baie Comeau, is the most powerful hydroelectric
power station in the Côte-Nord region, capable of generating 1,528
MW of hydroelectric power. This monolith, the building of which
started in 1960, is the most remarkable of its kind in Québec. Its
reservoir is twice the size of Lac Saint-Jean, and ranks as the sixth-
largest in the world.

Geophysicists claim that their study of the reservoir proves the
hypothesis that the crater from which it was created was formed by
the impact some 200-million years ago of a meteorite measuring
more than 5km in diameter.

Parc National du Saguenay   J.F. Bergeron, Sépaq

TADOUSSAC AND ITS WHALES

While the St. Lawrence River flows from the Great Lakes into the Atlantic, deep underwater currents also flow in the opposite direction in the Lower Estuary. As such, an underwater corridor that originates in the Gulf of St. Lawrence runs along the river's north shore and ends in a cul-de-sac at Tadoussac. In this corridor known as the Laurentian Channel, cold salt water flows upstream, carrying with it an abundance of plankton that then gets trapped at the mouth of the Saguenay, attracting fish that in turn create a toothsome buffet for whales.

According to scientists, the St. Lawrence is one of the world's top whale-watching spots. The river's rich waters accommodate 13 species, from small, common porpoises to great blue whales. It is also the southernmost habitat of beluga whales.

5. Pointe-des-Monts ★
Here, the river widens to resemble an ocean. Winds continuously buffet the coastal towns located farther and farther apart as you travel eastward.

6. Parc National du Saguenay ★★★
Parc National du Saguenay, a provincial park, is located along the St. Lawrence between Tadoussac and Baie des Ha!-Ha!. The park has three hiking trails that wind through the hilly countryside: the Fjord trail, the Colline de l'Anse à l'Eau trail and the Pointe de l'Islet trail. The last of these offers a magnificent view of the St. Lawrence.

7. Saguenay–St. Lawrence Marine Park ★★★
The **Saguenay–St. Lawrence Marine Park** features the Fjord du Saguenay, the southernmost fjord in the northern hemisphere, and part of the estuary of the St. Lawrence. The park was created to protect the area's exceptional aquatic wildlife.

Duplessis

This vast, remote region

The Rivière Moisie
APRM

is bordered to the south for almost 1,000km by the Gulf of St. Lawrence and to the north by Labrador. Duplessis's small population of francophones, anglophones and the Montagnais First Nation is concentrated along the St. Lawrence coast and in a few inland mining towns.

The region is far from any large urban centres, and its economy has always been based on natural resources. Aboriginals have lived in the region for thousands of years. In the 16th century, Basque and Breton fishers and whalers set up seasonal posts in the region.

The region's most celebrated son is popular Québec singer Gilles Vigneault, who has written songs that describe life in this corner of the province. From Natashquan eastward, the small towns that dot the coast are not linked to the rest of Québec by road.

Philippe Renault

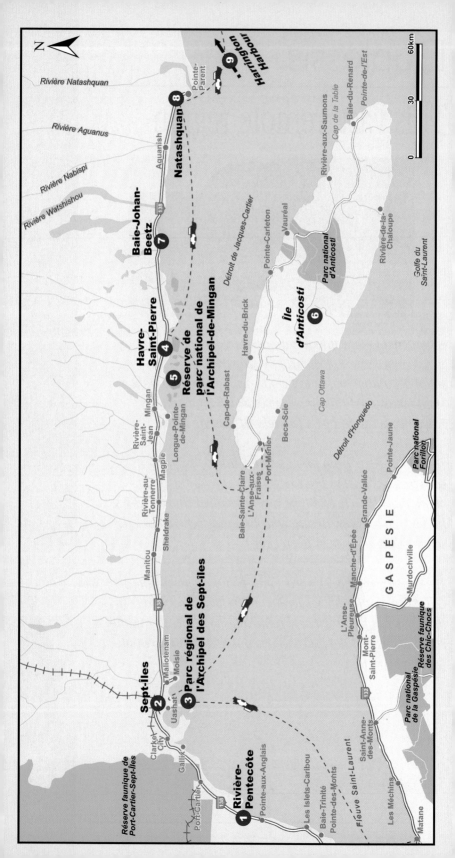

I. Rivière-Pentecôte

The British army attempted to take New France by force on several occasions. In 1711, during the Spanish Civil War, a large fleet commanded by Admiral Walker was sent from England to take Québec. However, due to fog on the St. Lawrence, the British ships ran aground on the Île-aux-Œufs reefs.

The **Musée Louis-Langlois★** features an exhibit on the shipwreck of Admiral Walker's fleet in 1711. Vestiges retrieved from the sunken ships help tell the story of this maritime catastrophe that, thankfully, was followed by many decades of peace.

2. Sept-Îles

The town of Sept-Îles is situated along the vast Baie de Sept-Îles (45km²). A fur-trading post under the French regime, Sept-Îles experienced an industrial boom in the early 20th century sparked by the development of the forestry industry.

Île au Marteau, Mingan Archipelago   ATRD - Stéphanie Élias

The **Musée Régional de la Côte-Nord ★** displays some 40,000 objects of anthropological and artistic importance found during the many archaeological excavations carried out along the Côte-Nord, as well as mounted wildlife, Aboriginal objects and contemporary artistic works (paintings, sculptures and photographs) from various regions of Québec.

3. The Parc Régional de l'Archipel des Sept Îles ★★

The **Parc Régional de l'Archipel des Sept Îles ★★** is an archipelago of several islands: Petite Boule, Grande Boule, Dequen, Manowin, Corossol, Grande Basque and Petite Basque. There is also an abundance of cod in the area, making fishing a popular activity. Trails and campsites have been set up on Île Grande Basque.

4. Havre-Saint-Pierre ★

This small picturesque town was founded in 1857 by fishers from the Îles-de-la-Madeleine. It is an excellent starting point for visitors who want to explore the Îles Mingan and the large Île d'Anticosti.

5. Mingan Archipelago National Park Reserve ★★

A series of islands and islets stretching over a 150km-long area, the **Mingan Archipelago National Park Reserve ★★** boasts incredible natural riches. The islands are characterized by distinctive rock formations, made up of very soft stratified limestone that has been sculpted by the waves.

THE CAJUNS

The inhabitants of Havre-Saint-Pierre, founded in 1857 by a handful of Acadian families from the Îles de la Madeleine who had previously been deported to Savannah, Georgia, are known as Cajuns. The term "Cajun" is a bastardization of "Acadian," shaped over time and by accent, and also designates Louisianians descended from Acadian-born French colonists.

Anticosti's white-tailed deer

ATRD - Jean-Guy Lavoie

6. Île d'Anticosti ★★

In 1895, Île d'Anticosti became the exclusive property of Henri Menier, a French chocolate tycoon. The "Cocoa Baron" introduced white-tailed deer and foxes to the island to create a personal hunting preserve. Menier governed the island like an absolute monarch reigning over his subjects.

The **Écomusée d'Anticosti** ★ displays photographs taken around the turn of the 20th century, when Menier owned Île d'Anticosti.

Measuring 222km in length and 56km in width, the **Parc National d'Anticosti** ★★, a provincial park, is big enough to accommodate a number of activities, including walking, swimming and fishing. Contributing to the magnificent scenery are breathtaking panoramas, long beaches, waterfalls, caves, cliffs, and rivers.

WHAT IS A "VIRGINIA DEER"?

Deer-watchers might be confused to see signs in French announcing the presence of *cerfs de Virginie*, or Virginia deer, in this region and others in the province. These are not exports from our southern neighbours, but rather white-tailed deer, or more specifically, and scientifically, *Odocoileus virginianus*.

Natashquan's Shoreline
ATRD - Denis Landry

ANTICOSTI, FORMER ESTATE OF HENRI MENIER

In 1895, Île d'Anticosti became the private playground of French chocolate magnate Henri Menier. The "chocolate baron" had white-tailed deer and red foxes shipped in to create a private hunting reserve for himself. He also built a first model village named Baie-Sainte-Claire (now a ghost town) and a second, Port-Menier, now the island's main settlement.

Menier ruled the island like an autocratic monarch reigning over his subjects and established a lumber company as well as a cod-fishing fleet here. In 1926, after the chocolate industry had been in a tailspin for a dozen years, Menier's heirs sold Île d'Anticosti to a consortium of Canadian logging companies, known as Wayagamack. The consortium continued its logging operations until 1974, when the Québec government purchased the island, part of which was then turned into a wildlife preserve... Only to have the selfsame government authorize logging again over two-thirds of the island in 2003 for the next 80 years, under the pretext of a development strategy to feed its 120,000 white-tailed deer!

Pointe Carleton Lighthouse on Île d'Anticosti

ATRD - Nick Gauthier

the Côte-Nord, and soon set up residence there. In 1898, he married a Canadian and built this charming Second Empire-style house, which has since been transformed into a museum and inn.

Johan Beetz contributed greatly to his neighbours' quality of life. Thanks to his university studies, he had learned the rudiments of medicine and became the man of science in whom the villagers placed their trust.

8. Natashquan ★

This small fishing village, with its wooden houses buffeted by the wind, is where the famous poet and songwriter Gilles Vigneault was born in 1928. Many of his songs describe the people and scenery of the Côte-Nord.

9. Harrington Harbour ★

Set apart by its makeshift wooden sidewalks, the modest anglophone fishing village of Harrington Harbour is located on a small island. The rocky terrain ruled out a conventional village layout, leading inhabitants to link their houses by slightly elevated wooden footbridges.

To get a taste of what you'll find here, check out the film *La Grande Séduction* or in English *Seducing Dr. Lewis* by Jean-François Pouliot, one of Québec cinema's 2003 successes and filmed in Harrington Harbour.

7. Baie-Johan-Beetz ★

The **Maison Johan-Beetz** ★ was the Canadian home of Johan Beetz, who was born in 1874 at the Oudenhouven castle in Brabant, Belgium. Grief-stricken over the death of his fiancée, he wanted to take off for the Congo, but a friend convinced him to emigrate to Canada instead. A hunting and fishing fanatic, he visited

GASPÉSIE

Patrick Escudero

Northern gannet

Gaspésie

A vast, mythical peninsula,

Gaspésie holds a cherished place in the memories of Quebecers and others as a favourite vacation spot. The shoreline of this easternmost part of Québec is washed by the waters of Baie des Chaleurs, the St. Lawrence River and the Gulf of St. Lawrence.

People dream of touring Gaspésie and discovering its magnificent coastal landscape, where the Chic-Choc mountains plunge abruptly into the cold waters of the St. Lawrence. They dream of going all the way to the famous Percé rock, heading out to sea toward Île Bonaventure, visiting the extraordinary Forillon National Park, and then slowly returning along Baie des Chaleurs and through the valley of Rivière Matapédia in the hinterland. This exceptional part of Québec, with its strikingly picturesque scenery, is inhabited by friendly, fascinating people, who still rely mainly on the sea for their living. The majority of Gaspesians live in small villages along the coast, leaving the centre of the peninsula covered with dense Boreal forest. The highest peak in southern Québec lies here, in the part of the Appalachians known as the Chic-Chocs.

The word Gaspé means "land's end" in the language of the Micmacs, who have been living in this region for thousands of years. Despite its isolation, the peninsula has attracted fishers from many different places over the centuries, particularly Acadians driven from their lands by the British in 1755. Its population is now primarily francophone.

Gaspésie's main attractions are its rugged, mountainous landscapes and the Gulf of St. Lawrence, which is so huge here that it might as well be the ocean. The coastline is studded with fishing villages, leaving the interior devoid of towns and roads, much as it was when Jacques Cartier arrived in 1534.

Patrick Escudero

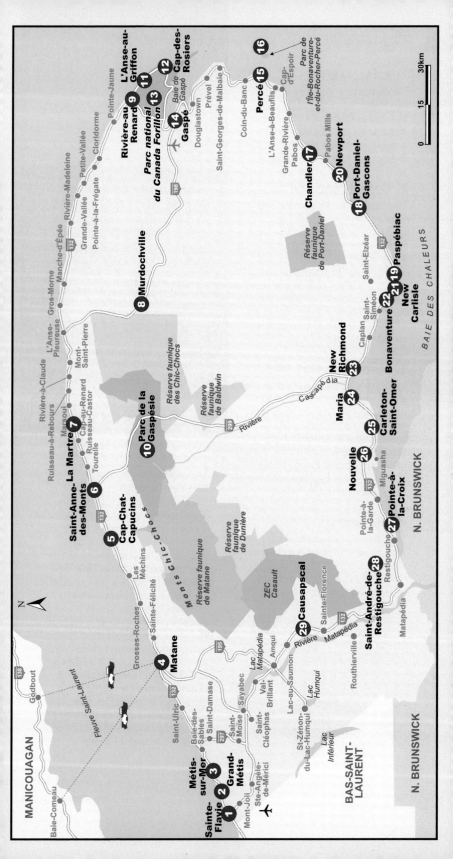

1. Sainte-Flavie

Nicknamed the gateway to Gaspésie, the village of Sainte-Flavie was founded in 1829. It owes its name to the Siegneuresse Angélique-Flavie Drapeau, daughter of Seigneur Joseph Drapeau.

2. Grand-Métis ★★

The **Jardins de Métis / Reford Gardens ★★★** are among Québec's most beautiful gardens, and their name is world-renowned. The gardens are also a national historic site. They are now owned by the grandson of their founder, Alexander Reford, who has infused them with new energy, thanks to achievements like the International Garden Festival.

3. Métis-sur-Mer ★

At the turn of the 20th century, this resort area, also known as Métis Beach, was a favourite among the professors of Montréal's McGill University, who rented elegant seaside cottages here for the summer vacation. Wealthy British families also built large New England–style homes in the area.

4. Matane

The main attractions in Matane, whose name means "Beaver Pond" in Micmac, are the salmon and the famous local shrimp, which are celebrated at an annual festival. The town is the region's administrative centre and economic mainspring, due to its diversified industry base of fishing, lumber, cement-making, oil refining and shipping.

Salmon

Fireweed   Patrick Escudero

5. Cap-Chat

Baie des Capucins is rich in flora and fauna (in particular birds) typical of saltwater marshes. This is actually the only saltwater marsh in the area. A lovely walk follows the bay's shoreline. The **Centre d'Interprétation de la Baie-des-Capucins** presents a small exhibit on the bay's natural environment.

The village of Cap-Chat is an ideal location for the production of wind energy and its many turbines create a somewhat supernatural landscape. The **Centre d'Interprétation de l'Énergie Éolienne (Éole) ★** is home to a 110m-high turbine, the tallest and strongest in the world, as well as the largest concentration of turbines in eastern Canada.

Windmill park in Cap-Chat
Patrick Escudero

GASPÉ IN THE WIND

The Gaspé has great wind-energy potential. Following the construction of a windmill park in Cap-Chat-Matane, new plans for wind-power-generation centres have landed on the drawing tables of engineering firms. Wind turbines have therefore been set up in the small village of Rivière-au-Renard and in the region of Murdochville, a former mining town. The 100-MW Le Nordais project in Cap-Chat-Matane boasts 133 wind turbines, making it the biggest windmill park in Canada.

To satisfy public curiosity, the town of Cap-Chat has built the Centre d'Interprétation de l'Énergie Éolienne (Éole). The centre reveals the secrets of Eole, the world's tallest vertical-axis windmill (110m), and of the one-of-a-kind Le Nordais windmill park.

6. Sainte-Anne-des-Monts ★

There are several interesting buildings in this town, including Église Sainte-Anne built by Louis-Napoléon Audet in 1939, and the former Palais de Justice (courthouse), now the Hôtel de Ville (town hall), erected in 1885. Visitors will also find a number of lovely homes, built for various ship captains and industrialists.

7. La Martre ★★

With its **wooden church** (1914) and **lighthouse** (1906), La Martre is a typical fishing village, located on the edge of the coastal plain. Beyond this point, the coast becomes much steeper and more jagged. The road zigzags into deep bays and out onto windswept capes.

8. Murdochville

Murdochville is located in the middle of the forest, 40km from civilization. It dates back only to 1951, when a company named Gaspésie Mines decided to mine the extensive copper deposits in this isolated region. Unfortunately, a sad page in the history of the town was written in 2000, when the mine was closed.

Nevertheless, visitors can still take in the **Centre d'Interprétation du Cuivre ★**, an unusual experience because visitors are required to don a miner's uniform supplied by the centre before heading into a real underground gallery. The objects on display illustrate the history of copper mining and the techniques involved in extracting the metal from the earth.

9. Rivière-au-Renard

The fish-processing centre (cleaning, preparing, canning) of Rivière-au-Renard is dominated by its factories. Its fishing port is the largest on the north shore of the Gaspé peninsula.

10. Parc National de la Gaspésie ★★★

Parc National de la Gaspésie, a provincial park, covers an area of 800km² and encompasses the famous Monts Chic-Chocs. It was established in 1937 in an effort to heighten public awareness regarding nature conservation in Gaspésie. The park is composed of conservation zones devoted to the protection of the region's natural riches, and an ambient zone, made up of a network of roads, trails and lodgings.

11. L'Anse-au-Griffon ★

Starting after the British conquest of New France in 1760, a small group of Anglo-Norman merchants from the Isle of Jersey took control of commercial fishing in Gaspésie. One of these individuals, John LeBoutillier, built warehouses for salt, flour and dried cod in L'Anse-au-Griffon around 1840, and then began exporting cod to Spain, Italy and Brazil.

12. Cap-des-Rosiers ★

Located in a magnificent setting, Cap-des-Rosiers has been the scene of many shipwrecks. Two monuments have been erected in memory of one in particular—that of the sailing ship *Karrik*, which claimed the lives of 87 of the 200 or so Irish immigrants aboard. The victims were buried in the local cemetery, while most of the survivors settled in Cap-des-Rosiers, giving the community a surprising new character.

Pic de l'Aube in Parc National de la Gaspésie
Jean-Pierre Huard, Sépaq

THE CHIC-CHOCS: QUÉBEC'S ROCKY MOUNTAINS

The Chic-Choc mountains derive their name from the Micmac word *sigsôg*, meaning "sheer cliffs" or "rocky mountains." Contrary to popular belief, the Gaspesian massif, formed by a high, narrow plateau, does not constitute the northernmost tip of the North American Appalachian range, which straddles the Gulf of St. Lawrence, but rather the Long Range Mountains, on the island of Newfoundland.

Inaccessible mountains, according to First Nations peoples of centuries past, the Chic-Chocs remain hard to reach and harbour very particular ecosystems. The loftiest part of the Appalachians in Québec—named here the Notre Dame Mountains—extend from the Canada-U.S. border in the Eastern Townships.

13. Forillon National Park ★★★

The motto of Forillon National Park is "harmony between man, land and sea." Many an outdoor enthusiast dreams about this series of forests, mountains and cliff-lined shores all crisscrossed by hiking trails. Home to a fairly wide range of animals, this federal park abounds in foxes, bears, moose, porcupines and other mammals.

14. Gaspé ★

It was here that Jacques Cartier claimed Canada for King Francis I of France in early July, 1534. However, it was not until the beginning of the 18th century that the first fishing post was established in Gaspé, and the town itself did not develop until the end of that century.

15. Percé ★★

A famous tourist destination, Percé lies in a beautiful setting, which has unfortunately been somewhat marred by the booming hotel industry. The majestic scenery features several natural phenomena, the most important being the famous Rocher Percé, which is to Québec what the Sugar Loaf is to Brazil.

The **Centre d'Interprétation du Parc National de l'Île-Bonaventure-et-du-Rocher-Percé** shows a short film on the history of Île Bonaventure and the gannets that nest there. Visitors will also find an exhibition area, saltwater aquariums and two short footpaths.

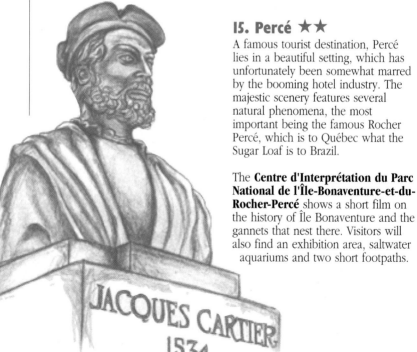

JACQUES CARTIER
1534

Seaside house in Forillon National Park

Patrick Escudero

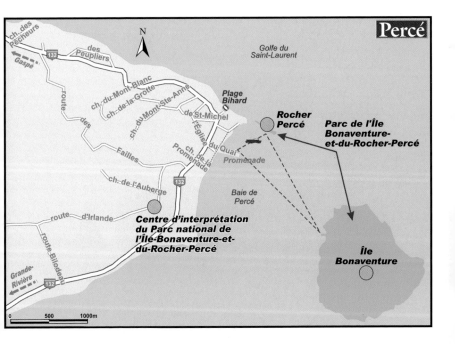

Percé

ch. des Pêcheurs

Gaspé

132

des Peupliers

route des

ch.-du-Mont-Blanc

ch.-de-la-Grotte

ch.-du-Mont-Ste-Anne

de-St-Michel

Failles

ch.-de-l'Auberge

ch. de la Promenade

Église du Quai

132

route d'Irlande

route Biodeau

Grande-Rivière

132

Golfe du Saint-Laurent

N

Plage Bihard

Rocher Percé

Parc de l'Île Bonaventure-et-du-Rocher-Percé

Promenade

Baie de Percé

Centre d'interprétation du Parc national de l'Île-Bonaventure-et-du-Rocher-Percé

Île Bonaventure

0   500   1000m

ROCHER PERCÉ

As its French name indicates, Rocher Percé consists of a pierced arch-shaped rock, for which it is world-famous, at least since the advent of photography. This huge monolith has always been a source of fascination, but will likely never reveal all its secrets, there being a few gaps in the story of its geomorphologic evolution with regard to the number of arches—and holes—it has had between the 16th and 19th centuries.

When Jacques Cartier first laid eyes on it in the 16th century, Rocher Percé was probably on terra firma—in Mont Joli— appearing as a cape jutting out into the sea rather than a mammoth rock sitting just offshore. However, Samuel de Champlain, who encountered it in 1603, noted the following in his journal: "We came upon Percé Island, which is like a very tall rock, with high sides and an archway through which boats and ships can pass from the high seas." Then, in the late 17th century, Father Leclerq referred to the "three or four arches of Percé Island." In the 19th century, Rocher Percé did indeed feature two arches—and two holes—the neighbouring obelisk being a result of the collapse of the second arch, which occurred in 1845.

More recently, Rocher Percé has lost 100 tonnes of rock due to torrential rains, and its hole has grown. But weighing in at four million tonnes, it should be able to withstand several more millennia!

Sunrise at the Rocher Percé

Philippe Renault

16. Parc National de l'Île-Bonaventure-et-du-Rocher-Percé ★★★

Upon arriving in Percé, visitors are greeted by the arresting sight of the famous **Rocher Percé ★★★**, a wall of rock measuring 400m in length and 88m in height at its tallest point. Its name, which translates as pierced rock, comes from the two entirely natural arched openings at its base. Only one of these openings remains today, since the eastern part of the rock collapsed in the mid-19th century.

Île Bonaventure ★★ harbours large bird colonies and a handful of rustic houses along its many hiking trails. In this exceptional bird reserve, some 200,000 birds, including **55,000 gannets**, constitute a veritable wildlife exhibit.

Parc National de l'Île-Bonaventure-et-du-Rocher-Percé
Jean-Pierre Huard, Sépaq

In 1977, upon the initiative of the local historical society, the **Musée de la Gaspésie ★★** was erected on Pointe Jacques Cartier, overlooking Baie de Gaspé. A museum of history and popular tradition, it houses a permanent exhibit entitled *Un Peuple de la Mer* (A People of the Sea), tracing life in Gaspésie from the first Aboriginal inhabitants, members of the Micmac nation, all the way up to the present day.

Northern gannets

LA BOLDUC

Il y en a qui sont jaloux
Ils veulent me mettr' des bois
dans les roues
Je vous dis tant que je vivrai
J' dirai toujours moé pis toé
Je parle comme l'ancien temps
J'ai pas honte de mes vieux
parents
Pourvu que j' mets pas d'anglais
Je nuis pas au bon parler français!

Excerpt from "La Chanson du
Bavard," 1931

Mary Travers

The songs, or *turlutes*, of Mary
Travers, better known as "La
Bolduc," stood out from those
of other folk musicians of the

Marie Travers, a.k.a. La Bolduc

National Library of Canada/
Fonds Philippe-Laframboise/MUS 281

time. Of Scottish and Irish inspiration, *turlutes* are reminiscent of the
refrains of traditional Irish or English songs. La Bolduc used her voice
as an instrument, creating refrains from vocables and using a
technique that dates back to the old ballads of the British Isles. This
is what is known in Scottish music as "mouth music," which is
frequently improvised, much like scat singing in jazz. Bolduc's
turlutage often replaced harmonica solos between verses, or vice
versa, especially in lively Scottish dances known as reels.

17. Chandler

The industrial city of Chandler is
dominated by the facilities of the
Gaspésia paper mill. The deepwater
port allows for the export of
newsprint used in the production of
the biggest daily newspapers in
Europe and the Americas.

18. Port-Daniel-Gascons

Besides offering a beautiful sandy
beach ideal for swimmers, Port-
Daniel-Gascons is home to a few
interesting buildings, including the
St. James Anglican Church, from
1907, and its presbytery, from 1912,
adorned with an octagonal tower and
large wooden balconies like those in
seaside villages along the east coast of
the United States.

Île Bonaventure
Patrick Escudero

19. Paspébiac

This little industrial town used to be the headquarters of the Robin company, which specialized in processing and exporting cod. The business was founded in 1766 by Charles Robin, a merchant from the Isle of Jersey.

The **Site Historique du Banc-de-Pêche-de-Paspébiac ★ ★**. A *banc* is a strip of sand and gravel used for drying fish. Paspébiac's *banc*, along with the town's deep, well-protected natural port, lent itself to the development of a fishing industry. In 1964, there were still some 70 buildings from the Robin and LeBoutillier companies on the *banc*. The eight surviving buildings have been carefully restored in this historic site and are open to the public.

20. Newport

Newport is a large commercial fishing port. This is also the birthplace of Marie Travers (1894-1941), renowned writer, composer and singer, better known as **La Bolduc**.

21. New Carlisle ★

The New Carlisle region was settled by American Loyalists, who came here after the 1783 signing of the Treaty of Versailles, under which Great Britain recognized the independence of the United States. A visit to New Carlisle wouldn't be complete without a tour of its three **Protestant churches ★**, which are a great source of pride to the villagers.

22. Bonaventure ★

This village at the mouth of the Rivière Bonaventure (one of the best salmon rivers in North America) was founded by Acadians taking refuge at the mouth of the Rivière Bonaventure (one of the best salmon rivers in North America) after Restigouche fell to the British in 1760. Today, Bonaventure is a bastion of Acadian culture in the Baie des Chaleurs area, as well as being home to a small seaside resort with a sandy beach and a deep water port. An estimated one million Quebecers are of Acadian descent. The **Musée Acadien du Québec ★** recounts the odyssey of Acadians living in Québec and elsewhere in North America.

ACADIANS

The odyssey of the Acadian people began in what would later become Nova Scotia, one of Canada's Atlantic Provinces. In 1605, a year after their arrival in North America, Pierre du Gua, Sieur de Monts, Samuel de Champlain and a few dozen men chose a site at the mouth of the Annapolis River on which to found Port-Royal, the first permanent settlement north of Florida. Port-Royal would be at the heart of Acadia's development until 1755, when the Acadians were forced into exile.

23. New Richmond
The first English colonists in Gaspésie settled here after the Conquest of 1760. They were soon joined by Loyalists, and then Irish and Scottish immigrants.

Located on Pointe Duthie, on your way into the village, the **Village Gaspésien d'Héritage Britannique** ★ is made up of buildings from the Baie des Chaleurs area, which were saved from demolition and transported to the grounds of the former Carswell estate.

24. Maria
Before reaching Carleton-Saint-Omer, you will cross the Rivière Cascapédia, at the mouth of which lies the village of Maria and the **Gesgapegiag Native Reserve**, with its tepee-shaped church.

25. Carleton-Saint-Omer ★
Carleton, like Bonaventure, is a stronghold of Acadian culture in Québec, and a seaside resort with a lovely sandy beach washed by calm waters that are warmer than elsewhere in Gaspésie and account for the name of the bay (*chaleur* means warmth). The mountains rising up behind the town give it a distinctive character.

26. Nouvelle
Palaeontology buffs will surely be interested in **Parc de Miguasha** ★★, a UNESCO World Heritage Site, and the second-largest fossil site in the world.

27. Pointe-à-la-Croix
On April 10, 1760, a French fleet set off from Bordeaux on its way to Canada, with the goal of liberating New France from the English. Only three ships reached Baie des Chaleurs, the others having fallen victim to English cannons as they headed out of the Gironde. The *Machault, Bienfaisant* and *Marquis-de-Malauze*, vessels weighing an

average of 350 tonnes, survived, but the English troops caught up with the French at the mouth of the Restigouche in Baie des Chaleurs. A battle broke out, and the English defeated the French fleet within a few hours.

At the **Battle of Restigouche National Historic Site** ★, visitors can see a collection of objects recovered from the wreckage of the battle between these ships, as well as a few pieces of the frigate *Machault*. An interesting audiovisual presentation illustrates the different stages of the confrontation.

Between Pointe-à-la-Croix and Restigouche, there is a bridge that stretches across Baie des Chaleurs, linking Québec to New Brunswick.

28. Saint-André-de-Restigouche

The Micmac village of Saint-André-de-Restigouche lies just north of the Matapédia and is the centre of the largest native reserve in Gaspésie. Many relics from the battle of Restigouche can be found here, as well as in **Matapédia**.

29. Causapscal

The Matapédia, one of the best salmon rivers in North America, flows through the centre of Causapscal with its towering sawmills. Every year, fans of sport fishing come to the area.

Site Historique Matamajaw ★. In 1873, Donald Smith, the future Lord Mount Stephen, acquired the fishing rights to the Matapédia. A few years later, he sold the rights to the Matamajaw Salmon Club. The club stopped operating around 1950; in 1984 the buildings on the Matamajaw property were listed as historic monuments and opened to the public.

Vallée de la Matapédia   Patrick Escudro

To fully appreciate the landscape of waterfalls, rapids and cliffs you will need to explore the surroundings along the secondary roads. Before **Amqui**, there is a covered bridge dating from 1931. Further along, in **Saint-Moise**, stands the most original church in Gaspésie. Built in 1914 according to plans by Bishop Georges Bouillon, its styling is Romano-Byzantine with a polygonal plan.

Sheep

House at the entrance to Forillon National Park
(next page)
Patrick Escudro

ÎLES DE LA MADELEINE

One of the islands' many lighthouses.

Îles de la Madeleine

Rising from the Gulf

of St. Lawrence more than 200km from the Gaspé Peninsula, the Îles de la Madeleine (sometimes referred to in English as the Magdalen Islands) constitute a 65km-long archipelago of about a dozen islands, many connected to one another by long sand dunes. Swept by winds from the open sea, these small islands offer superb, colourful scenery. The golden dunes and the long, untouched beaches blend with the red sandstone cliffs and the blue sea. Villages with brightly painted houses, lighthouses and harbours add the finishing touches to the islands' beautiful scenery.

The Îles de la Madeleine archipelago was first inhabited sporadically by Micmac peoples, also called the "Indians of the Sea." As of the 15th century, the islands were visited regularly by walrus and seal hunters, fishers and whalers, most of Breton or Basque descent. In 1534, Jacques Cartier came upon the islands during his first North American expedition. Permanent settlers did not arrive until after 1755, when Acadian families took refuge here after having escaped deportation. Following the British conquest, the Îles de la Madeleine were annexed to Newfoundland before being integrated into Québec territory in 1774. A few years later, in 1798, King George III granted Admiral Isaac Coffin the title of seigneur of the Îles de la Madeleine, ushering in a dismal period for the inhabitants of the archipelago. He and his family ruled the land despotically until 1895, when a Québec law allowed the Madelinots to buy back their land.

Tourisme Îles de la Madeleine

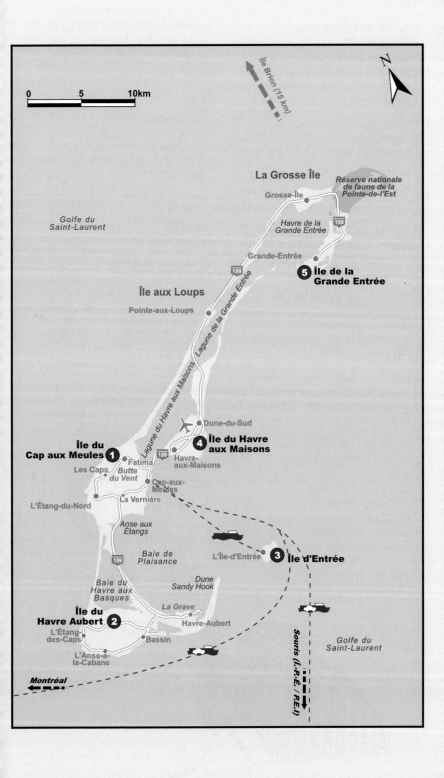

I. Île du Cap aux Meules ★

Cap-aux-Meules, the only urban centre of the archipelago, has experienced major development over the past few years. Since many buildings were constructed quickly, aesthetics were not a primary consideration. A few of the traditional houses still stand.

A climb to the top of the **Butte du Vent** ★★ reveals a superb panorama of the island and the gulf.

The beautiful **Chemin de Gros-Cap** ★★, south of Cap-aux-Meules, runs along the Baie de Plaisance and offers breathtaking scenery.

The imposing **Église de La Vernière** ★ lies next to the road with its interesting wooden construction and design; it has been classified as a historic monument.

North of L'Étang-du-Nord, visitors can take in the splendid view by walking along the magnificent **Falaises de La Belle Anse** ★★. The violent waves crashing relentlessly along the coast are an impressive sight from the top of this rocky escarpment.

2. Île du Havre Aubert ★★★

Beautiful Île du Havre Aubert, dotted with beaches, hills and forests, has managed to keep its picturesque charm. From early on it was home to various colonies. Even today, buildings testify to these early colonial years. Prior to this, it was populated by Micmac communities, and relics have been discovered.

Havre-Aubert, the first stop on the island, stretches along the sea and benefits from a large bay ideal for fishing. Apart from the magnificent scenery, the most interesting attraction is without a doubt the **La Grave** ★★★ area, which developed along a pebbly beach.

For anyone interested in the fascinating world of marine life, the **Aquarium des Îles** ★ is a real treat. Here, visitors can observe (and even touch) many different marine species, such as lobsters, crabs, sea urchins, eels, a ray, as well as a multitude of other fish and crustaceans.

The **Musée de la Mer** ★ recounts the history of the settlement of the islands as well as the relationship that links Madelinots to the sea. Visitors also have the opportunity to explore the world of fishing and navigation, as well as discover some of the myths and legends that surround the sea.

Like a long strip of sand stretching into the gulf, **Sandy Hook Dune** ★★★ is several kilometres long and its beach is among the nicest on the islands.

The road that runs along the sea between the Pointe à Marichite and L'Étang-des-Caps offers a **magnificent view** ★★ of the Gulf of St. Lawrence.

3. Île d'Entrée ★★

Île d'Entrée differs from the rest of the islands not only because of its geographic location (it is the only inhabited island that is not linked to the others), but also because of its population of some 200 residents, all of Scottish descent.

Fishing boats at rest
Philippe Renault

MADELEINE OF THE ISLANDS

Although Samuel de Champlain sailed past the Îles de la Madeleine in 1608 on his way to found Quebec City, there was no attempt to colonize them until the latter half of the 17th century. Indeed, it was not until 1663 that François Doublet was granted permission by the Compagnie de la Nouvelle-France to establish a colony on the islands. He then sailed there with two ships and everything required to fish, farm the land and build houses, with his crewmen as well as 25 military volunteers in tow.

On his arrival, Doublet encountered some 20 Basques who had already settled on the islands. He returned to France, leaving about 20 men behind. On his return, in the summer of 1664, he found the settlement in ruins. He then made his way to Percé, in the Gaspé, where he learned that his men had spent the better part of the winter drinking and carousing and, once provisions were exhausted, had robbed the Basques and set off for Québec City. This attempt at colonization was a failure, but Sieur Doublet nonetheless named the islands after his wife, Madeleine Fontaine.

THE "WHITECOATS"

The symbol of ecotourism in the Îles de la Madeleine, the "whitecoat" is the Greenland seal pup known to Madelinots as the "sea wolf." Indeed, Greenland seals give birth on the ice floes of the Îles de la Madeleine, after a long annual migration down the coast of Labrador and into the Gulf of St. Lawrence.

Come March, thousands of these little bundles of white fur, which moved the whole world in the 1970s when animal-rights activists—led by former French actress Brigitte Bardot—protested against the seal hunt, are born. Greenland seal pups do not venture into the water until they are about six weeks old, making them easy to observe. Sea-wolf meat, which is dark in colour, is considered a delicacy and even canned and sold in the islands.

A mother seal and her pup

Tourisme Îles-de-la-Madeleine

4. Île du Havre aux Maisons ★★

Île du Havre aux Maisons is characterized by its bare landscape and its small, attractive villages with pretty little houses scattered along the winding roads. The steep cliffs at the southern end of the island overlook the gulf and offer a fascinating view of this immense stretch of water.

5. Île de la Grande Entrée ★

Île de la Grande Entrée, colonized in 1870, was the last of the Îles de la Madeleine to be inhabited. Upon arriving, cross Pointe-Old-Harry to check out a striking view of the gulf.

To learn more about the lives of seals, visit the **Centre d'Interprétation du Phoque** ★ where various exhibits explain the comings and goings of these mammals.

Monoliths of the Îles de la Madeleine
Philippe Renault

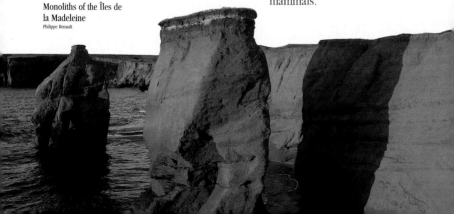

LANAUDIÈRE

Tourisme Lanaudière, Martin Savard

A mallard in full flight

Lanaudière

A peaceful region of lakes,

Saint-Donat

rivers, farmland, wild forests and huge open spaces, Lanaudière extends north of Montréal, from the plains of the St. Lawrence to the Laurentian plateau. This was one of the first colonized areas in New France, and possesses a rich architectural heritage. Though part of the region is engulfed in the urban sprawl of Montréal, you'll still find many traditions alive and well here.

For more than 25 years the region has hosted an important event: the Festival International de Lanaudière. Music-lovers from across Québec converge here for classical and popular music concerts performed by artists from around the globe. The city of Joliette is also home to one of Québec's most interesting regional museums, with an impressive collection of Québec art including many pieces of religious art.

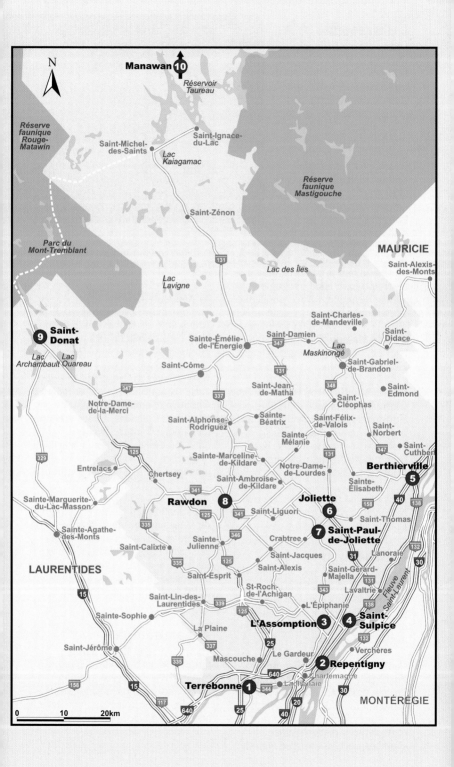

1. Terrebonne ★★

Located along the banks of the rushing Rivière des Mille-Îles, this municipality gets its name from the fertile soil (*terre* meaning earth, and *bonne* meaning good) from which it grew. Terrebonne is probably the best place in Québec to get an idea of what a prosperous 19th-century seigneury was really like.

Île des Moulins in Terrebonne   Tourisme Lanaudière, Luc Landry

Powerful Montréal banker Joseph Masson bought the seigneury of Terrebonne at auction in 1832, but the lean years that followed prevented him from developing it as he would have liked. His widow, Sophie Raymond, carried on his life's work, undertaking large-scale projects from 1848 on, including the imposing **Manoir Masson ★**, on Rue Saint-Louis, designed by French architect Pierre-Louis Morin.

Île des Moulins ★★ is an impressive concentration of mills and other pre-industrial equipment from the Terrebonne seigneury. Most of the buildings, located in a park, have been renovated and now serve as community and administrative buildings. Old Terrebonne, which also comprises Île des Moulins, is now protected, having been classified as a historic site.

2. Repentigny

The city of Repentigny was named after its first seigneur, Pierre Le Gardeur de Repentigny. It is pleasantly located at the confluence of the Rivière L'Assomption and the mighty St. Lawrence.

Construction of the **Église de la Purification-de-la-Bienheureuse-Vierge-Marie ★** began in 1723, making it the oldest church in the diocese of Montréal. It has many characteristics of New France churches, such as the apse with the corners cut off and the orientation of the building parallel to the river.

3. L'Assomption ★

The proximity of the carding mills in Terrebonne, as well as the frequent visits by the coureurs des bois, prompted the women of L'Assomption to design a special wool sash to be worn by French Canadians, to distinguish them from the Scottish, many of whom were employees of the Northwest Company. Hence was born the famous **ceinture fléchée** (chevron-design sash), now a symbol of Québec. L'Assomption had the monopoly on sash production from about 1805 to 1825.

The monumental facade of the **Église de L'Assomption-de-la-Sainte-Vierge ★** was designed by Victor Bourgeau (1863). The chancel was undertaken in 1819 and contains the tabernacle, the altar and the Baroque pulpit built by Urbain Brien dit Desrochers in 1834.

4. Saint-Sulpice

The present-day **Église Saint-Sulpice ★**, its third incarnation, was built in 1832, but refashioned in accordance with prevailing tastes in 1873 by Victor Bourgeau, who gave it an English gothic appearance.

LOUIS CYR, SAINT-JEAN-DE-MATHA'S ADOPTED SON

Louis Cyr, "the strongest man in the world," was born in 1863 in Napierville, in Montérégie. His family moved to the United States when he was only 10 years old, in the wake of a wave of emigration by French-Canadians to Lowell, Massachusetts. It was there that he met his wife-to-be, Mélina Comtois, a native of Saint-Jean-de-Matha who had also emigrated to the American city with her parents.

Louis Cyr

Archives nationales du Canada / C-08343

Cyr followed the Comtois family back to Québec and upon their return married Mélina in 1882 in Saint-Jean-de-Matha. Shortly thereafter, Cyr became a lumberjack and his prodigious strength increased tenfold. Throughout his short life, he challenged several of the world's strongmen and held several different jobs, including that of police officer in the old town of Sainte-Cunégonde.

Louis Cyr died of Bright's disease on his Saint-Jean-de-Matha farm at the age of 49. His body was first interred in the Notre-Dame-des-Neiges Cemetery, in Montréal, but was then repatriated to Saint-Jean-de-Matha, where he now rests alongside his wife, Mélina. A weightlifter, this modern-day Samson was recognized as an accomplished athlete by his peers throughout his life. In 2001, he was finally inducted into the Panthéon des sports du Québec (Quebec's sports hall of fame).

The town of Saint-Jean-de-Matha honoured its most celebrated resident when it opened the **Musée-Halte Louis Cyr** which recounts the strong man's history and storied life.

5. Berthierville ★

The **Église Sainte-Geneviève** ★★ is a Lanaudière treasure. Built in 1781, it is one of the oldest churches in the region. The Louis-XVI styling to the interior was designed by Amable Gauthier and Alexis Millette between 1821 and 1830. Many elements in the decor combine to make this building truly exceptional.

6. Joliette ★

At the beginning of the 19th century, notary Barthélémy Joliette (1789-1850) opened up logging camps in the northern section of the Lavaltrie seigneury, which was at the time still undeveloped land. In 1823, he founded "his" town around the saw-mills and called it "L'Industrie," a name synonymous with progress and prosperity. In 1864 it was renamed Joliette in honour of its founder.

Joliette owes its cultural vibrancy to the clerics of Saint-Viateur who established themselves here in the mid-19th century. In 1939, they undertook the construction of their new residence, the **Maison Provinciale des Clercs de Saint-Viateur ★**. The plans, by Montréal architect René Charbonneau, were inspired by a sketch done by Père Wilfrid Corbeil.

Père Wilfrid Corbeil founded the exceptional **Musée d'Art de Joliette ★ ★** with works collected during the 1940s by the clerics of Saint-Viateur that show Québec's place in the world.

7. Saint-Paul-de-Joliette

The exterior of the **Église Saint-Paul ★** has weathered the years quite well since its inauguration in 1804. Designed by Reverend Pierre Conefroy of Boucherville, architect of the famous plans that would influence church builders for 30 years, this place of worship is a typical example of Québec traditional religious architecture, austere but elegant.

8. Rawdon ★

After the Conquest of 1760, the British established a more familiar means of dividing the territory, namely the township system. The town-ships of Lanaudière were established in the foothills of the Laurentians, between the 19th-century seigneuries and the new territories opened up by the clergy after 1860.

Near Rawdon, two green spaces have been established to welcome visitors and are worth mentioning. First is the **Parc des Chutes-Dorwin ★**, with its two viewing stations offering views of the Rivière Ouareau's impressive 30-m-high falls.

The other spot of interest in the vicinity is **Parc des Cascades ★**. Located on the bank of Rivière Ouareau, which cascades prettily over the rocky riverbed here, this park includes a picnic area where sunbathers stretch out during the hot months of summer.

9. Saint-Donat ★

Minutes away from Mont-Tremblant, tucked between mountains reaching up to 900m and the shores of Lac Archambault, the small town of Saint-Donat extends east to the shores of Lac Ouareau.

10. Manawan ★

Manawan is one of three centres for the Atikamekw nation, along with Wemotaci and Obedjiwan. Certain traditional practices are still very much alive here, like the manufacture of canoes, snowshoes, moccasins and birchbark baskets.

Birchbark basket

Parc des Chutes-Dorwin, Rawdon
(page 114)

RAWDON: QUÉBEC'S LITTLE RUSSIA

Rawdon was already a multiethnic community when a handful of Russian-born Montrealers chose to set up their summer cottages here in the 1930s and '40s. Several years later, Orthodox priest Oleg Boldirev, seeking to cater to the Russians' spiritual needs, celebrated the "Divine Liturgy" in summer, in a chapel dedicated to St. Seraphim of Sarov, which he built here in 1956. A Russian cemetery was even laid out in "the Village of Sunshine" in 1962, and a skete (a monastery housing a few monks) as well as a small chapel were built on cemetery land.

In 1991, Bishop Seraphim of Ottawa and Canada (Orthodox Church in America) founded the Monastic Community of St. Seraphim of Sarov (though it only became known as such in 1999), which brings together French-speaking Canadian monks and nuns, in Rawdon. Other monks as well as Orthodox lay persons have since settled in the St. Seraphim of Sarov Orthodox Community. Services are held in French, English and Slavonic, the liturgical language of Orthodox Slavs since the Middle Ages.

Parc National du Mont-Tremblant

THE LAURENTIANS

A young fisher in Parc National d'Oka

The Laurentians

Renowned as a resort area

Parc National du Mont-Tremblant

J.P. Danguin, Sépaq

in Québec, the beautiful Laurentides region, also called the Laurentians, attracts a great many visitors all year round. For generations now, people have been "going up north" to relax and enjoy the beauty of the Laurentian landscape. The lakes, mountains and forests provide a particularly good setting for a variety of physical activities or outings. As the region boasts the highest concentration of ski resorts in North America, skiing gets top billing here when winter rolls around. The villages scattered at the foot of the mountains are both charming and friendly.

The southern part of the region, known as the Basses-Laurentides (lower Laurentians), was settled early on by French colonists, who came here to cultivate the rich farmland. A number of local villages reveal this history through their architectural heritage.

The settling of the Laurentian plateau, initiated by the now legendary Curé Labelle, began much later, toward the middle of the 19th century. The development of the Pays d'En Haut, or upper Laurentians, was part of an ambitious plan to colonize the outlying areas of Québec in an effort to counter the exodus of French Canadians to industrial towns in the north-eastern United States. Given the poor soil, farming here was hardly profitable, but Curé Labelle nevertheless succeeded in founding about 20 villages and attracting a good number of French Canadian colonists to the region.

Guillaume Pouliot

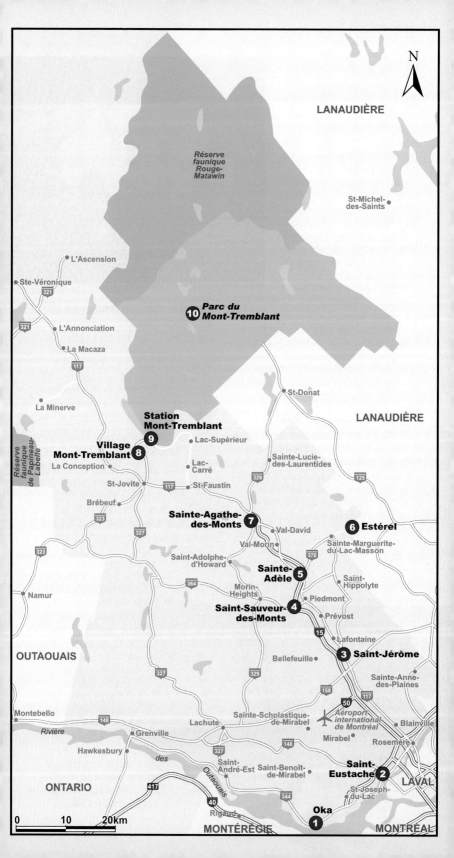

I. Oka ★

The Sulpicians, like the Jesuits, established missions in the Montréal area with the goal of converting local natives to Catholicism. The disciples of Ignatius Loyola settled permanently in Kahnawake in 1716, and those of Jean-Jacques Olier followed in their footsteps in 1721, settling on the shores of Lac des Deux-Montagnes in a lovely spot named Oka, which means "golden fish."

On the calvary trail   ATR Laurentides

At the end of the 18th century, a number of Iroquois from New York State supplanted the original Aboriginal inhabitants of the mission, giving an anglophone character and, more recently, a new name (Kanesatake) to a whole section of territory located upriver from the village.

Abbaye Cistercienne d'Oka ★. In 1881, a few Cistercian monks left the Abbaye de Bellefontaine in France to found a new abbey in Canada. The Sulpicians, who had already donated several pieces of their extensive territorial holdings in Montréal to various religious communities, granted the new arrivals a hillside in the seigneury of Deux-Montagnes.

The **Parc National d'Oka** with its **Calvaire d'Oka ★** encompasses trails for hikers in the summer (22km) and cross-country skiers (50km) in the winter. The Calvaire d'Oka trail (5.5km) guides visitors past the oldest stations of the cross in the Americas. This calvary was set up by the Sulpicians back in 1740, in an effort to stimulate the faith of Aboriginals recently converted to Catholicism. Humble and dignified at the same time, the calvary is made up of four trapezoidal oratories and three rectangular chapels built of whitewashed stone. These little buildings, now empty, once housed wooden bas-reliefs depicting the Passion of Christ.

The **Église d'Oka ★**, an eclectic church built in 1878 in the Romanesque Revival style, stands in front of the lake, on the same site once occupied by the church of the Sulpician mission (1733). Its bas-reliefs were severely damaged by vandals in 1970 before being removed from the oratories and chapels and hung in the Chapelle Kateri Tekakwitha, adjacent to the Église d'Oka.

A pair of snowshoers in Parc National d'Oka   Charles Grégoire, Sépaq

2. Saint-Eustache

In the early 19th century, Saint-Eustache was a prosperous farming community that had produced a French Canadian intellectual and political elite. These individuals played a major role in the Patriote Rebellion of 1837-38, making Saint-Eustache one of the main arenas of the tragic events that took place at the time.

L'église Saint-Eustache   Agatha Lopez

The **Église Saint-Eustache** ★★ is remarkable mainly for its high Palladian facade built out of cut stone between 1831 and 1836. Its two bell towers bear witness to the prosperity of local residents in the years leading up to the rebellion. As expected, this church occupies an important place in the heart of French Canadians. Beside the church, visitors will find the presbytery, the convent (1898) and the **Monument aux Patriotes**. The church was severely damaged during the Rebellion of 1837-38, damage that was repaired the day after the fight.

THE PATRIOTES OF SAINT-EUSTACHE

In the midst of the Rebellion of 1837, the Patriotes of Saint-Eustache were forced to seek refuge in the village church on December 14. General John Colborne, nicknamed "Vieux Brûlot" (Old Fire Ship), commander of 1,000 British troops, then gave the order to fire cannons on the church. The Patriotes had not harmed a soul, however, having merely played at being soldiers and given themselves the fleeting illusion of power and purpose. These young Quebecers dreamed of a better world... Some 70 idealistic Patriotes died in the attack.

The memoirs of Jacques Paquin reveal the full-blown horror of the massacre. He described the bones of so many wretched souls burned beyond recognition in the conflagration, dragging themselves along and being cut to pieces by the troops. Still other suffering and blood-soaked Patriotes were finished off with rifle-butt blows to the head and their bodies burnt to a crisp. The sight of the lifeless bodies of all these poor wretches strewn here and there—by turns mutilated and burnt to a cinder, some fallen with their heads thrown back in a ditch, others with their skulls bashed in and still others with their hair singed like animals on a butcher's chopping block—was horrifying to behold.

THE LAURENTIANS: MONTRÉAL'S PLAYGROUND

As soon as Montrealers hear the word "Laurentians," images of their favourite getaway, a huge swath of mountainous, lake-studded territory, dance through their heads. Moreover, "their" Laurentians lie just an hour's drive from Québec's metropolis. And yet, the Laurentian mountain range extends across the Ontario border into Ottawa, runs all the way to Charlevoix and ends in the hinterland of the Côte-Nord. The Laurentian playground therefore only covers part of the eponymous mountains. Finally, the highways leading there make the journey considerably shorter since the days of the train known as the P'tit Train du Nord, which was put out of commission some time ago.

The Laurentians extend from the Rivière des Milles Îles, a waterway that hugs the shore of Île Jesus north of Laval, to north of Mont Laurier between the Outaouais and Lanaudière regions. They are drained by three large rivers: the Rivière Lièvre, the Rivière Rouge and the Rivière du Nord. These moving thoroughfares crisscross the region, taking you anywhere you want to go, and once served as vital arteries for the fur trade as well as for logging. Today, a fair share of urbanites come to frolic in their waters with canoes, kayaks and rafts.

Canoeing in the Laurentians

J.F. Bergeron, Sépaq

3. Saint-Jérôme

This administrative and industrial town is nicknamed "La Porte du Nord" (The Gateway to the North), because it marks the passage from the St. Lawrence valley into the mountainous region that stretches north of Montréal and Québec City. The Laurentians are one of the oldest mountain ranges on earth. Compressed by successive glaciations, the mountains are low, rounded, and composed of sandy soil. Colonization of this region began in the second half of the 19th century, with Saint-Jérôme as the starting point.

The **Cathédrale de Saint-Jérôme** ★, a simple parish church when it was erected in 1899, is now a large Roman Byzantine-style edifice reflecting Saint-Jérôme's prestigious status as the "headquarters" of the colonization of the Laurentians. A bronze statue of Curé Labelle, sculpted by Alfred Laliberté, stands in front of the cathedral.

4. Saint-Sauveur-des-Monts ★

Located perhaps a little too close to Montréal, Saint-Sauveur-des-Monts has been over-developed in recent years, and condominiums, restaurants and art galleries have sprung up like mushrooms. This resort is a favourite among entertainers, who own luxurious second homes on the mountainside.

5. Sainte-Adèle ★

The Laurentians were nicknamed the Pays-d'En-Haut (the Highlands) by 19th-century colonists heading for these northern lands, far from the St. Lawrence Valley. Writer and journalist Claude-Henri Grignon, born in Sainte-

Snowboarder in Saint-Sauveur-des-Monts   Ville de Saint-Sauveur

Adèle in 1894, used the region as the setting for his books. His famous novel, *Un homme et son péché* (A Man and his Sin), depicts the wretchedness of life in the Laurentians back in those days.

Grignon asked his good friend, architect Lucien Parent, to design the village church, which graces Rue Principale to this day. In 1989, Québec businessman Pierre Péladeau, deceased in 1997, converted the old Anglican chapel into a sumptuous concert hall, the **Pavillon des Arts de Sainte-Adèle**.

6. Estérel ★

In Belgium, the name Empain is synonymous with financial success. Baron Louis Empain, who inherited the family fortune in the early 20th century, was an important builder. During a trip to Canada in 1935, Baron Louis purchased Pointe Bleue, a strip of land that extends out into Lac Masson. In two years, from 1936 to 1938, he erected about 20 buildings on the site, all designed by Belgian architect Antoine Courtens. Empain named the development **Domaine de l'Estérel**.

A cross between Streamlined Art Deco and the modern Le Corbusier movement, the estate of Baron Empain pays eloquent homage to the elegant modernity of the inter-war years. Notably it encompasses the **old Pointe Bleue hotel**, a long rectangular-shaped building made of concrete and white stucco that accommodated a good number of celebrities over the years—including Georges Simenon, who penned three novels here—a glassed-in sports club, now integrated into the Esterel Resort, and a shopping centre built on piles (surrounded by a parking lot). The latter comprised a gas station, shops, a movie theatre and a dance hall enlivened by the Benny Goodman Orchestra. This 1936 building, now in a pitiful state, can be deemed the first real shopping centre in North America.

7. Sainte-Agathe-des-Monts ★

Located at the meeting point of two colonization movements, the British settling of the county of Argenteuil and the French-Canadian settling of Saint-Jérôme, the town of Sainte-Agathe-des-Monts succeeded in attracting wealthy vacationers, who, lured by **Lac des Sables**, built several

MONT TREMBLANT: THE TREMBLING MOUNTAIN

The area's first inhabitants, the Algonquins, named Mont Tremblant Manitonga Soutana, "mountain of the devil" (or of the spirits), for they claimed the mountain rumbled and that natives who climbed it felt the earth tremble beneath their feet; in French this became "Mont Tremblant" (literally "trembling mountain"). Legend has it that the Great Manitou would make the mountain tremble whenever anyone dared to flout the sacred laws of nature. Those who respected these laws, however, would breathe in the scent of flowers, drink from clear spring waters, enjoy the fresh morning air and rejoice in bird song.

In 1894, the Québec government created Parc de la Montagne-Tremblante. Although the name "Mont Tremblant" was already in use in 1936—the village of Mont Tremblant was founded in 1940—the park's name was only changed to Parc de Récréation de Mont-Tremblant in 1962. It has since been renamed Parc National du Mont-Tremblant, one of 23 provincial parks in Québec.

Parc National du Mont-Tremblant

Heiko Wittenborn, Sépaq

beautiful villas around the lake and near the Anglican church.

Lac des Sables can be toured by land or by water ★. The Chemin du Lac (11km) can be followed by bicycle or by car. Short cruises on the lake are also available.

8. Village Mont-Tremblant ★

On the shores of Lac Tremblant lies charming Mont-Tremblant Village, not to be confused with the resort area.

9. Station Mont-Tremblant ★★★

Some of the largest resorts in the Laurentians were built by wealthy American families with a passion for downhill skiing. They chose this region for the beauty of the land-scape, the province's French charm and above all for the northern

climate, which makes for a longer ski season than in the United States. Station Mont-Tremblant was founded by Philadelphia millionaire Joseph Ryan in 1938.

Since 1991, the resort has been owned by Intrawest, which also owns Whistler Resort in British Columbia. Intrawest has built a veritable village at the foot of the ski hill as well as two magnificent golf courses. The colourful buildings of the village are quite a sight in this pristine wilderness area.

JACK RABBIT JOHANNSEN

Born in Norway in 1875, Herman Smith-Johannsen immigrated to Canada in 1901. An engineer by profession, he started selling railroad equipment, which enabled him to visit a number of remote areas. He would ski to these places, meeting many Aboriginals along the way, who dubbed him "Wapoos," or Jack Rabbit. This nickname was then picked up by Smith-Johannsen's friends at the Montréal Ski Club.

Jack Rabbit Johannsen explored the Laurentians throughout the 1920s and 1930s. He even set up residence here and developed a network of cross-country ski trails. It took him four years to clear a 128km trail known as the Maple Leaf, which stretches between the towns of Prévost and Labelle. Unfortunately, this lovely trail has since been interrupted by Autoroute 15 (Autoroute des Laurentides).

By founding a number of cross-country ski centres and opening numerous trails, Jack Rabbit Johannsen is remembered as a pioneer of sorts. This living legend hung up his skis, so to speak, at the age of 106 and passed away in 1987, at the age of 111. His legacy is the history of cross-country skiing in Québec.

10. Parc National du Mont-Tremblant ★★

Created in 1894, this provincial park was originally known as Parc de la Montagne Tremblante (Trembling Mountain Park) in reference to an Algonquian legend. It covers an area of 1,510km², encompassing the mountain, seven rivers and about 400 lakes. The ski resort opened in 1938, and has been welcoming skiers ever since.

11. Parc Linéaire le P'tit Train du Nord ★★

The **Parc Linéaire le P'tit Train du Nord ★★** follows the course of the old Laurentian railroad. It stretches 200km between Saint-Jérôme and Mont-Laurier. Since its inception in 1990, this extraordinary park has become a top attraction in the region. During summer, it is taken over by thousands of cyclists, while in winter, cross-country skiers and snowmobilers (north of Sainte-Agathe) take to the trail.

The Parc Linéaire le P'tit Train du Nord   ATR Laurentides

Saint-Jérôme   Diane Leblond (AL)

MAURICIE AND CENTRE-DU-QUÉBEC

A pair of snow geese

Mauricie and Centre-du-Québec

Straddling the St. Lawrence

La Mauricie National Park

River, the Mauricie and Centre-du-Québec are an amalgamation of diverse regions that together formed one huge tourism region until 2000. Since then, they have split in two, each with its own tourism infrastructure. Located about halfway between Montréal and Québec City, these two regions form a north-south axis that includes the three types of terrain that make up the province: the Canadian Shield, the St. Lawrence plains, and part of the Appalachian Mountain range.

The city of Trois-Rivières, the second city founded in New France (1634), is generally considered the heart of Mauricie. First a fur trading post, it became an industrial centre with the founding of the Saint-Maurice ironworks in 1730. Further up the Rivière Saint-Maurice, the towns of Shawinigan and Grand-Mère, also major industrial sites, serve as centres for the production of hydroelectric power, and for the major industries that consume that power. To the north lies a vast untamed expanse of lakes, rivers and forests.

To the south of the St. Lawrence River lie the rural zones of Centre-du-Québec. Opened up very early to colonization, the land is still divided according to the old seigneurial system. In the extreme south of the region, the gently rolling hills of this countryside herald the Appalachian Mountains.

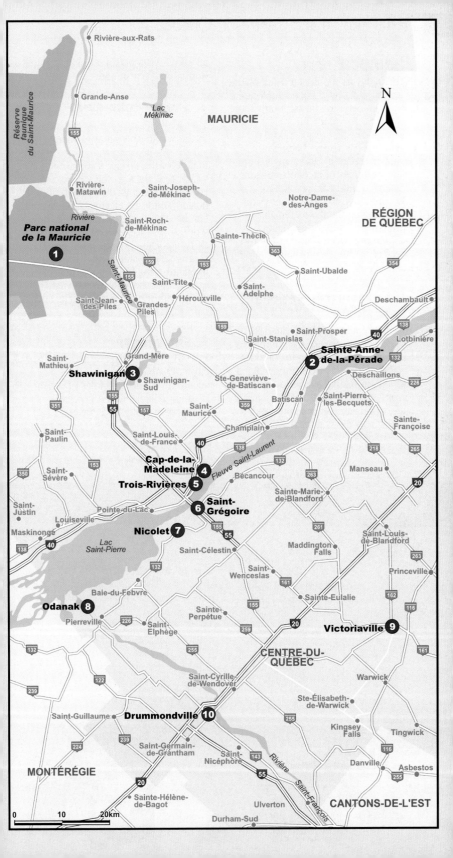

MAURICIE ★★

The valley of the Rivière Saint-Maurice is located halfway between Montréal and Québec City, on the north shore of the St. Lawrence River. The cradle of Canada's first major industry, Mauricie has always been an industrial region. Its towns feature fine examples of architecture from Québec's industrial revolution. Nevertheless, the vast countryside surrounding the towns remains primarily an area of mountain wilderness covered in dense forest, perfect for hunting, fishing, camping and hiking.

1. La Mauricie National Park ★★

This federal park was created in 1970 to preserve a part of the Laurentians. It is the perfect setting for outdoor activities such as canoeing, walking, mountain biking, snowshoeing and cross-country skiing. Hidden among the woods are several lakes and rivers, as well as natural wonders of all kinds. Visitors can stay in dormitories year-round.

2. Sainte-Anne-de-la-Pérade ★

In the winter, this pretty farming village sprouts a second village in the middle of the Rivière Sainte-Anne, which runs through the village. Hundreds of multicoloured shacks, heated and lit by electricity, shelter families that come from all over the world to fish for tomcod, also known as *petit poisson des chenaux*, which means "little channel fish." Ice-fishing in Sainte-Anne has become part of Québecois folklore over the years, along with trips to sugar shacks and corn-roasts.

3. Shawinigan

In 1901, Shawinigan became the first city in Québec to be laid out according to the principles of urban planning, thanks to the powerful Shawinigan Water and Power

Ice-fishing in Sainte-Anne-de-la-Pérade

Philippe Renault

La Mauricie National Park
Patrick Escudero

Company, which supplied electricity to all of Montréal. The name of this hilly town means "portage at the peak" in Algonquian. The town itself was hard hit by the recession of 1989-93, which left indelible marks on its urban landscape.

Inaugurated in the spring of 1997, the **Cité de l'Énergie** ★★ acquaints visitors, children and adults alike with the history of industrial development in Québec in general, and Mauricie in particular. A huge theme park, the Cité de l'Énergie, features several attractions: two hydroelectric power stations, one of which, the Centrale Shawinigan 2, is still in operation; a science pavilion; and a 115m-high observation tower, which, needless to say, offers a sweeping view of the area, including the frothy Shawinigan Falls.

4. Cap-de-la-Madeleine

The heartland of Catholicism in North America, Québec is home to a number of major pilgrimage destinations visited every year by millions from all over the world.

Sanctuaire Notre-Dame-du-Cap
Fondation du Patrimoine Religieux du Québec

The **Sanctuaire Notre-Dame-du-Cap** ★★, a shrine under the auspices of the Oblate Missionaries of the Virgin Mary, is consecrated to the worship of the Virgin. Visitors can participate in a symbolic candlelit march from May to October, weather permitting.

5. Trois-Rivières ★★

Trois-Rivières is a city redolent with Old World charm, with its many cafés, restaurants and bars on Rue des Forges, and the terrace overlooking the St. Lawrence River. Trois-Rivières was founded in 1634 by Sieur de Laviolette at the confluence of the St. Lawrence and Saint-Maurice rivers, where the latter divides into three branches, hence the town's name.

South of Rue Hart is the new **Musée Québécois de Culture Populaire ★★**. The general themes of the museum's new exhibits are the material (objects, environments) and the non-material (traditions, customs). Among others, is an exhibit on museum conservation methods.

The **Forges du Saint-Maurice National Historic Site ★★** commemorates the founding of the ironworks in 1730, when Louis XV granted permission to François Poulin de Francheville to work the rich veins of iron ore that lay under his land. The presence of dense wood lots from which charcoal is made, limestone, and a swift-running waterway, favoured the production of iron. After the British Conquest, the plant passed into the hands of the British colonial government, who in turn ceded it to a private enterprise. The works were in use until 1883.

Trois-Rivières hosts the **Festival International de la Poésie** (the International poetry festival) every fall, which has given it the well-deserved title of the poetry capital of Québec. The town had the brilliant idea of building a walkway, which it named **Promenade de la Poésie ★**, with 300 plaques featuring excerpts from poets across Québec.

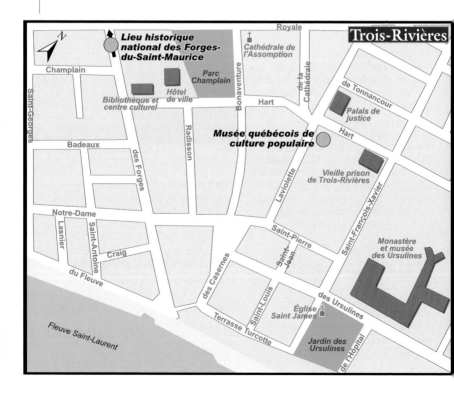

LAC SAINT-PIERRE BIOSPHERE RESERVE

In November 2000, Lac Saint-Pierre was declared a UNESCO Biosphere Reserve. The largest flood plain, largest rest stop for migrating wildfowl, first spring rest stop for migrating snow geese on the St. Lawrence and largest heron site in North America, Lac Saint-Pierre includes the largest archipelago in the St. Lawrence River (with some 100 islands), 20% of all its marshes and half its wetlands.

Snow goose

CENTRE-DU-QUÉBEC ★

The population of Centre-du-Québec is a mix of French, British, Acadian and Loyalist colonists. Up until the mid-19th century, there was not much going on here. However, the arrival of the Grand Trunk Railway began a process of industrialization that has yet to taper off. In the course of the last quarter century, some of Canada's largest and most modern factories have been built here.

6. Saint-Grégoire

The **Église Saint-Grégoire ★★** is in the middle of the old village of Saint-Grégoire, founded in 1757 by a group of Acadians originally from Beaubassin. The parishioners began the construction of the present church in 1803. Since then the church has been touched up by two famous Québécois architects, Thomas Baillairgé, who designed the 1851 neoclassical facade, and Victor Bourgeau, who remodelled the bell towers before decorating the chancel arch.

7. Nicolet

The St. Lawrence Valley shelters some towns and villages that were founded by the Acadians after their deportation from the Maritimes by the British army in 1755. Nicolet is one of these towns.

The **Cathédrale de Nicolet ★** replaced the church destroyed by the landslide of 1955. The curved shape of the reinforced concrete building, designed by Gérard Malouin in 1962, evokes the sail of a ship. Jean-Paul Charland's gigantic stained glass window (21m by 50m) for the church's facade is best appreciated from the inside.

The **Musée des Religions ★** presents interesting thematic exhibits on different religious traditions from around the world.

8. Odanak

Marguerite Hertel, the owner of the Saint-François seigneury at the beginning of the 18th century, ceded a portion of her land on the east bank of the Rivière Saint-François to the government of Trois-Rivières for the creation of an Aboriginal village. The goal of resettling the Abenaki nation of Maine, who were allies of the French, was attained in 1700. Subsequently, at the time of the British conquest in 1759, the village was laid to waste by the British seeking retaliation.

The **Musée des Abénaquis ★** was founded in 1962, and allows visitors to explore Abenaki culture. A permanent exhibit depicts the ancestral way of life of the Abenakis and their relations with the French. The museum's animators bring to life the artifacts on display with traditional songs, legends and dances. The **village church**, with its native carvings, is also well worth a visit.

9. Victoriaville

The economic heartland of the Centre-du-Québec, Victoriaville owes its development to the forestry and steel industries.

Arthabaska ★, the southern portion of Victoriaville, means "place of bulrushes and reeds" in the native language. It has produced or welcomed more than its share of prominent figures in the worlds of art and politics, including Canada's seventh Prime Minister, Wilfrid Laurier, the painter Marc-Aurèle Suzor-Côté and the lawyer and poet Adolphe Poisson. Its residential sectors have always boasted a refined architecture, notably in the European and American styles.

The **Maison Wilfrid-Laurier National Historic Site ★** occupies the house of the first French-Canadian Prime

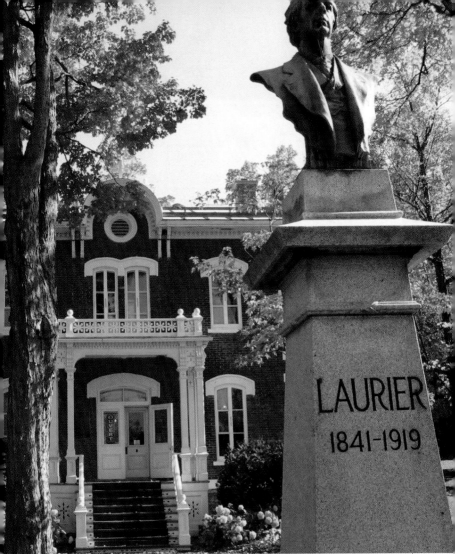

Maison Wilfrid-Laurier National Historic Site

Minister (1896 to 1911), Sir Wilfrid Laurier (1841-1919). Born in Saint-Lin in the Basses-Laurentides, Laurier moved to Arthabaska as soon as he finished his legal studies. His house was turned into a museum in 1929 by two admirers.

10. Drummondville

Drummondville was founded in the wake of the War of 1812 by Frederick George Heriot, who gave it the name of the British Governor of the time, Sir Gordon Drummond. The colony was at first a military outpost on the Rivière Saint-François, but the building of mills and factories soon made it a major industrial centre.

The **Village Québécois d'Antan** ★★ traces 100 years of history. Some 70 colonial-era buildings have been reproduced to evoke the atmosphere of village life from 1810 to 1910. People in period costume make **ceintures fléchées** (chevron-design sashes), candles and bread. Many historical television shows are shot on location here.

MAPLE SYRUP

By the time the first colonists arrived in America, the various indigenous cultures had already been enjoying maple syrup for a long time.

According to an Iroquois legend, it happened like this: Woksis, the Great Chief, headed out hunting one morning. The night had been cold, but the day promised to be warm. The day before, he had left his tomahawk stuck in a maple tree, and when he removed it, sap began to flow from the crack in the wood. The sap flowed into a bucket that happened to be sitting under the hole. Later, Woksis's wife needed water to prepare the evening meal. Upon seeing the bucket full of sap, she thought it would spare her a trip to the river. An intelligent and conscientious woman who hated waste, she tasted the water and found it a bit on the sweet side, but nevertheless good, and used it to make the meal. On his way home, Woksis smelled the sweet scent of maple from far away and knew something extra special was cooking. The sap had turned into syrup, making the meal positively succulent. And thus was born one of North America's sweetest traditions.

Natives did not have the necessary materials to heat a cauldron at very high temperatures, so they used heated rocks, which they dropped into the water to make it boil. Another method was to let the maple water freeze overnight, then remove the layer of ice the following morning, repeating this process until nothing remained but a thick syrup. Maple syrup played a prominent role in the Aboriginal diet, culture and religion. The syrup-making methods used today were handed down by Europeans, who taught them to the natives.

Maple grove
Sucrerie Jean-Louis Massicotte
101, route 159,
Saint-Prosper

A pair of snowshoers
(next page)
Jean Sylvain - Sépaq

MONTÉRÉGIE

J.-F. Bergeron, Sépaq

Hiking in Parc National du Mont-Saint-Bruno

Montérégie

Rich in history

Manoir Rouville-Campbell, Mont-Saint-Hilaire

François Rivard, Tourisme Montérégie

and harbouring several heritage buildings, the Montérégie region is above all a beautiful plain located between Ontario, New England and the foothills of the Appalachians in the Eastern Townships. Located just south of Montréal, with many natural transportation routes, such as the majestic Rivière Richelieu, Montérégie has always played an important military and strategic role.

The six hills in Montérégie, Mont Saint-Bruno, Mont Saint-Hilaire, Mont Yamaska, Mont Rigaud, Mont Saint-Grégoire and Mont Rougemont, are the only large hills in this otherwise flat region. The hills, which do not rise much over 500m, are spread out and were long considered ancient volcanoes. Actually, they are metamorphic rocks that did not break through the upper layer of the earth's crust and became visible as the neighbouring land eroded over a long period of time.

The ancient fortifications dotting the region and which are now open to the public were once a first line of defense against the Iroquois, the English and then the Americans. The young American country actually suffered its first military defeat here in 1812. The Patriotes and British also met here in Saint-Charles-sur-Richelieu and Saint-Denis during the Rebellion of 1837-1838.

M. Pitre, Sépaq

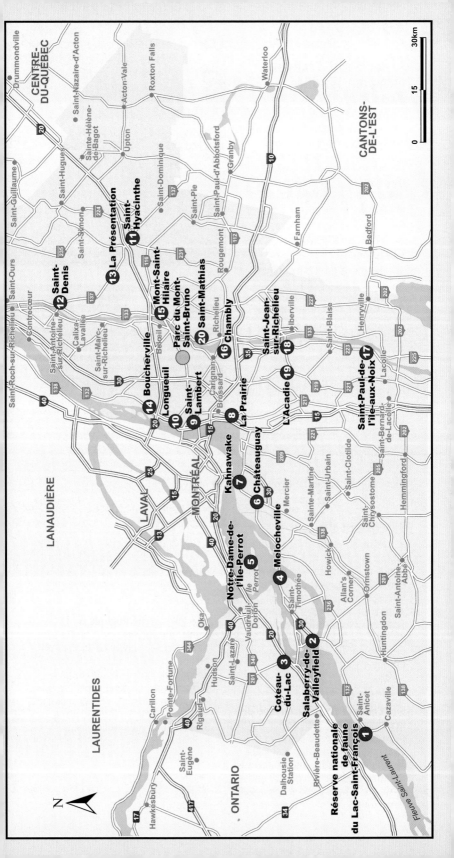

1. Lac-Saint-François National Wildlife Area★★

On the south shore of the St. Lawrence River, this federal park is a wetland recognized by the Ramsar Convention (a worldwide list of protected sites). Visitors can observe 220 species of birds, 600 plants and over 40 species of mammals.

Snow geese

François Rivard, Tourisme Montérégie

2. Salaberry-de-Valleyfield

The **Battle of the Châteauguay National Historic Site** ★. In October 1813, the 2,000 troops of U.S. General Hampton gathered at the border. They entered Canadian territory during the night along the Rivière Châteauguay. But Charles Michel d'Irumberry de Salaberry, seigneur of Chambly, was waiting for them along with 300 militiamen and a few dozen Aboriginals. On October 26, the battle began. Salaberry's tactics got the better of the Americans, who retreated, putting an end to a series of conflicts and inaugurating a lasting friendship between the two countries.

3. Coteau-du-Lac ★

A narrowing of the river at Coteau-du-Lac combined with a series of rapids makes navigation impossible here. The St. Lawrence reaches its lowest level after a change in altitude of 25m over a distance of just 12.8km. Coteau-du-Lac therefore became a rallying and portage point even before the arrival of the Europeans.

4. Melocheville

The **Centrale Hydroélectrique de Beauharnois** ★, with its 5,000 MW of power, was once the jewel in the crown of the large Montréal Light, Heat and Power Electric Company. Built in stages between 1929 and 1956, the power plant is a sprawling 864m long.

Battle of the Châteauguay National Historic Site

Parks Canada / S.Grenier

The **Parc Archéologique de la Pointe-du-Buisson** ★. The Buisson headland was inhabited sporadically for thousands of years by Aboriginals, leaving the area rich with artifacts (arrowheads, cooking pots, harpoons, etc). There is an active archaeological site here, along with trails, picnic areas and an interpretive centre.

5. Notre-Dame-de-l'Île-Perrot

The **Église Sainte-Jeanne-de-Chantal** ★★ is often described as the perfect example of a French Canadian church in the Montréal region. In fact, its modest dimensions, reminiscent of the first churches of the French regime, as well as its interior decor in the Louis XV and Louis XVI styles, make the church an excellent example of traditional Québec architecture.

Église Sainte-Jeanne-de-Chantal
Fondation du Patrimoine Religieux du Québec

6. Châteauguay

When the first church in Châteauguay was built in 1735, it was the westernmost parish on the south shore of the St. Lawrence. Work on the present **Église Saint-Joachim** ★★ began in 1775 in order to better serve a growing number of parishioners.

7. Kahnawake

The **Enceinte, Musée Kateri Tekakwitha** and **Église Saint-François-Xavier** ★★. Under the French regime, villages and missions were required to surround themselves with fortifications. Very few of these walls have survived. The *enceinte*, or wall, of the Kahnawake mission, still partially standing, is the kind of ruin rarely found north of Mexico.

Église Saint-Joachim
Fondation du Patrimoine Religieux du Québec

Église Saint-François-Xavier was modified in 1845 according to the plans of Jesuit Félix Martin, and redecorated by Vincent Chartrand (1845-47), who also made some of the furniture. Guido Nincheri designed the polychromatic vaulted ceiling in the 20th century. Also found here is the tomb of Kateri Tekakwitha, a young Aboriginal who was beatified in 1980. The convent houses the Kateri Tekakwitha museum, where visitors can see some of the objects that belonged to the Jesuits.

8. La Prairie ★

La Prairie's strategic location led its authorities to fortify the village in 1684. Very little remains today of the stone-and-wood enclosure that was dismantled by the Americans during the 1775 invasion. A pier was built in 1835, where steam-ships linking the South Shore to Montréal docked. The following year saw the inauguration of Canada's first railway, linking Saint-Jean-sur-Richelieu to La Prairie.

The streets of **Vieux-La Prairie** ★★ have an urban character rarely found in Québec villages during the 19th century. Several houses were carefully restored after the Québec government declared the area a historic district in 1975.

Victoria Bridge   François Rivard, Tourisme Montérégie

9. Saint-Lambert

The **Victoria Bridge** ★ is the oldest bridge linking the island of Montréal to the mainland. It was built with difficulty by hundreds of Irish and French Canadian workers between 1854 and 1860 for the Grand Trunk railway company.

The **Écluse de Saint-Lambert** ★, or locks, are the gateway to the seaway, which begins here and ends 3,800km upstream, at the tip of the Great Lakes. The seaway allows ships to bypass the natural obstacles posed by the St. Lawrence and to provide a direct route to the centre of the continent.

10. Longueuil ★

Longueuil experienced continuous growth during the 19th century with the introduction of the railway (1846) and the arrival of many summer vacationers who built beautiful villas along the river banks. At the beginning of the 20th century, the powerful Pratt and Whitney company opened a small factory that has since grown and has created an important industrial centre specializing in engineering and airplane technology.

The site of the **Église Saint-Antoine-de-Padoue** ★★ was once occupied by a 17th century castle known as the Château de Longueuil. After being besieged by American rebels during the 1775 invasion, it was requisitioned by the British army. A fire broke out while a garrison was stationed here in 1792, destroying a good part of the building. In 1810, the ruins were used as a quarry during the building of a second Catholic church. A few years later, Rue Saint-Charles was built right through the rest of the site, forcing the complete destruction of this unique North American building. The 1810 church was demolished in 1884 to make room for the present building, completed in 1887, according to plans drawn up by Montréal architects Perrault and Mesnard.

11. Saint-Hyacinthe ★★

Saint-Hyacinthe was settled in the late 18th century, around the mills on the Rivière Yamaska. The surrounding fertile soil helped the town expand rapidly, attracting several religious institutions, businesses and industries.

Rue Girouard Ouest ★ is the main street in the upper part of Saint-Hyacinthe. This opulent residential neighbourhood reflects the success of local entrepreneurs. It lies between the gates known as the Portes des Anciens Maires, erected in 1927 to honour the memory of the 11 first magistrates of the city, and the Église Notre-Dame-du-Rosaire.

12. Saint-Denis ★

Throughout the 1830s, Saint-Denis was home to large political gatherings as well as the headquarters of the Fils de la Liberté (Sons of Freedom), a group of young French Canadians who wanted Lower Canada (Québec) to become an independent country. But even more important, Saint-Denis was the site of the only Patriotes victory over the British during the Rebellion of 1837-38.

QUEBEC'S BREADBASKET

St-Hyacinthe's residents - called *Maskoutains* because the region is crossed by the Rivière Yamaska - occupy a rural area that is among the most fertile in the province. The provincial farming capital, Saint-Hyacinthe is also home to Québec's leading agricultural college as well as the veterinary school of the Université de Montréal.

The region's rich farmland is essentially made up of clay, the result of deposits left behind by age-old vestiges of the post-glacial Champlain Sea, formed by a retreating glacier that covered a vast area, including the St. Lawrence Lowlands.

Sunset in Montérégie

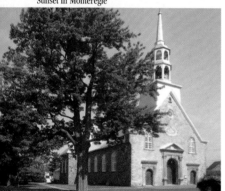

Église de La Présentation Fondation du Patrimoine Religieux du Québec

To the south of the Parc des Patriotes stands a former inn built of stone for Jean-Baptiste Mâsse in 1810, and now the **Maison Nationale des Patriotes ★**. The building's irregular shape is characteristic of urban homes of the late 18th century. It is one of the rare examples of this type found outside of Montréal and Québec City.

13. La Présentation

The **Église de La Présentation ★★** is unique among places of worship built in Montérégie during the same era because of its finely sculpted stone facade, completed in 1819. Note the inscriptions written in Old French above the entrances.

14. Boucherville ★

Unlike many seigneuries in New France that were granted to servicemen or tradesmen, the Boucherville seigneury was handed over by Intendant Talon to a settler from Trois-Rivières, Pierre Boucher, in 1672. Rather than speculate or use it as a hunting reserve, Boucher made sustained efforts to develop his seigneury, an act that earned him a title of nobility from the king.

The **Manoir de Boucherville ★** is one of the rare manors dating back to the French regime to have survived in the Montréal area. The large stone house was built in 1741 for François-Pierre Boucher, the third seigneur of Boucherville.

15. Mont-Saint-Hilaire ★

This small town, located at the foot of Mont Saint-Hilaire, was originally part of the seigneury of Rouville, granted to Jean-Baptiste Hertel in 1694.

The **Musée d'Art de Mont-Saint-Hilaire ★** promotes the development of contemporary visual arts and highlights the works of famous artists who have lived in Mont-Saint-Hilaire including Ozias Leduc, Paul-Émile Borduas and Jordi Bonet.

Fort Chambly National Historic Site

Sandra Fabris

The **Maison des Cultures Amérindiennes** ★ is the brainchild of the Ushket-André Michel foundation, which has made it its mission to foster a better understanding of First Nations peoples. The cultural centre therefore seeks to encourage interaction and sharing and to bring people together through environmental, agricultural, cultural and gastronomic activities.

Situated on the upper half of Mont Saint-Hilaire, the **Centre de la Nature du Mont-Saint-Hilaire** ★★ is a former estate that Brigadier Andrew Hamilton Gault passed on to Montréal's McGill University in 1958. The Centre was recognized as a Biosphere Reserve by UNESCO in 1978 for its virgin forest.

16. Chambly ★★

The town of Chambly occupies a privileged site alongside the Richelieu. The river widens here to form the Bassin de Chambly at the end of the rapids, which once hindered navigation on the river and made the area a key element in New France's defence system.

Bird's-eye view of Fort Chambly

Parks Canada / J. Audet

Fort Chambly National Historic Site ★★★ is the largest remaining fortification of the French regime. It was built between 1709 and 1711 according to plans drawn by engineer Josué Boisberthelot de Beaucours at the request of the marquis of Vaudreuil. It replaced three wooden forts that had occupied the site since 1665.

17. Saint-Paul-de-l'Île-aux-Noix

Fort Lennox National Historic Site ★★ takes up two-thirds of Île aux Noix and significantly alters its

Fort Lennox National Historic Site and Île aux Noix

Parks Canada, J. Audet

shape. It was built on the ruins of previous forts between 1819 and 1829 by the British, prompting the construction by the Americans of Fort Montgomery just south of the border.

18. Saint-Jean-sur-Richelieu ★

This industrial city was, for a long time, an important gateway into Canada from the United States, as well as an essential rest stop on the road from Montréal. Three features made this city important: its port on the Richelieu, active from the end of the 18th century onwards; its railway, the first in Canada, which linked the town to La Prairie as of 1836; and the opening of the Canal de Chambly in 1843.

The **Musée du Haut-Richelieu** ★ is located inside the former public market, built in 1859. Apart from various objects relating to the history of the upper Richelieu, the museum boasts an interesting collection of pottery and earthenware produced in the region during the 19th century.

19. L'Acadie ★

During the Seven Years War between France and England, Acadia (part of present-day Nova Scotia and New Brunswick) was conquered, and in 1755, the Acadians, who owned the best lands, were deported to faraway places. Between 1764 and 1768, some of them returned from exile and established themselves on the shore of Petite Rivière. They formed "Petite Acadie," which later became the village of L'Acadie.

In L'Acadie, the **Église Sainte-Marguerite-de-Blairfindie** ★ ★, the presbytery and the old school are some of the most picturesque and best-kept institutional buildings in the Montérégie area. The present-day stone church was completed in 1801.

20. Saint-Mathias

Noted for its outstanding interior decor and its stone cemetery enclosure, the **Église Saint-Mathias** ★ ★ also boasts a charming exterior that reflects traditional Québec architecture. It was built in 1784 by mason François Châteauneuf.

Kayaking in Parc National des Îles-de-Boucherville *(page 148)*
Jean-Sébastien Perron, Sépaq

Parc National du Mont-Saint-Bruno
M. Pitre, Sépaq

MONTÉRÉGIE'S PROVINCIAL PARKS

Mont Saint-Bruno was once a popular holiday resort for wealthy English-speaking Montrealers. Several families, such as the Birks, the Drummonds and the Merediths, built summer homes here, in what is now the **Parc National Mont Saint-Bruno**. At the top of the mountain lie two lakes, Lac Seigneurial and Lac du Moulin, near which stands a 19th-century watermill. The park is a pleasant place for a stroll or a little R&R.

River shuttle boats that depart from the Promenade René-Lévesque, in Longueuil, or the Promenade Bellerive, in eastern Montreal, travel to the **Parc National des Îles-de-Boucherville** in summer. Some of the islands are still dotted with farms, but most of the archipelago, a string of islands linked by cable ferries, is open to visitors. The park is devoted to outdoor activities, particularly hiking and cycling. It is also home to an amazing variety of bird species and thus favoured by budding ornithologists.

Porcupine

MONTRÉAL

The Illuminated Crowd, by Raymond Mason, and the Tour BNP

Montréal

At the crossroads

*of America and Europe, with a soul both Latin and northern,
Montréal is a city of paradoxes that holds nothing back. It succeeds in
delighting American tourists with its "European charm", but also
manages to surprise overseas travellers with its haphazard character
and nonchalance. Montréal is enchanting and exhilarating; it is
generous, friendly and not at all mundane.*

*Montréal's richly varied urban landscape illustrates the different
stages of the city's evolution. The oldest buildings in Vieux-Montréal,
or Old Montréal, pre-date the glass skyscrapers downtown by over
three centuries, during which time the city was in constant expansion.
The splendour of Montréal's countless churches, the neoclassical
facades of the banks along Rue Saint-Jacques, the flat-roofed little
houses in the working-class neighbourhoods and the sumptuous
residences of the "Golden Square Mile" all bear witness, like so much
else here, to the city's history. Montréal's important role, both past and
present, as the province's main centre of artistic and intellectual
activity, and as a large industrial, financial, commercial and port
city, is eloquently reflected in its rich architectural heritage.*

*Though it has the appearance of a big North American city, Montréal
is above all a city of narrow streets, of neighbourhoods, each with its
own church, handful of businesses, corner delicatessen, brasserie or
tavern. Over the years, the city has also been shaped by an
increasingly cosmopolitan population. The division between the east
and west (between French-speakers and English-speakers, respectively)
still exists to a certain degree, although it no longer stirs up the same
feelings. Over the past century, immigrants from all over the world
have joined these two main elements of Montréal society. The great
diversity of these neighbourhoods and their inhabitants help give
Montréal a unique charm and a character that is markedly different
from that of the rest of Québec.*

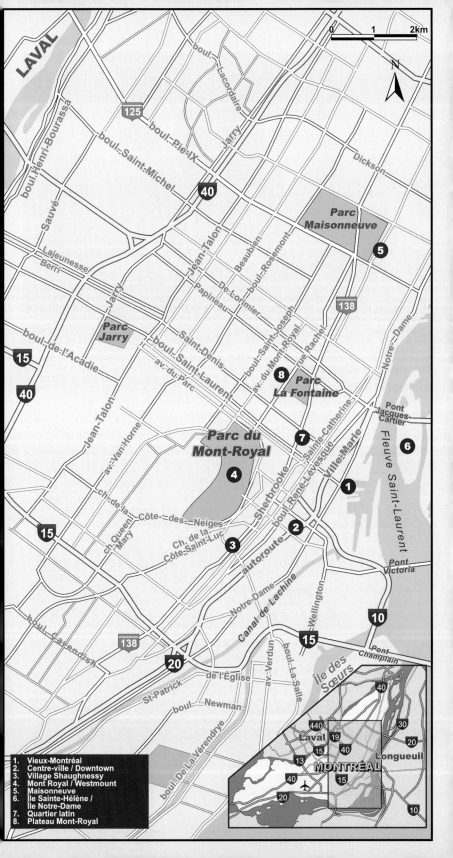

Old Montréal

Phillippe Renault

VIEUX-MONTRÉAL (OLD MONTRÉAL) ★★★

In the 18th century, Montréal, like Québec City, was surrounded by stone fortifications. Between 1801 and 1817, these ramparts were demolished due to the efforts of local merchants, who saw them as an obstacle to the city's development. The network of old streets, compressed after nearly a century of confinement, nevertheless remained in place. Today's Vieux-Montréal, or Old Montréal, thus corresponds quite closely to the area covered by the fortified city.

In the 19th century, **Square Victoria** ★ was a Victorian garden surrounded by Second Empire and Renaissance Revival stores and office buildings. Only the narrow building at 751 Rue McGill survives from that era. Square Victoria has been completely restored to its original splendour, and is one of the centrepieces of the Quartier International de Montréal.

The **Tour de la Bourse** ★, or the stock exchange tower, dominates the surroundings to Square Victoria. Its construction was intended to breathe new life into the business section of the old city, which was deserted after the stock market crash of 1929 in favour of the area around Square Dorchester downtown. According to the initial plan, there were supposed to be three identical towers.

World trade centres are exchange organizations intended to promote international trade. Montréal's **Centre de Commerce Mondial / World Trade Centre** ★, completed in 1991, is a new structure hidden behind an entire block of old façades. An impressive glassed-in passageway stretches 180m through the centre of the building.

Begun in 1928 according to plans by New York skyscraper specialists York and Sawyer, the former head office of the **Banque Royale / Royal Bank** ★★, was one of the last buildings erected during this era of prosperity. The 22-storey tower has a base inspired by Florentine palazzos, which corresponds to the scale of the neighbouring buildings.

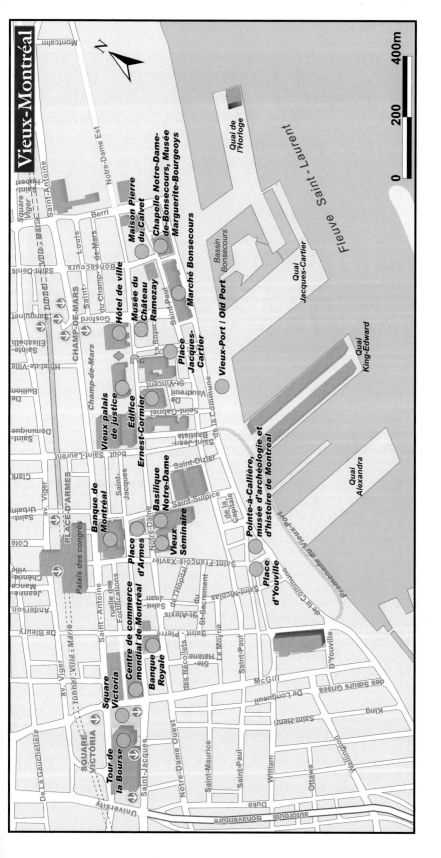

Basilique Notre-Dame   Phillippe Renault

Under the French regime, **Place d'Armes** ★ ★ was the heart of the city. Used for military manoeuvres and religious processions, the square was also the location of the Gadoys well, the city's main source of potable water. In 1847, the square was transformed into a lovely, fenced-in Victorian garden, which was destroyed at the beginning of the 20th century in order to make room for a tramway terminal. In the meantime, a **monument to Maisonneuve** ★ ★ was erected in 1895. Executed by sculptor Philippe Hébert, it shows the founder of Montréal, Paul de Chomedey, Sieur de Maisonneuve, surrounded by prominent figures from the city's early history, namely Jeanne Mance, founder of the Hôtel-Dieu (hospital), Lambert Closse, along with his dog Pilote, and Charles Lemoyne, head of a family of famous explorers. An Iroquois warrior completes the tableau.

The square, which is in fact shaped more like a trapezoid, is surrounded by several noteworthy buildings. The **Banque de Montréal / Bank of Montréal** ★ ★, founded in 1817 by a group of merchants, is the country's oldest banking institution. Its present

head office takes up an entire block on the north side of Place d'Armes. A magnificent building by John Wells, built in 1847 and modelled after the Roman Pantheon, it occupies the place of honour in the centre of the block.

The **Basilique Notre-Dame** ★ ★ ★, built between 1824 and 1829, is a true North American masterpiece of Gothic Revival architecture. It should be seen not as a replica of a European cathedral, but rather as a fundamentally neoclassical structure characteristic of the Industrial Revolution, complemented by a medieval-style decor which foreshadowed the historicism of the Victorian era. These elements make the building remarkable.

Between 1874 and 1880, the original interior, considered too austere, was replaced by the fabulous polychromatic decorations found today. Executed by the then leading architect of religious buildings in the Montréal region, Victor Bourgeau, along with about 50 artists, it is made entirely of wood, painted and gilded with gold leaf. Particularly noteworthy features include the baptistery,

MAISONNEUVE, FOUNDER OF MONTRÉAL

In the 17th century, the fur trade was the driving force behind France's bid to colonize Canada. Yet this lucrative trade was not the initial cause of the founding of Montréal, but rather it was the religious conversion of First Nations peoples.

Paul de Chomedey, Sieur de Maisonneuve, born in 1612 south-east of Paris, was not only chosen to carry out this mission, but also designated the new colony's first governor. Maisonneuve left France in May 1641 leading an expedition of some 50 people, the Montréalistes de la Société Notre-Dame, a group that included Jeanne Mance. Jeanne Mance's ship reached Québec three months later without incident.

Maisonneuve was not so fortunate, however, encountering violent storms along the way. In fact, he arrived so late that the founding of Montréal was postponed to the following year. The group spent the winter in Québec City. On May 17, 1642, Maisonneuve founded Ville-Marie, on the island of Montréal. A few years later, the name Montréal supplanted that of Ville-Marie.

In 1665, the governor of Montréal was summoned back to France indefinitely. He returned to Paris with a heavy heart, abandoning his duties and his beloved city and retiring among the Doctrine Chrétienne order of priests, where he died in 1676. He was likely buried in the order's former chapel, which was located in the vicinity of 17 Rue de Cardinal-Lemoine, in the 5e Arrondissement of Paris.

The founder of Montréal was a warm-hearted man of great intelligence and virtue. A monument to Paul de Chomedey, Sieur de Maisonneuve, erected in 1895, stands in Place d'Armes, in the heart of Old Montréal.

decorated with frescoes by Ozias Leduc, and the powerful electro-pneumatic Casavant organ with its 5,772 pipes, often used during the numerous concerts given at the basilica. Lastly, there are the stained glass windows by Francis Chigot, a master glass artist from France, which depict various episodes in the history of Montréal. They were installed in honour of the church's centennial.

The small **Musée de la Basilique** displays various treasures, including embroidered liturgical clothing as well as the episcopal throne and personal effects of Monseigneur de Pontbriand, the last bishop of New France.

The **Vieux Séminaire** ★ was built in 1683 in the style of a Parisian *hôtel particulier*, with a courtyard in front and a garden in back. It is the oldest building in the city. For more than three centuries, it has been occupied by Sulpician priests, who, under the French regime, used it as a manor from which they managed their vast seigneury.

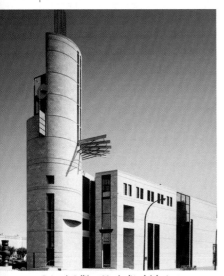

Pointe-à-Callière, Musée d'Archéologie et d'Histoire de Montréal
Roderick Chen

The **Musée d'Archéologie et d'Histoire de Montréal / Montréal Museum of Archaeology and History** ★★, lies on the exact site where Ville-Marie (Montréal) was founded on May 18, 1642, the **Pointe-à-Callière**. The museum uses the most advanced techniques available to provide visitors with a survey of the city's history.

Stretching from Place Royale to Rue McGill, **Place d'Youville** ★ owes its elongated shape to its location over the bed of the Rivière Saint-Pierre, which was canalized in 1832.

The Port of Montréal is the largest inland port on the continent. It stretches 25km along the St. Lawrence, from Cité du Havre to the refineries in the east end. **The Vieux-Port de Montréal / Old Port** ★★ corresponds to the historic portion of the port, located in front of the old city. Abandoned because of its obsolescence, it was revamped between 1983 and 1992, following the example of various other centrally located North American ports.

From the time it was inaugurated in 1926 until it closed in 1970, the **Édifice Ernest-Cormier** ★ was used for criminal proceedings. The former courthouse was converted into a conservatory and was named after its architect, the illustrious Ernest Cormier, who also designed the main pavilion of the Université de Montréal and the doors of the United Nations Headquarters in New York City. The building returned to its original function as the Québec Court of Appeal in 2004.

The **Vieux Palais de Justice** ★, the oldest courthouse in Montréal, was built between 1849 and 1856, according to a design by John Ostell and Henri-Maurice Perrault, on the site of the first courthouse, which was erected in 1800. It is another fine example of Canadian neoclassical architecture.

Place Jacques-Cartier ★ was laid out on the site once occupied by the Château de Vaudreuil, which burned down in 1803. The property was

THE LACHINE CANAL:
THEN AND NOW

The mainspring of Montréal's industrialization, the 13.5km-long Lachine Canal has been part of the city's heritage since the 19th and 20th centuries when its excavation and the building of its sluice gates made it possible to bypass the tumultuous Lachine Rapids, after a few fruitless attempts.

François Dollier de Casson, the Superior of the Sulpician order, was the first, in 1689, to believe in the project of a canal bypassing the rapids and leading to the Great Lakes. The project was ultimately abandoned in midstream due to high costs. After the conquest of New France, a similar project was undertaken by the British and, after seven years of studies, negotiations and petitions, was completed between 1812 and 1819.

It was then that Montréal merchants formed the Company of the Lachine Canal in order to finally complete the present canal. The company went bankrupt in 1821, but the project was taken over and the work completed by the government of Lower Canada. The widening of the canal as well as the restoration and addition of locks would proceed without interruption between its opening in 1825, and that of the St. Lawrence Seaway in 1959. The Lachine Canal was closed to maritime traffic between 1970 and 2002, when it re-opened to pleasure-boats for the summer.

The Lachine Canal

Montréal City Hall   Patrick Escudero

Chapelle Notre-Dame-de-Bonsecours   Normand Rajotte

The **hôtel de ville** ★, or city hall, a fine example of the Second Empire, or Napoleon III, style, is the work of Henri-Maurice Perrault, who also designed the neighbouring courthouse. It was from the balcony of the city hall that France's General de Gaulle cried out his famous "*Vive le Québec libre!*" ("Freedom for Québec!") in 1967, to the great delight of the crowd gathered in front of the building.

The humblest of all the "châteaux" built in Montréal, the **Château Ramezay** ★ ★ is the only one still standing. It was built in 1705 for the governor of Montréal, Claude de Ramezay, and his family. In 1895, after serving as the first building of the Montréal branch of the Université Laval in Québec City, the château was converted into a museum, under the patronage of the Société d'Histoire et de Numismatique de Montréal (Montréal Numismatic and Antiquarian Society), founded by Jacques Viger.

This site was originally occupied by another chapel, built in 1657 upon the recommendation of Saint Marguerite Bourgeoys, founder of the congregation of Notre-Dame. The present **Chapelle Notre-Dame-de-Bonsecours** ★ dates back to 1771, when the Sulpicians wanted to establish a branch of the main parish in the eastern part of the fortified city. In 1890, the chapel was modified to suit contemporary tastes, and the present stone façade was added, along with the "aerial" chapel looking out on the port. Parishioners asked God's blessing on ships and their crews bound for Europe from this chapel. The interior, redone at the same time, contains a large number of votive offerings from sailors saved from shipwrecks. Some are in the form of model ships, hung from the ceiling of the nave.

purchased by local merchants, who decided to give the government a small strip of land, on the condition that a public market be established there, thus increasing the value of the adjacent property, which remained in private hands. This explains Place Jacques-Cartier's oblong shape.

Between 1996 and 1998, excavations below the nave of the chapel uncovered several artifacts, including some dating from the colony's early days. Today, the **Musée Marguerite-**

The Marché Bonsecours

Bourgeoys ★ adjoining the Notre-Dame-de-Bonsecours chapel displays these interesting archaeological finds. But there is even more to explore: extends from the top of the tower, where the view is breathtaking, to the depths of the crypt.

Built in 1725, the **Maison Pierre-du-Calvet** ★★, at the corner of Rue

Bonsecours, is representative of 18th-century French urban architecture adapted to the local setting, with thick walls made of fieldstone embedded in mortar, storm windows doubling the casement windows with their little squares of glass imported from France, and high firebreak walls, then required by local regulations as a means of limiting the spread of fire from one building to the next.

Montréal's oldest street, the course of which was mapped in 1672 by town planner and historian François Dollier de Casson along a winding aboriginal trail, **Rue Saint-Paul** was long Montréal's main commercial thorough-fare. The lovely greystone neoclassical **Marché Bonsecours** ★★★ with its sash windows was erected on Rue Saint-Paul between 1845 and 1850.

The True Likeness Room at the Musée Marguerite-Bourgeoys

Downtown Montréal

DOWNTOWN ★★★

The downtown skyscrapers give Montréal a typically North American look. Nevertheless, unlike most other cities on the continent, there is a certain Latin spirit here, which seeps in between the towering buildings, livening up this part of Montréal both day and night. Bars, cafés, department stores, shops and head offices, along with two universities and numerous colleges, all lie clustered within a limited area at the foot of Mont Royal.

The lovely Presbyterian **Church of St. Andrew and St. Paul ★★** was one of the most important institutions of the Scottish elite in Montréal. Built in 1932 according to plans by architect Harold Lea Fetherstonaugh as the community's third place of worship, it illustrates the endurance of the medieval style in religious architecture.

The **Musée des Beaux-Arts de Montréal / Montreal Museum of Fine Arts ★★** is the oldest and largest museum in Québec. It houses a variety of collections that illustrate the evolution of the fine arts from antiquity up until the present day. The museum occupies two separate buildings on either side of Rue Sherbrooke Ouest.

The small **Musée des Arts Décoratifs de Montréal ★** moved to the Pavillon Jean-Noël Desmarais of the Montreal Museum of Fine Arts in 1997 and is now part of the museum's permanent collection. The collection is made up of furniture and decorative objects in the International Style (from 1935 on) donated by Liliane and David Stewart.

The last of Montréal's old hotels, **the Ritz-Carlton ★** was inaugurated in 1911 by César Ritz himself. For many

The Musée des Beaux-Arts de Montréal, Pavillon Michal et Renata Hornstein

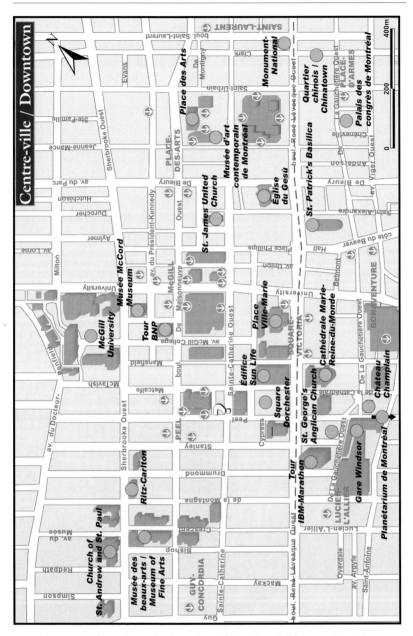

years, it was the favourite gathering place of the Montréal bourgeoisie. Many celebrities have stayed at this sophisticated luxury hotel over the years, including Richard Burton and Elizabeth Taylor, who were married here in 1964.

The **Édifice Sun Life** ★ ★, erected between 1913 and 1933 for the powerful Sun Life insurance company, was for many years the largest building in the British Empire. It was in this "fortress" of the Anglo-Saxon establishment, with its colonnades reminiscent of ancient mythology, that the British Crown Jewels were hidden during World War II.

SPOTLIGHT ON THE CITY

For almost five years now, Montréal has had its own "Plan Lumière," a lighting program whose mission is to illuminate the city after dark and make it as attractive by nightfall as it is by daylight. The concept of highlighting the city's architectural heritage in this way, which has been all the rage in Europe for the last 20 years or so, is the work of Gilles Arpin, the leading Québec expert in urban lighting.

Lampposts and carefully positioned floodlights make Montréal's monuments and public squares emerge out of the shadows and reveal aspects of their architecture that might otherwise pass unnoticed in the light of day. The whole program is controlled by computer. You need only walk around downtown or Old Montréal to appreciate most of these permanent night-time landscapes.

From 1799 to 1854, **Square Dorchester** ★ was occupied by Montréal's Catholic cemetery, which was then moved to Mont Royal, where it is still located. In 1945-1950, the city turned the free space into two squares, one on either side of Dorchester Street (now Boulevard René-Lévesque). The northern portion is called Square Dorchester, while the southern part was renamed Place du Canada in 1964.

The Planétarium de Montréal

A number of churches clustered around Square Dorchester before it was even laid out in 1872. Unfortunately, only two of the eight churches built in the area between 1865 and 1875 have survived. One of these is the beautiful Gothic Revival-style **St. George's Anglican Church** ★★.

The other is **Cathédrale Marie-Reine-du-Monde** ★★, the seat of the archdiocese of Montréal and a reminder of the tremendous power wielded by the clergy up until the Quiet Revolution. It is exactly one third the size of St. Peter's in Rome. Its construction began in 1870 and was finally completed in 1894.

The elegant 47-storey **Tour IBM-Marathon** ★, forming part of the backdrop of St. George's, was completed in 1991 according to a design by the famous New York architects Kohn, Pedersen and Fox. Its winter bamboo garden is open to the public.

In 1887, the head of Canadian Pacific, William Cornelius Van Horne, asked his New York friend Bruce Price (1845-1903) to draw up the plans for

Gare Windsor ★, a modern train station that would serve as the terminus of the transcontinental railroad, completed the previous year.

Built in 1966, the **Château Champlain** ★, nicknamed the "cheese grater" by Montrealers due to its many arched, convex openings, was designed by Québec architects Jean-Paul Pothier and Roger D'Astou. The latter is a disciple of American architect Frank Lloyd Wright, with whom he studied for several years.

The **Planétarium de Montréal** ★ projects astronomy films into a 20m hemispheric dome. The universe and its mysteries are explained in a way that makes this marvellous, often poorly understood world accessible to all.

Place Ville-Marie ★★★ was erected in 1959. The famous Chinese-American architect Ieoh Ming Pei (Louvre Pyramid, Paris; East Building of the National Gallery, Washington, D.C.) designed the multi-purpose complex built over the railway tracks and containing vast shopping arcades

St. George's Anglican Church

now linked to most of the surrounding edifices. It also encompasses a number of office buildings, including the famous cruciform aluminium tower.

The **Tour BNP ★**, certainly the best designed building on Avenue McGill College, was built for the Banque Nationale de Paris in 1981 by the architectural firm Webb, Zerafa, Menkès, Housden Partnership (Tour Elf-Aquitaine, Paris; Royal Bank, Toronto).

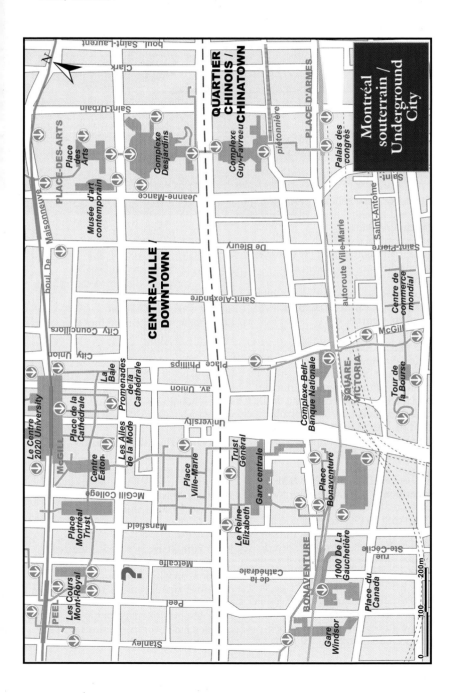

The **Musée McCord d'Histoire Canadienne / McCord Museum of Canadian History** ★★ occupies a building formerly used by the McGill University Students' Association. Designed by architect Percy Nobbs (1906), this handsome building of English baroque inspiration was enlarged at the rear in 1991. For anyone interested in the First Nations and daily life in Canada in the 18th and 19th centuries, this is the museum to see in Montréal.

McCord Museum of Canadian History

© McCord Museum

McGill University ★★ was founded in 1821, thanks to a donation by fur trader James McGill. It is the oldest of Montréal's four universities. Throughout the 19th century, the institution was one of the finest jewels of the Golden Square Mile's Scottish bourgeoisie. The university's main campus lies nestled in greenery at the foot of Mont Royal.

A former Methodist church designed in the shape of an auditorium, **St. James United Church** ★ originally had a complete façade looking out onto a garden. In 1926, in an effort to counter the decrease in its revenue, the community built a group of stores and offices along the front of the building on Rue Sainte-Catherine, leaving only a narrow passageway into the church.

After a 40-year absence, the Jesuits returned to Montréal in 1842 at Monseigneur Ignace Bourget's invitation. Six years later, they founded Collège Sainte-Marie, where several generations of boys would receive an outstanding education. **Église du Gesù** ★★ was originally designed as the college chapel.

Fleeing misery and potato blight, a large number of Irish immigrants came to Montréal between 1820 and 1860, and helped construct the Lachine Canal and the Victoria Bridge. **St. Patrick's Basilica** ★★ was thus built to meet a pressing new demand for a church to serve the Irish Catholic community.

During the rush of the Quiet Revolution, the government of Québec, inspired by cultural complexes like New York's Lincoln Center, built **Place des Arts** ★, a collection of five halls for the performing arts.

Erected in 1893 for the Société Saint-Jean-Baptiste, which is devoted to protecting the rights of French-speakers, the **Monument National** ★ was intended to be a cultural centre dedicated to the French Canadian cause. The building was sold to the National Theatre School of Canada in 1971. As Canada's oldest theatre, it was carefully restored for its 100th anniversary.

Musée d'Art Contemporain de Montréal and Place des Arts
Stéphane-Emmanuel Cocke

Sculpture garden at the MACM   Stéphane-Emmanuel Cocke

The **Musée d'Art Contemporain de Montréal** ★★ or MACM, Montréal's modern art museum, opened in 1992. The long, low building, erected on top of the Place des Arts parking lot, contains eight rooms, where post-1940 works of art from both Québec and abroad are exhibited.

Montréal's **Chinatown** ★ may be rather small, but it is nonetheless a pleasant place to walk around. Rue de la Gauchetière has been converted into a pedestrian street lined with restaurants and framed by lovely Chinese-style gates.

To the west of Rue Saint-Urbain lies Montreal's convention centre, the **Palais des Congrès de Montréal** ★, a forbidding mass of concrete erected over the Autoroute Ville-Marie, which contributes to the isolation of the old city from downtown. Following large-scale extension work in 2002, the convention centre has doubled in size and now has two means of entry: the main entrance, on Avenue Viger, and a second, on Rue De Bleury. The Palais de Congrès' new wing stands in the heart of the Quartier International de Montréal and its entrance is now at street level. The huge coloured-glass facade overlooking Rue De Bleury creates an interplay of light and colour both inside and outside the convention centre. It faces a new public square, **Place Jean-Paul Riopelle** ★★, located at the corner of Saint-Antoine and Bleury streets, which features a monumental bronze sculpture by the famous artist entitled "La Joute" (The Joust).

THE *REFUS GLOBAL*

"Supporters of the status quo suspect us of endorsing the 'Revolution,' supporters of the 'Revolution' of being mere rebels: '... we oppose the established order, but only to transform it, not change it."

Extract from the *Refus Global* manifesto, 1948
Paul-Émile Borduas and 15 other signatories

The Refus Global, which spawned the Quiet Revolution of the 1960s, is a manifesto denouncing the political and religious conformity of the 1940s, which made Québec a stifling and hostile environment hindering individual and collective creativity. Signed in 1948 by painter Paul-Émile Borduas (1905-1960) and 15 other artists, including Jean-Paul Riopelle, the manifesto marked the beginning of a radical shift in Québec society. Following its publication, which caused a huge uproar, Borduas was fired from his teaching post at Montréal's École du Meuble and, a few years later, sought exile in Paris.

Chinatown

JEAN-PAUL RIOPELLE

Jean-Paul Riopelle was one of Québec's most renowned painters, and its best-known internationally. Many of the impressive number of paintings he created are exhibited throughout the world. This legendary character, an abstract painter famous for his huge mosaics, left his mark on the world of contemporary art. He was born in Montréal in 1932, and his career took off with the Automatism movement in the 1940s.

He was also one of the 16 co-signatories of the *Refus Global*, an artistic manifesto. He lived in Paris for several years but returned to the province of Québec during the last years of his life. He died on March 12, 2002, in his manor on Île aux Grues, on the St. Lawrence River, in the migration path of the snow geese he held so dear to his heart.

SHAUGHNESSY VILLAGE ★★

Shaughnessy Village lies close to downtown, bordered by Ste-Catherine, Guy, Atwater and René-Lévesque streets. Since 1960, the number of inhabitants in this neighbourhood has increased considerably, making Shaughnessy Village the most densely populated area in Québec.

The Sulpicians' farmhouse was surrounded by a wall linked to four stone corner towers, earning it the name Fort des Messieurs. The house was destroyed when the **Grand Séminaire** ★★ (1854-1860) was built, but two towers, erected in the 17th century according to plans by François Vachon de Belmont, superior of the Montréal Sulpicians, can still be found in the institution's shady gardens.

Founded in 1979 by Phyllis Lambert, the **Centre Canadien d'Architecture / Canadian Centre for Architecture** ★★★ is both a museum and a centre for the study of world architecture. Its collections of plans, drawings, models, books and photographs are the most important of their kind in the entire world. The amusing **architecture garden** ★, by artist Melvin Charney, lies across from Shaughnessy House between two highway on-ramps.

The **Couvent des Sœurs Grises** ★★ is the product of an architectural tradition developed over the centuries in Québec. The chapel alone reveals a foreign influence, namely the Romanesque Revival style favoured by the Sulpicians, as opposed to the Renaissance and Baroque Revival styles preferred by the church.

THE TAM-TAMS

The slope of Mont Royal facing Avenue du Parc has been the site of a colourful, impromptu party, known simply as the Tam Tams, every Sunday afternoon in summer for over 20 years now. Weather permitting, people of all stripes and ages gather here in a bohemian atmosphere.

Dozens of percussionists then settle in at the foot of the huge monument to Sir George-Étienne Cartier—one of the fathers of Confederation—and improvise increasingly lively world-beat rhythms throughout the afternoon. Hordes of dancers groove to the frenzied beat of African congas and other drums, while a merry crowd of onlookers enjoys a picnic or sunbathes on the grass.

MONT ROYAL AND WESTMOUNT ★★

Montréal's central neighbourhoods were built around Mont Royal, an important landmark in the cityscape. Known simply as "the mountain" by anglophone Montrealers, this squat mass, measuring 234m at its highest point, is in fact Montréal's "green lung".

From the **Belvédère Camillien-Houde** ★★, a lovely scenic lookout, visitors can look out over the entire eastern portion of Montréal. The Plateau Mont-Royal lies in the foreground, a uniform mass of duplexes and triplexes, pierced in a few places by the oxidized copper bell towers of parish churches, while the Rosemont and Maisonneuve districts lie in the background, with the Olympic Stadium towering over them.

Pressured by the residents of the Golden Square Mile, who saw their favourite playground being deforested by various firewood companies, the City of Montréal created **Parc du Mont-Royal** ★★★ in 1870. Frederick Law Olmsted (1822-1903), the celebrated designer of New York's

Parc du Mont Royal   Tourisme Montréal, Stéphan Poulin

Central Park, was commissioned to design the park.

The **Chalet du Mont Royal** ★★★, located in the centre of the park, was designed by Aristide Beaugrand-Champagne in 1932 as a replacement for the original structure, which was about to collapse. The interior is decorated with remounted paintings depicting scenes from Canadian history. They were commissioned from some of Québec's great painters, such as Marc-Aurèle Fortin and Paul-Émile Borduas. Nevertheless, people go to the chalet mainly to stroll along the lookout and take in the exceptional view of downtown from the **Belvédère Kondiaronk** (named for the Huron Chief who negotiated the 1701 peace), best in the late afternoon and in the evening, when the skyscrapers light up the darkening sky.

The **Mount Royal Cemetery** ★★ is a Protestant cemetery that ranks among the most beautiful spots in the city. Designed as an Eden for the living visiting the deceased, it is laid out like a landscape garden in an isolated valley, giving visitors the impression that they are a thousand miles from the city, though they are in fact right in the centre of it. The wide variety of hardwood and fruit trees attract species of birds found nowhere else in Québec.

The **Cimetière Notre-Dame-des-Neiges** ★★, Montréal's largest cemetery, is a veritable city of the dead, as more than a million people have been buried here since it opened in 1855. It replaced the cemetery in Square Dominion, which was deemed too close to the neighbouring houses. Unlike the Protestant cemetery, it has a conspicuously religious character, clearly identifying it with the Catholic faith.

Both the cemetery and the roads leading to it offer a number of views of the **Oratoire Saint-Joseph** ★★. The enormous building topped by a copper dome, the second-largest dome in the world after that of St. Peter's in Rome, stands on a hillside, accentuating its mystical aura. From the gate at the entrance, there are over 300 steps to climb to reach the oratory.

The **Université de Montréal** ★ became autonomous in 1920, enabling its directors to develop grandiose plans. Ernest Cormier (1885-1980) was approached about designing a campus on the north side of Mont Royal. Plans for the main building called for a streamlined Art Deco design with a central tower. In 1943, the building welcomed its first students. Since then the Université de Montréal has become the second largest French-language university in the world.

Westmount is like a piece of Great Britain in North America. Its **City Hall** ★ was built in the Neo-Tudor style, inspired by the architecture of the age of Henry VIII and Elizabeth I, which was regarded during the 1920s as the national style of England because it originated in the British Isles.

At the corner of Avenue Clarke stands **Église Saint-Léon** ★, the only French-language Catholic parish in Westmount. The sober, elegant Romanesque Revival façade

The Oratoire Saint-Joseph

Fondation du Patrimoine Religieux du Québec

NOTRE-DAME-DES-NEIGES

Cimetière Notre-Dame-des-Neiges (Notre Dame des Neiges Cemetery) opened in 1855. It stretches over land that was once the north shore of a lost island in the ancient Champlain Sea (the site of present-day Mont Royal) following the thaw of the Inlandsis Laurentidien (a 3km-thick continental glacier) 10,000 years ago.

On May 29, 1855, Mrs. Jane Gilroy, wife of Thomas McCready, then a Montréal municipal councillor, was the first person to be buried in the new cemetery. Since the burial of Mrs. Gilroy, almost one million people have been laid to rest here, making Cimetière Notre-Dame-des-Neiges the second-largest cemetery in North America after Arlington Cemetery in Washington. A walk through the 55km of trails that crisscross the site proves that this cemetery is a unique treasure, as much for its architectural, cultural and historical aspects as for its natural setting.

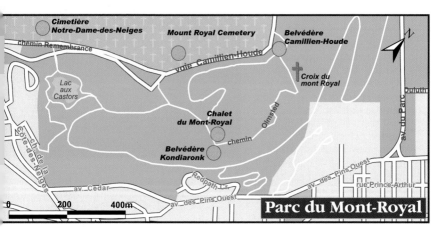

conceals an exceptionally rich interior decor begun in 1928 by artist Guido Nincheri.

Architect Ludwig Mies van der Rohe (1886-1969), one of the leading masters of the modernist movement and the head of Bauhaus in Germany, designed **Westmount Square ★★** in 1964. The complex is typical of the architect's North American work, characterized by the use of black metal and tinted glass.

MAISONNEUVE ★★★

In 1883, the city of Maisonneuve was founded in eastern Montréal by farmers and French Canadian merchants; port facilities expanded into the area and the city's development picked up. Then, in 1918, the formerly autonomous city was annexed to Montréal, becoming one of its major working-class neighbourhoods, with a 90% francophone population

The Jardin Botanique de Montréal / Montréal's Botanical Garden ★★★, covering an area of 73ha, was begun during the economic crisis of the 1930s on the site of Mont-de-La-Salle, home base of the brothers of the Écoles Chrétiennes, by Frère Marie-Victorin, a well-known Québec botanist. Behind the Art Deco building occupied by the Université de Montréal's institute of biology, visitors will find 10 connected greenhouses, that shelter a precious collection of orchids and the largest grouping of bonsais and *penjings* outside of Asia. Thirty outdoor thematic gardens stretch to the north and west of the greenhouses, including the **Japanese Garden** and stunning **Chinese Garden**. Another must-see is the **First Nations Garden**, which explores Aboriginals' relationship with the plant world. The northern part of the botanical garden is occupied by an arboretum. The **Maison de l'Arbre** was established in this area to educate people about the life of a tree. The interactive, permanent exhibit is actually set up in an old tree trunk. The **Insectarium** is located to the east of the greenhouses. This innovative, living museum invites visitors to discover the fascinating world of insects.

The **Château Dufresne ★★** is in fact two 22-room private mansions behind

Chinese Garden at Montréal's Botanical Gardens   Philippe Renault

Butterfly at the Insectarium   René Limoges

the same façade, built in 1916 for brothers Marius and Oscar Dufresne, shoe-manufacturers and authors of a grandiose plan to develop Maisonneuve. The plan was abandoned after the onset of World War I, causing the municipality to go bankrupt.

The **Stade Olympique / Olympic Stadium ★★★** is also known as the "Big O." The 56,000-seat oval stadium is covered with a Kevlar roof supported by cables stretching from the 190m-high leaning tower. In the distance, visitors will see the two pyramid-shaped towers of the **Olympic Village**, where the athletes were housed in 1976. Each year, the stadium hosts different events. The stadium's tower, which is the tallest leaning tower in the world, was renamed the **Tour de Montréal**.

The former cycling track, known as the Vélodrome, located nearby, has been converted into an artificial habitat for plants and animals called the **Biodôme** ★ ★ ★. This new type of museum, associated with the Jardin Botanique, contains four very different ecosystems: the Tropical Rainforest, the Laurentian Forest, the St. Lawrence Marine Ecosystem and the Polar World, within a space of 10,000m².

Behind the somewhat drab Romanesque Revival façade of the **Église du Très-Saint-Nom-de-Jésus** ★, built in 1906, visitors will discover a rich, polychromatic decor, created in part by artist Guido Nincheri, whose studio was located in Maisonneuve.

Montréal's Botanical Garden Philippe Renault

Penguins at the Biodôme Sean O' Neill

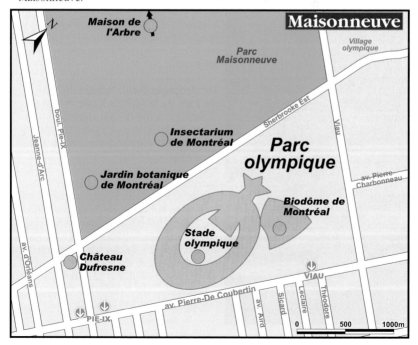

Habitat 67   Philippe Renault

ÎLE SAINTE-HÉLÈNE AND ÎLE NOTRE-DAME ★★

When Samuel de Champlain reached the island of Montréal in 1611, he found a small rocky archipelago located in front of it. He named the largest of these islands in the channel after his wife, Hélène Boulé. **Île Sainte-Hélène** later became part of the seigneury of Longueuil. Around 1720, the Baroness of Longueuil chose the island as the site for a country house surrounded by a garden.

The **Tropique Nord, Habitat '67** and the **Parc de la Cité du Havre ★★** were all built on a spit of land created to protect the port of Montréal from ice and currents. From here, visitors can spot the large glass wall of the Tropique Nord, a residential complex composed of apartments with a view of the outdoors on one side, and an interior tropical garden on the other. Next, visitors will see Habitat '67, an experimental housing development built for Expo '67 by architect Moishe Safdie, who was only 23 at the time. At the Parc de la Cité du Havre, visitors will find 12 panels containing a brief description of the history of the St. Lawrence River.

Marina in the Vieux-Port de Montréal   Patrick Escudero

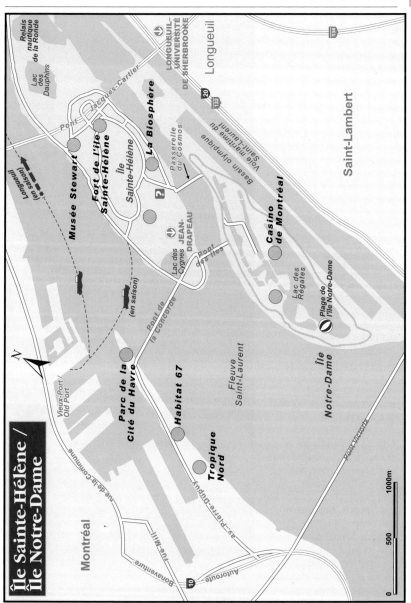

Île Sainte-Hélène / Île Notre-Dame

Parc Jean-Drapeau ★★ lies on Île Sainte- Hélène, which originally covered an area of 50ha but was enlarged to over 120ha for Expo '67. The original portion corresponds to the raised area studded with breccia stone boulders. Peculiar to the island, breccia is a very hard, ferrous stone that takes on an orange colour when exposed to air for a long time. In this lovely riverside park, visitors will find **L'Homme** ("Humankind"), a large metal sculpture by Alexandre Calder, created for Expo '67.

After the War of 1812 between the United States and Great Britain, the **Fort de l'Île Sainte-Hélène** ★★ was built so that Montréal could be properly defended if ever a new conflict were to erupt. Built of breccia stone, the fort is in the shape of a jagged U, surrounding a drill ground, used today by the Compagnie Franche de la Marine and the 78th Regiment of the Fraser Highlanders as a parade ground.

The arsenal is now occupied by the **Musée Stewart** ★★, which is dedicated to colonial history and the exploration of the New World. The museum exhibits objects from past centuries, including interesting collections of maps, firearms, and scientific and navigational instruments collected by Montréal industrialist David Stewart and his wife Liliane.

The Biosphere ★★, built of tubular aluminium and measuring 80m in diameter, unfortunately lost its translucent acrylic skin in a fire back in 1978. An environmental interpretive centre on the St. Lawrence River, the Great Lakes and the different Canadian ecosystems is now located in the dome.

Casino de Montréal ★ occupies the former French and Québec pavilions of Expo '67. The main building corresponds to the old **French Pavilion** ★, an aluminium structure designed by architect Jean Faugeron. The upper galleries offer some lovely views of downtown Montréal and the St. Lawrence Seaway. Immediately to the west of the former French pavilion, the building shaped like a truncated pyramid is the former **Québec pavilion** ★.

18th-century soldiers at the Musée Stewart   Philippe Renault

The Musée Stewart at the Fort de l'Île Sainte-Hélène   La Compagnie Franche de la Marine

The Biosphère   Environment Canada's Biosphère

The **Bibliothèque Nationale** ★, the national library, was originally built for the Sulpicians, who looked unfavourably upon the construction of a public library on Rue Sherbrooke. Even though many works were still on the Index, and thus forbidden reading for the clergy, the new library was seen as unfair competition. Known in the past as Bibliothèque Saint-Sulpice, this branch of the Bibliothèque Nationale du Québec was designed in the Beaux-Arts style by architect Eugène Payette in 1914.

Unlike most North American universities, with buildings contained within a specific campus, the campus of the **Université du Québec à Montréal (UQAM)** ★ is integrated into the city fabric like French and German universities built during the Renaissance. The university is located on the site once occupied by the buildings of the Université de Montréal and the Église Saint-Jacques, which was rebuilt after the fire of 1852.

Artist Napoléon Bourassa lived in a large house on Rue Saint-Denis. **Chapelle Notre-Dame-de-Lourdes** ★, erected in 1876, was his greatest achievement. It was commissioned by the Sulpicians, who wanted to secure their presence in this part of the city.

A symbol of the social ascent of a certain class of French Canadian businessmen in the early 20th century, the former business school, the **École des Hautes Études Commerciales** ★★, profoundly altered Montréal's managerial and

Houses on Square Saint-Louis

Philippe Renault

QUARTIER LATIN ★★

The area's origins date back to 1823, when Montréal's first Catholic cathedral, Église Saint-Jacques, opened on Rue Saint-Denis. This prestigious edifice quickly attracted the cream of French Canadian society—mainly old noble families who had remained in Canada after the Conquest—to the area. In 1852, a fire ravaged the neighbourhood, destroying the cathedral and Monseigneur Bourget's bishop's palace in the process.

After the great fire of 1852, a reservoir was built at the top of the hill known as Côte-à-Barron. In 1879, it was dismantled and the site was converted into a park by the name of **Square Saint-Louis** ★★. Developers built beautiful Second Empire-style homes around the square, making it the nucleus of the French Canadian bourgeois neighbourhood.

"TÊTE À PAPINEAU"

The son-in-law of Louis-Joseph Papineau, artist Napoléon Bourassa—whose masterpiece Notre-Dame-de-Lourdes chapel, erected on Sainte-Catherine street in Montreal in 1876—lived in a large house located on Rue St-Denis (no. 1242), near the aforementioned chapel. An interesting titbit: on the house's facade is Papineau's head (tête à Papineau). A joke? Certainly not!

Heroic instigator of the Patriote movement, Louis-Joseph Papineau remains, without question, a major player in the dismantling of a political regime unacceptable to the people of Lower Canada. His reputation as a man of high intelligence survives to this day in the popular French-language expression "*Ça ne prends pas la tête à Papineau!*" (meaning "It doesn't take Papineau's brains!" or "It's not rocket science!").

Rue Saint-Denis

Philippe Renault

financial circles. Prior to the school's existence, these circles were dominated by Canadians of British extraction. Today, this magnificent building is home to the Montréal archives branch of the Archives Nationales du Québec.

PLATEAU MONT-ROYAL ★

If there is one neighbourhood typical of Montréal, it is definitely the Plateau Mont-Royal. Thrown into the spotlight by writer Michel Tremblay, one of its illustrious sons, the "Plateau," as its inhabitants refer to it, is a neighbourhood of penniless intellectuals, young professionals and old Francophone working-class families.

The **Bibliothèque Centrale de Montréal**, the city's public library, was inaugurated in 1917 by Maréchal Joffre. Even back in the early 20th century, the edifice was of modest size, given the number of people it was intended to serve, a result of the clergy's reservations about a non-religious library opening in Montréal.

Parc Lafontaine ★, the Plateau's main green space, was laid out in 1908 on the site of an old military shooting range. Monuments to Sir Louis-Hippolyte Lafontaine, Félix Leclerc and Dollard des Ormeaux have been erected here. The park covers an area of 40ha and is embellished with two artificial lakes and shady paths for pedestrians and cyclists.

Église Saint-Jean-Baptiste ★★, dedicated to the patron saint of French Canadians, is a gigantic symbol of the solid faith of the Catholic working-class inhabitants of the Plateau Mont-Royal at the turn of the 20th century, who, despite their poverty and large families, managed to amass considerable amounts of money for the construction of sumptuous churches.

Stairways in the Quartier Latin   Patrick Escudero

Outdoor skating rink   Philippe Renault

LAVAL

Laval, Québec's second-largest city, is located on a large island north of Montréal called Île Jésus. The island is surrounded by three bodies of water: Lac des Deux-Montagnes to the east, Rivière des Prairies to the south and Rivière des Mille Îles to the north. Laval is now a residential and industrial suburb, but it has managed to preserve some of its architectural heritage and farmland, and also has set aside several large spaces for outdoor activities.

Sainte-Rose ★

Old Sainte-Rose features a surprising array of neoclassical buildings graced with sizeable stone facades with wooden footings. Art galleries, antique shops and pleasant restaurants are housed in the former dwellings lining Boulevard Sainte-Rose.

Parc de la Rivière-des-Mille-Îles ★

Parc de la Rivière-des-Mille-Îles takes skilful advantage of the host of islands scattered throughout this stretch of the Rivière des Mille Îles. Visitors can explore the area by canoe, kayak or rabaska (a large voyager canoe) from a quiet bay, which also serves as a play and rest area. Boaters can put in at one of the many islands for a picnic or to contemplate the local flora and fauna, particularly abundant in this humid environment. In winter, a skating rink, and cross-country ski and walking trails among the islands provide fun for the whole family.

Sainte-Dorothée

In Sainte-Dorothée, follow what is now known as the **Route des Fleurs (Flower Trail)** ★. Blessed with some of the most fertile land in Québec, Sainte-Dorothée has built an enviable reputation for itself over the years as "Québec's horticultural capital."

The Cosmodôme   Tourisme Laval

Historic house in Sainte-Rose   Tourisme Laval

Chomedey

The **Cosmodôme** ★ is a space museum. A tour of the premises starts with a fascinating multimedia presentation on the history of the discovery of outer space.

Centre de la Nature ★★

Laid out on the site of a former quarry, the sprawling Centre de la Nature, a 47ha park, is an outstanding example of a successful urban renewal project. Over the course of its existence, it has become a major multipurpose recreational facility.

Canoeing on the Rivière des Mille Îles
(page 182)

Tourisme Laval

ROUTE DES FLEURS

Laval is home to the Route des Fleurs, a 11.5km-long agro-tourism route that winds its way through the village of Sainte-Dorothée. This suburban route is dotted with, among other things, countless flower-producing greenhouses in a contemporary setting, something unique in itself.

Drivers seeking a change of scenery close to the city are sure to enjoy and be dazzled by this singular tour. The Route des Fleurs, boasting state-of-the-art horticulture, is not only open to drivers and tour-bus groups, but also to walkers, cyclists, cross-country skiers and snowmobilers.

To top it all off, in the fall, Laval hosts the Bal des Fleurs, a great flower festival featuring models draped from head to toe in fabrics and flowers of all kinds. Every year brings a new theme to the event.

The Route des Fleurs

Tourisme Laval

NORD-DU-QUÉBEC

Woodland caribou

Nord-du-Québec

A gigantic northern territory

The Cratère du Nouveau-Québec

stretching north from the 49th parallel to the 62nd parallel, the tourist region of Nord-du-Québec (Northern Québec) covers more than half of Québec's total area. The rough beauty of this barren landscape, its harsh winter climate and its unique tundra vegetation giving way to taiga and then boreal forest, create a region completely different from the rest of Québec.

The 14 communities along the shores of Hudson Bay, Hudson Strait and Ungava Bay are home to the Inuit. In Inuktitut, the language of the Inuit, this territory is known as Nunavik. The Cree live in nine villages on the taiga, mostly along the shores of James Bay.

From the first days of North American colonization, English and French forces fought for the control of the fur trade in this vast region. Today, and for the last 30 years, it is the government of Québec that has taken a keen interest in the resources of these lands, namely the massive potential for hydroelectric power contained in certain rivers.

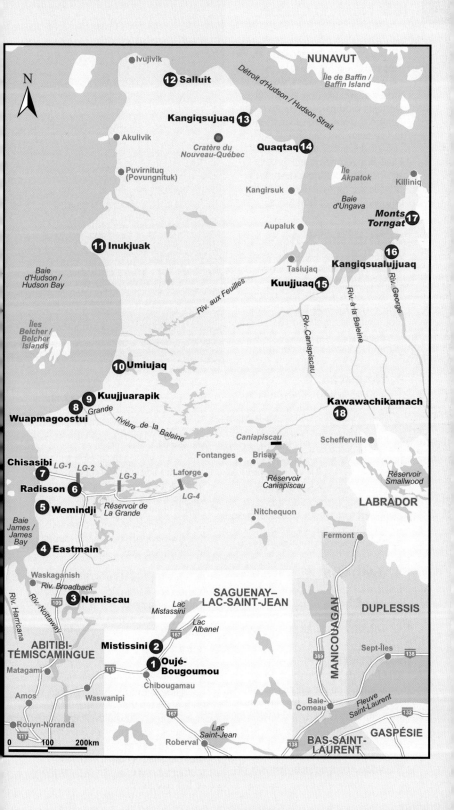

1. Oujé-Bougoumou ★★

This most recently established Cree village is in many ways also the most remarkable one. Architect Douglas Cardinal, the creative mind behind the Museum of Civilization in Gatineau, was entrusted with the task of designing the settlement. Oujé-Bougoumou's architecture is profoundly traditional despite the prevalence of symbolism and the emphasis on vanishing lines.

2. Mistissini ★★

At the heart of what was known as Le Domaine du Roi (the king's domain) during the fur trade, halfway between the St. Lawrence Valley and Hudson Bay, Mistissini, along with its immense lake, has been a tremendously important cultural crossroads for centuries.

Day of fishing in northern Québec   Tourisme Baie-James

3. Nemiscau ★

The French began trading furs as early as 1661 at this historic crossroads, and commerce continued to play a determining role in the history of Nemiscau, mainly thanks to the Hudson's Bay Company, which maintained a post here until 1970. At that point, this centre of economic activity disappeared and the Cree dispersed to found a beautiful, brand-new village on the shores of marvellous Lac Champion in 1979.

4. Eastmain ★

Eastmain enjoys a striking view of the mouth of the Rivière de Rupert and exudes the warmth and welcome of an isolated community.

5. Wemindji ★

The Cree did not establish this community, on the shores of James Bay at the mouth of the Maquatua river, until 1959 when they left Vieux-Comptoir, 45km to the south. The name Wemindji means "ochre mountain," and the hills surrounding the village contain rich deposits of

this mineral, which is mixed with grease to make paint.

6. Radisson ★★

This town was built in 1974 to accommodate the workers from the south who were arriving as part of the James Bay hydroelectric project. During the boom years of construction on the hydro project, there were more than 6,000 people living on the site.

Radisson's main draw is its impressive hydroelectric complex: the **Centrale Robert-Bourassa ★★★** formerly known as La Grande 2, and **La Grande-1**.

7. Chisasibi ★★

A Cree word meaning "the big river," Chisasibi is a modern village that was built in 1981, after the Cree left Île de Fort George. This little village was laid out in keeping with the Cree's matriarchal society, so that the houses stand in small groups, with the mother's house surrounded by those of her daughters.

NOUVEAU-QUÉBEC, KATIVIK OR NUNAVIK?

In 1912, the federal government divided Rupert's Land among Manitoba, Ontario and Québec. Thus the northern border of Québec changed from the Eastmain River to the Hudson Strait, 1,110km further north. This region was called Nouveau Québec. With the James Bay and Northern Québec Agreement the government of Québec created a new region called Kativik, to designate those villages located north of the 55th parallel. However, in 1986, the Inuit community held a referendum and chose to adopt the name Nunavik, which means "place to live."

8-9. Whapmagoostui ★★ and Kuujjuarapik ★★

Here is a truly unique community, as much for its history and geographic location as for its social makeup. The Cree village of Whapmagoostui sits across from the Inuit village of Kuujjuarapik at the mouth of Grande Rivière de la Baleine on Hudson Bay. This coexistence has lasted for about two centuries around the trading post known as Great Whale or Poste-de-la-Baleine.

10. Umiujaq ★

Situated 160km north of Kuujjuarapik, the village of Umiujaq was inaugurated in December 1986. Sitting at the foot of a hill that resembles an umiak (a large sealskin boat), Umiujaq looks out onto Hudson Bay.

11. Inukjuak ★

Nunavik's second-largest village, Inukjuak is set 360km north of Kuujjuarapik, at the mouth of the Innuksuac river, facing the Hopewell Islands. The lives of the residents of Inukjuak remain strongly tied to traditional activities.

12. Salluit ★★

Situated 250km north of Puvirnituq, 115km east of Ivujivik and 2,125km from Québec City, Salluit is nestled in a valley formed by steep mountains, about 10km from the mouth of the fjord of the same name.

The actual site of Salluit, dominated by jagged mountains and steep hills, is absolutely spectacular. Located between the sea and the mountains on a magnificent **fjord ★★** , it is one of the most picturesque villages in Nunavik.

13. Kangiqsujuaq ★★

Surrounded by majestic mountains at the bottom of a superb valley, Kangiqsujuaq, an Inuktitut word that means "the large bay," stands proudly over the fjord of immense Wakeham Bay.

The most impressive natural tourist attraction of the area, and of Nunavik in general, is without question the **Cratère du Nouveau-Québec ★★**, which the Inuit call Pingualuit. Less than 100km from the village, this gigantic crater has imposing dimensions: its diameter measures 3,770m and it is 446m deep.

14. Quaqtaq

Quaqtaq (an Inuktitut word meaning "intestinal worm") is bounded to the north by mountainous terrain and to

PINGUALUIT: WHERE THE LAND RISES

In 2003, the Québec government finally recognized the importance to the Inuit of the Cratère du Nouveau Québec's (New Québec Crater), officially designating it by its rightful Inuit-language name, Pingualuit, which means "where the land rises," and creating the first park in Nunavik: Parc National Pingualuit. Thus it is seeking to preserve this environment and its ecosystems for future generations. Until the establishment of an autonomous government in Nunavik, the Québec government has entrusted the management of the park to the Inuit.

The Pingualuit Crater, a circular depression measuring about 3km in diameter and more than 400m deep, was created by the impact of a huge meteorite roughly 1.4 million years ago. Purportedly the deepest in North America, the lake that formed within the crater is made up of fresh water of unmatched purity supplied exclusively by rainwater and melting snow.

The Cratère du Nouveau-Québec

Jean Boisclair
Société de la faune et
des parcs du Québec

the south and east by low rocky hills. Located 157km from its nearest neighbour, Kangiqsujjuaq, and 350km north of Kuujjuaq, the village stretches over a peninsula that juts into Hudson Strait and forms the coast of **Diana Bay** ★, known among the Inuit as Tuvaaluk, "the large ice floe".

15. Kuujjuaq ★

Today, Kuujjuaq (Inuktitut for "big river") is the administrative centre of the territory of Nunavik and the headquarters of the Administration Régionale de Kativik. Various governmental and regional organizations have offices here, as well.

Majestic **Rivière Koksoak** ★ is one the marvels of the area. It adds a unique and very picturesque dimension to Kuujjuaq's setting, and its tides shape landscapes of fascinating beauty.

Sea kayaking in LG4 sector

Tourisme-Baie James

16.
Kangiqsualujjuaq ★★★

The hamlet was created on the initiative of local Inuit who founded the first cooperative in Nouveau-Québec here with the goal of creating a commercial char fishery. Construction of the village began at the very beginning of the 1960s, and the first public services were organized here at that time. The region attracts one of the largest herds of caribou in the world.

17. The Monts
Torngat ★★★

The Torngats are situated about 100km east of the village, between Ungava Bay and the Atlantic Ocean, at the Québec-Labrador border. At over 220km long and 100km wide, they are the highest mountains in Québec, making the chain as vast as the Alps. Many of the summits reach altitudes of 1,700m, including majestic **Mont d'Iberville ★** (the highest summit in Québec), which dominates the range with its height of 1,768m.

18. Kawawachikamach ★

Situated 15km from Schefferville, some 1,000km north of Montréal and right next to the Labrador border, Kawawachikamach is the only

Naskapi community in Québec. Related to the Cree and the Montagnais, the Naskapi are also part of the Algonquian language family. Kawawachikamach, a Naskapi word that means "the place where the sinuous river becomes a great lake," is located in a region of exceptional natural beauty and innumerable lakes and rivers.

Inuit woman and baby

OUTAOUAIS

Champlain Lookout in Gatineau Park

Outaouais
The realm of explorers

Gatineau Park

National Capital Commission

and trappers from early on, the Outaouais region was not settled by Europeans until the arrival of Loyalists from the United States in the early 19th century. Forestry was long the region's main economic activity. Of particular importance to the industry were red and white pine, trees used for ship building. The logs were sent down the Ottawa and St. Lawrence Rivers to Québec City, where they were loaded onto ships headed for Great Britain.

Directly north of the new city of Gatineau, which combines the former cities of Hull, Aylmer and Gatineau, lies an expanse of rolling hills, lakes and rivers, including the magnificent Gatineau Park. The park is the location of the official summer residence of the Canadian Prime Minister. The city also has one of the best museums in the country: the Canadian Museum of Civilization.

Andrew Van Beek

Lac Fortune, Gatineau Park
(page 190)
National Capital Commission

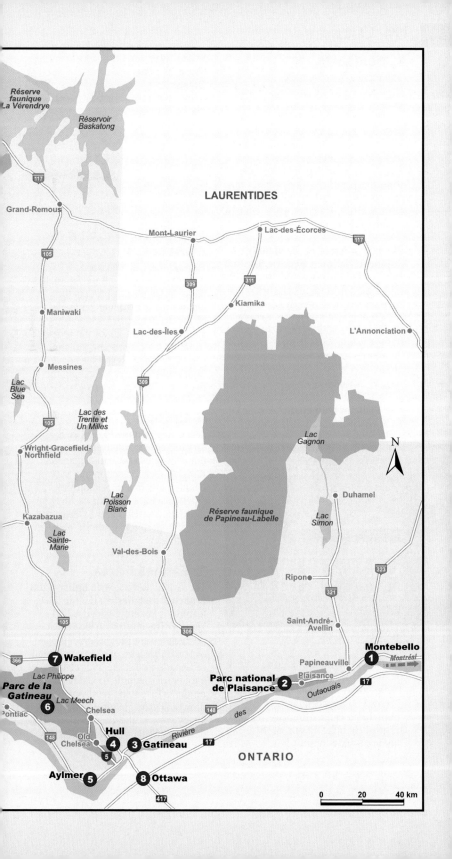

I. Montebello ★

The Outaouais region did not experience significant development under the French regime. Located upstream of the Lachine Rapids, the area was not easily accessible by water, and was thus left to hunters and trappers until the early 19th century and the beginning of the forestry operations. The Petite-Nation seigneury, granted to Monseigneur de Laval in 1674, was the only attempt at colonization in this vast region.

The manor house of the **Manoir Papineau National Historic Site ★★** was erected between 1846 and 1849 in the monumental neoclassical villa style. It was designed by Louis Aubertin, a visiting French architect. The towers added in the 1850s give the house a medieval appearance. One of the towers houses a precious library that Papineau placed here to protect it from fire.

The **Château Montebello ★★** is a large resort hotel on the Papineau

Manoir Papineau National Historic Site
Parks Canada/N. Rajotte

estate. It is the largest log building in the world. The hotel was erected in 1929 (Lawson and Little, architects) in a record 90 days. The impressive lobby has a central fireplace with six hearths, each facing one of the building's six wings.

Spread over 600ha, the **Parc Oméga ★** is home to many different animal species that can be observed from within one's vehicle, including bison, wild sheep, elk, wild goats, wild boar and deer.

White-tailed deer

2. The Parc National de Plaisance ★

Parc National de Plaisance, a provincial park, is one of the smallest parks in Québec. It borders the Ottawa River for some 27km and its goal is to introduce visitors to the animal and plant life of the region. To better observe birds and aquatic plants, wooden footbridges have been built above the marshes along the river.

Gatineau

While Anglophone federal civil servants reside mainly in Ontario municipalities (Nepean, Uplands, Kanata), their Francophone counterparts live mostly on the Québec side of the Ottawa River, in the Gatineau, Hull and Aylmer areas, which collectively form the megacity of Gatineau.

3. Gatineau Area

The Gothic Revival-style **Église Saint-François-de-Sales ★**, built in 1866, features a beautiful gilded-wood interior. The church's bell was bequeathed by Lady Aberdeen, wife of Lord Aberdeen, Governor-General of Canada in the late 19th century, as a token of gratitude to Gatineau residents for saving her from drowning. The church square offers a lovely view of the Ottawa River and Parliament Hill, in Ottawa, Ontario.

THE COUREUR DES BOIS

The coureur des bois is a legendary figure in Québec culture. When the colony was first established, Champlain left a young man named Étienne Brûlé in this region. Brûlé learned the language of the Algonquins and travelled inland. In those days, men like him—who in some way were sent out to measure the impact that the French had on the natives, be it positive or negative—were known as *truchements* or "go-betweens."

Upon his return, Champlain found Brûlé dressed like the Aboriginals and completely adapted to their way of life. The *truchements* originally adopted the native lifestyle for economic reasons, as they did not want to offend their hosts and thus imperil the fur trade. However, as the months went by, they came to appreciate the Aboriginals' daily routines, which were in direct response to the environment. They thus learned to eat corn, wear snowshoes and use bark canoes. They also started using toboggans to carry their cargo. Removed from church and state as they were, however, these *truchements* did have a tendency to let themselves go altogether, and their unfettered liberty led to some rather dubious practices. This side of their life is clearly exemplified by Étienne Brûlé's death; he was killed and eaten by the Hurons, with whom he had lived for a long time.

Be that as it may, these *truchements*-turned-coureurs-des-bois were still the first Europeans to adopt and begin to understand the traditional native way of life. They chose this lifestyle because it corresponded to the geographic, climatic, economic and social conditions in the New World. Their behaviour may not always have been exemplary, but they nevertheless played a crucial role in Canada's development by serving as a link between the European and Aboriginal cultures.

4. Hull Area

Although the road leading into Hull is named after an important post-war town planner, the city is certainly not a model of enlightened urban development. Its architecture is very unlike that of Ottawa, just across the river. Hull is a mixture of old factories, typical working-class houses, tall, modern government office buildings, and barren land awaiting future government expansion.

Canadian Museum of Civilization   Harry Foster

As part of a large redevelopment program in the National Capital Region between 1983 and 1989, parks and museums were created on both sides of the Québec-Ontario border. Hull became the site of the magnificent **Canadian Museum of Civilization ★ ★ ★**, dedicated to the history of Canada's various cultural groups. Douglas Cardinal, a First Nations architect from Alberta, drew up the plans for the museum's two striking curved buildings.

The **Casino du Lac-Leamy ★ ★** has an impressive location between two lakes; Leamy Lake, in the park of the same name, and Lac de la Carrière, which is in the basin of an old limestone quarry. The theme of water is omnipresent around the superb building, completed in 1996. The magnificent walkway leading to the main entrance is dotted with towering fountains, and the harbour has 20 slips for boaters.

Imagine contemplating the magnificent landscapes of the Gatineau Park and River from the comfort of a steam-powered train dating from 1907... Well, this memorable excursion is precisely what the **Hull-Chelsea-Wakefield Steam Train ★** offers.

5. Aylmer Area ★

Aylmer was once the administrative centre of the Outaouais region. The city was founded by Charles Symmes, an American from Boston who arrived in Canada in 1814. The Hudson's Bay Company, then a major player in the fur trade, centred its activities in this region. Today, Aylmer, with its residential streets lined with middle-class homes, is a suburb of Ottawa.

Prompted by his uncle, Philemon Wright, Charles Symmes settled in the Aylmer region in 1824. In 1830, he built the **old Symmes Inn ★**, which became very popular with fur-trappers heading out to the Canadian Shield.

6. Gatineau Park ★ ★

This 35,000-ha park was founded during the Depression in 1934 to protect the forests from people looking for firewood. It is crossed by a 34km-long road dotted with panoramic lookout points, including the **Champlain Lookout**, which offer superb views of the lakes, rivers and hills of the region of Pontiac.

Andrew Van Beek

Hull-Chelsea-Wakefield steam train

DOUGLAS CARDINAL, METIS ARCHITECT

A true native of Alberta, world-famous Metis architect Douglas Cardinal is renowned as the innovator of a unique, organic style of architecture. His best-known work, the Canadian Museum of Civilization (1989), is located in the new megacity of Gatineau, on the Ottawa River.

Douglas Cardinal studied architecture at the University of British Columbia and the University of Texas. He established his unconventional, fluid architectural style, inspired by forms found in nature and blending in with the surrounding landscape, as early as 1969 with St. Mary's Church, in Alberta. More recently, he designed the public buildings of the Cree village Oujé-Bougoumou, in northern Québec; they received official recognition from the United Nations in 1995 with the *We The People - Fifty Communities Award*.

The opening of the Smithsonian Institute's National Museum of the American Indian in Washington D.C. coincides with the fall equinox of 2004. The most recent work of Douglas Cardinal, the NMAI is an excellent example of Cardinal's reconciliation of his native roots and his architectural vision.

Champlain Lookout in Gatineau Park

National Capital Commission

False ruins at the Domaine Mackenzie-King

Québec en images

The **Domaine Mackenzie-King ★ ★**. William Lyon Mackenzie King was Prime Minister of Canada from 1921 to 1930, and again from 1935 to 1948. He was always happy to get away to his summer residence near Lac Kingsmere, which today is part of Gatineau Park. The estate consists of two houses (one of which is now a charming tea room), a landscaped garden and follies, false ruins that were popular at the time.

7. Wakefield ★

Wakefield is a charming little town located at the mouth of Rivière La Pêche. It is quite pleasant to stroll down its main avenue, with shops and cafés on one side and the beautiful Gatineau River on the other. The Gendron covered bridge, painted a striking brick red, stands out in the distance, particularly in summer when it is surrounded by leafy trees.

8. Ottawa (Ontario) ★ ★ ★

Canada has one federal capital and 13 provincial and territorial capitals corresponding to 10 provinces and 3 territories. Ottawa, the federal capital, was founded in 1827 by Colonel By, who first named the city Bytown.

Following the 1849 Montréal riots and the lack of consensus on a location for a permanent capital for the British colony, Queen Victoria decided in 1857 to place the seat of the colonial government on the border of anglophone Upper Canada and francophone Lower Canada. Specifically, she chose the small Ontario city of Ottawa, on the Ottawa River. Ten years later, in 1867, the agreement that created the independent Dominion of Canada was finally signed, and the House of Commons sat for the first time in the new Parliament Buildings.

Ottawa has several interesting museums, including the **National Gallery of Canada ★ ★ ★**, located on the left when coming off the Alexandra Bridge. Also of interest in the city are the Gothic Revival buildings on **Parliament Hill ★ ★ ★**, and the **Parliament Buildings ★ ★ ★**, dominated by the **Peace Tower** and surrounded by greenery and public gardens.

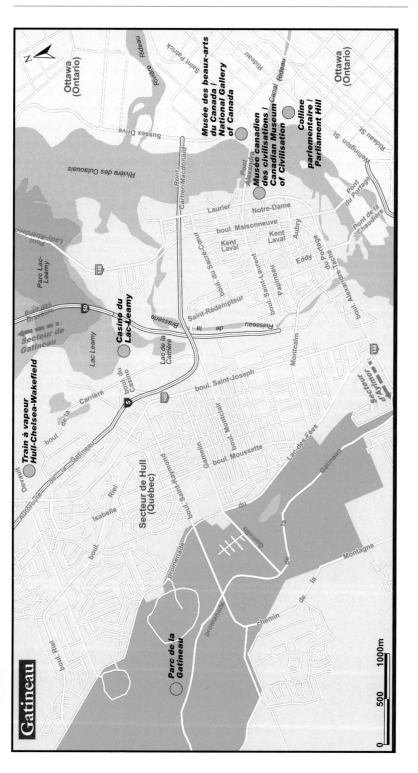

Gatineau

Musée des beaux-arts du Canada / National Gallery of Canada

Musée canadien des civilisations / Canadian Museum of Civilisation

Colline parlementaire / Parliament Hill

Casino du Lac-Leamy

Train à vapeur Hull-Chelsea-Wakefield

Parc de la Gatineau

Ottawa (Ontario)

Rivière des Outaouais

Secteur de Gatineau

Secteur de Hull (Québec)

Secteur d'Aylmer

0   500   1000m

QUÉBEC CITY

Château Frontenac

Québec City

A magical place

whatever the season, Québec City stands out as much for the stunning richness of its architectural heritage as for the beauty of its location.

The Haute-Ville quarter covers a promontory more than 98m high, known as Cap Diamant, and juts out over the St. Lawrence River, which narrows here to a mere 1km. In fact, it is this narrowing of the river that gave the city its name: in Algonquian, kebec means "place where the river narrows". Affording an impregnable vantage point, the heights of Cap Diamant dominate the river and the surrounding countryside. From the inception of New France, this rocky peak played a strategic role and was the site of major fortifications early on. Dubbed the "Gibraltar of North America," today Québec is the only walled city north of Mexico.

The cradle of New France, Québec City's atmosphere and architecture are more reminiscent of Europe than of America. The stone houses that flank its narrow streets and the many spires of its churches and religious institutions evoke the France of old. In addition, the old fortifications of the Haute-Ville, the Parliament and the grandiose administrative buildings attest eloquently to the importance of Québec City in the history of the country. Indeed, its historical and architectural richness is such that the city and its historic surroundings were recognized by UNESCO in 1985 as a World Heritage Site, the first in North America.

Ice Hotel
(page 200)
Ice Hotel Québec-Canada

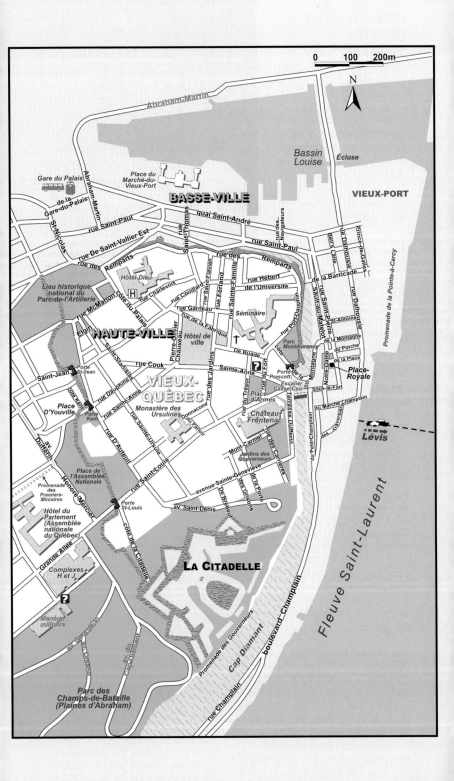

VIEUX-QUÉBEC (HAUTE-VILLE) ★★★

As the administrative and institutional centre, the upper part of Old Québec is adorned with convents, chapels and public buildings the construction of which date back, in some cases, to the 17th century. The walls of Haute-Ville, dominated by the citadel, surround this section of Vieux-Québec and give it the characteristic look of a fortress. These same walls long contained the development of the town, resulting in a densely built bourgeois and aristocratic milieu. With time, the picturesque urban planning of the 19th century contributed to the present-day image of Québec City through the construction of such fantastical buildings as the Château Frontenac and the creation of public spaces like Terrasse Dufferin, spirit of the Belle Époque.

Château Frontenac   Patrick Escudero

At the **Fortifications of Québec National Historic Site ★**, you can visit the **Poudrière de l'Esplanade**, which houses the **Centre d'Initiation aux Fortifications et à la Poudrière de l'Esplanade**. This centre displays models and maps outlining the development of Québec City's defence system. Information plaques have been placed along the wall, providing another means of discovering the city's history. The walkway on top of the wall can be reached by taking the stairs next to the city gates.

The **Maison Cirice-Têtu ★** was built in 1852. It was designed by Charles Baillairgé, a member of a celebrated family of architects who, beginning in the 18th century, left an important mark on the architecture of Québec City and its surroundings. The Greek Revival facade of the house, a masterpiece of the genre, is tastefully and discreetly decorated with palmettes and laurel wreaths.

The charming square known as **Jardin des Gouverneurs ★** was originally the private garden of the governor of New France. The square was laid out in 1647 for Charles Huaut de Montmagny, to the west of Château Saint-Louis, the governor's residence.

Walking along the wooden planks of **Terrasse Dufferin ★★★**, overlooking the St. Lawrence, provides an interesting sensation compared to the pavement most of us are used to. It was built in 1879 at the request of the governor general of the time, Lord Dufferin. The boardwalk's open-air pavilions and ornate streetlamps were designed by Charles Baillairgé and were inspired by the style of French urban architecture common under Napoleon III.

In 1890, the Canadian Pacific Railway company, under Cornelius Van Horne, decided to create a chain of distinguished hotels across Canada. The first of these hotels was the **Château Frontenac ★★★**, named in honour of one of the best-known governors of New France, Louis de Buade, Comte de Frontenac (1622-1698).

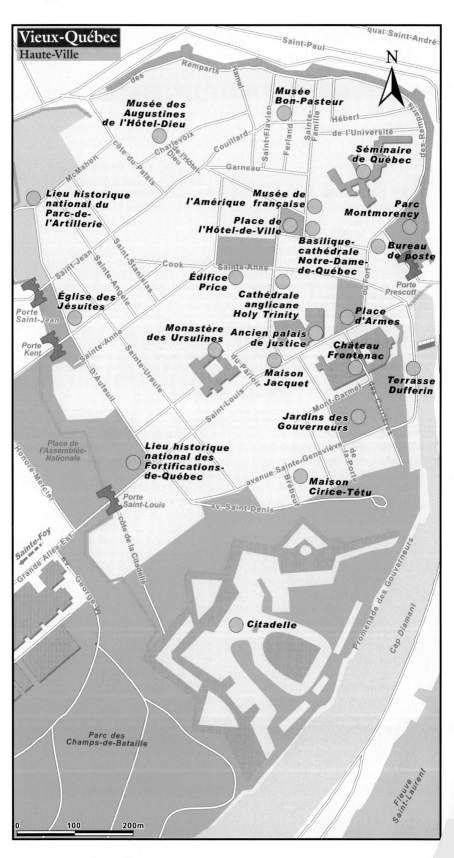

Until the construction of the citadel, **Place d'Armes** ★ was a military parade ground. It became a public square in 1832. In 1916, the Monument de la Foi (Monument of Faith) was erected in Place d'Armes to mark the tri-centennial anniversary of the arrival of the Récollets religious order in Québec.

The **Ancien Palais de Justice** ★ is the city's original courthouse, built in 1883 by Eugène-Étienne Taché, architect of the parliament buildings. The courthouse resembles the parliament in a number of ways. Its French Renaissance Revival design preceded the Château style as the "official" style of the city's major building projects.

Maison Jacquet ★, a small, red-roofed building covered in white roughcast dating from 1677, is the oldest house in Haute-Ville; it is the only house in Vieux-Québec that still looks just as it did in the 17th century. The house is distinguished from those built during the following century by its high steep roof covering a living area with a very low ceiling.

With the help of a benefactor, Madame de la Peltrie, the Ursulines arrived in Québec in 1639 and, in 1641, founded a monastery and convent where generations of young girls have received a good education. The **Monastère des Ursulines** ★★★, or Ursuline convent, is the longest-operating girls' school in North America.

The **Holy Trinity Anglican Cathedral** ★★ was built following the British conquest of Québec, when a small group of British administrators and military officers established themselves in Québec City. These men wanted to distinguish their presence through the construction of prestigious buildings with typically British designs. However, their small numbers resulted in the slow progress of this vision until the beginning of the 19th century, when work began on an Anglican cathedral designed by Majors Robe and Hall, two military engineers inspired by St. Martin-in-the-Fields Church in London.

The design of the **Édifice Price** ★ manages to adhere to traditional North American skyscraper architecture and yet does not look out of place among the historic buildings of Haute-Ville.

Place de l'Hôtel-de-Ville ★, a small square, was the location of the Notre-Dame market in the 18th century. A monument in honour of Cardinal Taschereau, created by André Vermare, was erected here in 1923.

The history of Québec City's cathedral, the **Basilique-Cathédrale Notre-Dame-de-Québec** ★★★, underscores the problems faced by builders in New France and the determination of Quebecers in the face of the worst circumstances. The cathedral as it exists today is the result of numerous phases of construction and a number of tragedies that left the church in ruins on two occasions.

The **Séminaire de Québec** ★★★ was founded in 1663 by Monseigneur Francois de Laval, on orders from the Séminaire des Missions Étrangères de Paris (Seminary of Foreign Missions), with which it remained affiliated until 1763. Headquarters for the clergy throughout the colony, the seminary was where future priests studied, parochial funds were administered and ministerial appointments were made. Louis XIV's Minister, Colbert, further required the seminary to establish a smaller school devoted to the conversion and education of Aboriginals.

Period Québec house

Philippe Renault

SMALL PANES OF GLASS

Why do the windows of the old houses in Québec City and the rest of the province have many small panes instead of large panes of glass? You might think it is because of the cold and the snow. But the answer is even more down-to-earth. During colonial times, glass was imported from France. Needless to say, much of it broke en route. As a result, the merchants decided to import smaller pieces of glass so there would be less risk of breakage. Even so, in order to protect the glass it was sometimes transported in large barrels of molasses!

The Musée Bon-Pasteur

Patrick Escudero

there will come a time when those who bit me will be paid in kind". It is said that the message was intended for Intendant Bigot, a swindler if ever there was one, who was so outraged he had the Bordeaux merchant killed.

Parc Montmorency ★ was laid out in 1875 after the city walls were lowered along Rue des Remparts and the Governor General of Canada, Lord Dufferin, discovered the magnificent view from the promontory.

The halls of the old **Université Laval** ★ can be seen through a gap in the wall of the ramparts. Built in 1856 in the gardens of the seminary, they were completed in 1875 with the addition of an impressive mansard roof surmounted by three silver lanterns.

The **Musée de l'Amérique Française** ★★ is dedicated to the seven North American communities that were formed by French immigration. Other than Quebecers, they are the Acadians, Franco-Ontarians, francophones from the West, Metis and francophones from Louisiana and New England.

The **Bureau de Poste** ★, Canada's first post office, opened in Québec City in 1837. For many years it occupied old Hôtel du Chien d'Or, a solid dwelling built around 1753 for a wealthy Bordeaux merchant, who ordered a bas-relief for above the doorway, depicting a dog gnawing a bone.

The following inscription appeared underneath the bas-relief, which was relocated to the pediment of the present post office in 1872: "I am a dog gnawing a bone, as I gnaw, I rest at home. Though it's not yet here,

The **Musée Bon-Pasteur** ★ tells the story of the Bon Pasteur (meaning "Good Shepherd") community of nuns, which has been serving the poor of Québec City since 1850. The museum is located in the Béthanie house, an eclectic brick structure built around 1887 to shelter unwed mothers and their children.

The **Musée des Augustines de l'Hôtel-Dieu** ★★ traces the history of the Augustinian community in New France through items of furniture, paintings and medical instruments. On display in the museum is the chest that contained the meagre belongings of the founders (pre-1639), as well as pieces from the Château Saint-Louis, the residence of the first governors under the French regime, including portraits of Louis XIV and Cardinal Richelieu.

The Citadelle   Jacques Lessard

Artillery Park National Historic Site   Parks Canada / E. Kedl

Artillery Park National Historic Site ★★, also called Lieu Historique National du Parc-de-l'Artillerie, occupies an enormous military emplacement running alongside the walls of the city. On display is a fascinating model of Québec City built between 1795 and 1810 by military engineer Jean-Baptiste Duberger for strategic planning. The model has only recently been returned to

Québec City, after having been sent to England in 1813. It shows the layout of the city in the years following the British conquest.

The last of Québec's Jesuits died in 1800, his community having been banished by the British and then, in 1774, by the Pope himself. The community was resuscitated in 1814, however, and returned to Québec in 1840. François Baillairgé designed the plans for the **Église des Jésuites ★**, which was completed in 1818.

The **Citadelle ★★★** represents three centuries of North American military history and is still in use. Since 1920, it has housed the Royal 22nd Regiment of the Canadian Army, a regiment distinguished for its bravery during World War II. Within the circumference of the enclosure are some 25 buildings including the officers' mess, the hospital, the prison, and the official residence of the Governor General of Canada, as well as the first observatory in Canada.

Hôtel Jean-Baptiste-Chevalier

Jacques Lessard

VIEUX-QUÉBEC (BASSE-VILLE) ★★★

Québec's port and commercial area is a narrow U-shaped piece of land wedged near the waters of the St. Lawrence. This area is sometimes called the Basse-Ville of Vieux-Québec because of its location just at the foot of the Cap Diamant escarpment. The cradle of New France, Place-Royale is where, in 1608, Samuel de Champlain (1567-1635) founded the settlement he called "Abitation," which would become Québec City. In the summer of 1759, three-quarters of the city was badly damaged by British bombardment.

Maison Louis-Jolliet ★ is one of the earliest houses of Vieux-Québec (1683) and one of the few works of Claude Baillif still standing. The house was built after the great fire of 1682, which destroyed Basse-Ville. It was Louis Jolliet (1645-1700), along with Father Marquette, who discovered the Mississippi and explored Hudson Bay. During the last years of his life, he

taught hydrography at the Séminaire de Québec.

Maison Demers ★ was built in 1689 by mason Jean Lerouge. This impressive residence is an example of the bourgeois style of Québec's Basse-Ville. A two-storey residential facade looks on to Rue du Petit-Champlain while the rear, which was used as a warehouse, extends down another two storeys to open directly onto l'Anse du Cul-de-Sac.

Hôtel Jean-Baptiste-Chevalier ★★ is not a hotel but rather the townhouse of a wealthy family. The first building in the Place-Royale area to be restored, the hôtel is really three separate houses from three different periods: the square-shaped Maison de l'Armateur Chevalier (1752); Maison Frérot, with a mansard roof (1683); and Maison Dolbec (1713).

With no walls to protect Basse-Ville, other means of defending it from the cannon-fire of ships in the river had to be found. Following the attack by Admiral Phipps in 1690, it was

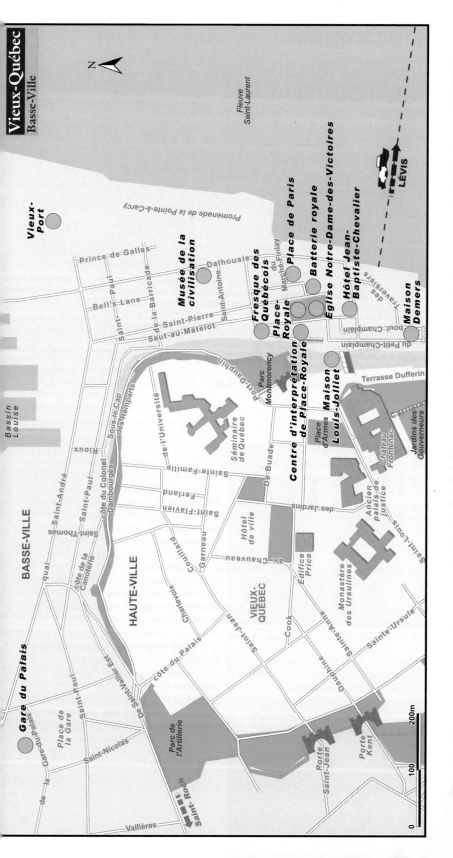

RUE DU TRÉSOR

This pretty little street where artists work during the summer has been called Rue du Trésor since the time of the French regime. In fact, the colonists passed through this street on the way to pay their taxes to the treasury, which was situated where Maison Maillou now stands. Strangely enough, this building now houses the Chambre de Commerce de Québec. One could say that true callings are not always lost with time!

decided to set up the **Batterie Royale** ★, according to a plan drawn up by Claude Baillif. The strategic position of the battery allowed for the bombardment of any enemy ships foolhardy enough to venture into the narrows in front of the city.

Place-Royale ★★★ is the most European quarter of any city in North America. It resembles a village in northwestern France. Place-Royale is laden with symbolism, as it was on this very spot that New France was founded in 1608. After many unsuccessful attempts, this became the official departure point for French exploits in America.

Small, unpretentious **Église Notre-Dame-des-Victoires** ★★ is the oldest church in Canada. Designed by Claude Baillif, it dates from 1688. It was built on the foundations of Champlain's Abitation and incorporates some of its walls. Beside the church, black granite marks the foundation remains from the second Abitation de Champlain. These vestiges were discovered in 1976.

On the blind wall of Maison Soumande, in front of Parc de la Cetière, the colours of the **Fresque des Québécois** ★★ are displayed. From top to bottom and from left to right, you will see Marie Guyart, Catherine de Longpré, François-Xavier Garneau, Louis-Joseph Papineau, Jean Talon, Comte de Frontenac, Marie Fitzbach, Marcelle Mallet, Louis Jolliet, Alphonse Desjardins, Lord Dufferin, Félix Leclerc and finally, Samuel de Champlain, who started it all.

The **Centre d'Interprétation de Place-Royale** ★★ opened in 1999. To accommodate the centre, both the Hazeur and Smith houses, which had burned down, were rebuilt in a modern style while using a large portion of the original materials. You will learn, among other things, that the first inn to be established in Québec City was opened

The Gare du Palais   CCNQ, Jean-Philippe Servant

The Fresque des Québécois
Commission de la Capitale Nationale du Québec

in 1648 by a Mr. Boidon. Coincidentally, his name in French (Bois donc) means "have a drink!".

Place de Paris ★ is an elegant and sophisticated combination of contemporary art and traditional surroundings conceived by Québec architect Jean Jobin in 1987. From the square, which was once a market, there is a splendid view of the Batterie Royale, the Château Frontenac and the St. Lawrence River.

The **Vieux-Port** ★ (old port) is often criticized for being overly American in a city with such a pronounced European flavour. It was refurbished by the Canadian government on the occasion of the maritime celebration, "Québec 1534-1984."

Designed by New York architect Harry Edward Prindle in the same style as the Château Frontenac, the **Gare du Palais** ★ gives visitors a taste of the romance and charm that await them in Québec City. Opposite it, **Place de la Gare** is a lovely spot to relax in and contains an impressive fountain designed by Charles Daudelin.

The **Musée de la Civilisation** ★ ★ is housed in a building that was completed in 1988 in the traditional architectural style of Québec City, with its stylized roof, dormer windows and a bell tower like those common to the area. Architect Moshe Safdie, who also designed the revolutionary Habitat '67 in Montréal, Ottawa's National Gallery and Vancouver's Public Library, designed a sculptural building with a monumental outdoor staircase at its centre.

VAULTS

The houses in Vieux-Québec often had vaulted cellars to support the building; because of their cool temperature, food and drink were often stored there. Some of these cellars have survived and can be visited. Maison Fornel, on Place-Royale, which houses the Association Québec-France, opens its vaults to visitors and even presents small exhibitions.

S-SHAPED TIES

You have perhaps noticed the S-shaped pieces of iron that decorate the walls of some of this neighbourhood's old houses. These objects are ties that hold the stones to the walls upon which the weight of the roof rests.

Musée de la Civilisation   Jacques Lessard

GRANDE ALLÉE ★★

Grande Allée appears on 17th-century maps, but it was not built up until the first half of the 19th century, when the city grew beyond its walls. The Grande Allée was originally a country road linking the town to the Chemin du Roi and thereby to Montréal. At that time, it was bordered by the large agricultural properties of the nobility and clergy of the French regime.

The **Hôtel du Parlement ★★★** is known to Quebecers as l'Assemblée Nationale, the National Assembly. The seat of the government of Québec, this imposing building was erected between 1877 and 1886. It has a lavish French Renaissance Revival exterior intended to reflect the unique cultural status of Québec in the North American context.

RUE DES PAINS-BÉNITS

If you visit the city during the Christmas holidays, consider visiting Place-Royale, especially on January 3. This is the feast day of Saint Geneviève, patron saint of the chapel adjoining Église Notre-Dame-des-Victoires. Every year since the colony was established, bread rolls that have been blessed are distributed to the people to celebrate this event. The little street that runs along the east side of the church is called Rue des Pains-Bénits (blessed-bread street). While eating your bread, take a look at the nativity scene inside the church.

The **Jardin Jeanne-d'Arc ★★** offers walkers some beautiful flowerbeds as well as a statue of the young girl from Orléans set on a fiery charger. The monument honours the memory of soldiers killed in New France during the Seven Years War.

Behind the austere facade of the motherhouse of the Soeurs du Bon-Pasteur, a community devoted to the education of abandoned and delinquent girls, is the charming, Baroque Revival style **Chapelle Historique Bon-Pasteur ★★**, designed by Charles Baillairgé in 1866.

Chapelle des Franciscaines de Marie ★ is the chapel of a community of nuns devoted to the adoration of the Lord. They commissioned the Sanctuaire de l'Adoration Perpétuelle (Sanctuary of Perpetual Adoration) in 1901. This exuberant Baroque Revival chapel invites the faithful to prayer and celebrates the everlasting presence of God.

Monastère des Dominicains ★ and its church are relatively recent realizations that testify to the persistence and historical exactitude of 20th-century Gothic Revival architecture. This sober building of British character incites reverence and meditation.

The **Musée National des Beaux-Arts du Québec ★★★** previously called "Musée du Québec", was renovated and enlarged in 1992. The older, west-facing building, called the Pavillon Gérard-Morisset, is on the right. Parallel to Avenue Wolfe-Montcalm, the new entrance is dominated by a glass tower similar to that of the Musée de la Civilisation. The 1933 neoclassical edifice is linked underground with the old prison on the left. The latter has been cleverly restored to house exhibits, and has been renamed the Pavillon Charles-Baillairgé in honour of its architect. Some of the cells have been preserved.

THE PROVINCIAL CAPITAL IN THE SPOTLIGHT

Like a number of the world's other major cities, the provincial capital has wisely instituted a plan that seeks to illuminate local monuments and historic sites after sundown. Indeed, an "enlightened" lighting system now highlights Québec City's most beautiful locales and buildings. The Parliament buildings, the Château Frontenac and the Pont de Québec, as well as Cap Diamant, thus come alive when night falls.

Château Frontenac in the spotlight

Patrick Escudero

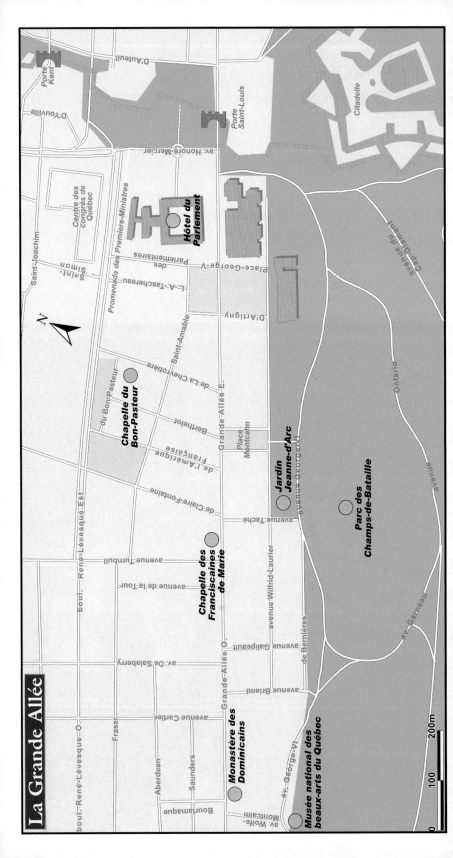

La Grande Allée

QUÉBEC'S EMBLEMS

In 1999, the Québec government adopted the *iris versicolor* (blue flag) as its floral emblem. Until then, the province's official flower had been the white lily (fleur-de-lys) that adorns its flag, commemorating the French origins of the founders of Québec. But because the white lily doesn't actually grow here, the iris was chosen. Indeed, not only is the iris indigenous to the province, it symbolizes its people in several ways: it grows in wet environments, which are omnipresent in Québec; it blossoms in late June, in time for St-Jean-Baptiste Day, Québec's national holiday; and while it is usually blue, the colour of the Québec flag, it also comes in many different varieties, just like the province's various cultural communities. Québec's official tree is the yellow birch, while its avian emblem is the beautiful snowy owl.

Iris versicolor

Sylvie Bouchard - CCBB

Parc des Champs-de-Bataille ★ ★ ★ , commonly known as the Plaines d'Abraham or Plains of Abraham, is where the battle of Québec took place in 1759. The park was created in 1908 to commemorate the event. With its 101ha, extending right up to the cliff overlooking the river, it offers Québec City residents a superb spot to enjoy all kinds of recreational activities.

THE TRANSFER OF MONTCALM'S REMAINS

In 1759, the Marquis de Montcalm, commander in chief of the French army in North America, lost New France, and his life, to the British in the Battle for Québec on the Plains of Abraham. Montcalm's remains were kept in the chapel of the Ursulines, located in the heart of the old fortified city on Rue Donnaconna, for 242 years. Then, one morning in 2001, a funeral cortege transported them to a new burial site, a mausoleum built in his honour in the Hôpital-Général cemetery. He now rests there alongside more than 1,000 of his fallen comrades, whom the hospital's Augustine nuns had endeavoured in vain to nurse back to health. More than 4,000 other people are also buried here, including victims of the Seven Years War, in whose memory a memorial was built.

The transfer of Montcalm's remains

CCNQ, Marc-André Grenier

Cemetery of St. Matthew's Church

Fondation du patrimoine religieux du Québec

FAUBOURG SAINT-JEAN-BAPTISTE ★

A hangout for young people, complete with bars, cafés and boutiques, the Saint-Jean-Baptiste quarter is perched on a hillside between Haute-Ville and Basse-Ville. The abundance of pitched and mansard roofs is reminiscent of parts of the old city, but the orthogonal layout of the streets is quintessentially North American.

Centre des Congrès de Québec ★ was inaugurated in 1996 and is situated north of the Hôtel du Parlement. This large, modern convention centre features glass walls that let the daylight stream in. It has an exhibition hall, several conference rooms and even a ballroom.

There has been a cemetery on the site of the **Church and Cemetery of Saint Matthew ★** since 1771, when Protestants, whether French Huguenot, English Anglican or Scottish Presbyterian, banded together to found a Protestant graveyard.

The **Église Saint-Jean-Baptiste ★** stands out as Joseph Ferdinand Peachy's masterpiece. A disciple of French eclecticism, Peachy was a wholehearted admirer of the Église de la Trinité in Paris. The resemblance here is striking, as much in the portico as in the interior.

ELSEWHERE IN QUÉBEC CITY

The **Chapelle** and **Musée de l'Hôpital Général ★★**. The Récollets built the first stone church in New France in 1621 on the site of this hospital. Their plan was to bring 300 families from France and settle on the banks of Rivière Saint-Charles in a village called Ludovica. Although this project was never realized, the institution slowly grew and took root. In 2001, the Marquis de Montcalm's remains were transferred from the Ursulines chapel in Haute-Ville to the cemetery of the Hôpital Général. The **Mausolée de Montcalm ★★** and a **monument to the victims of the Seven Years War ★★** can now be found here.

Streetscape in Vieux-Québec
(next page)
Patrick Escudero

QUÉBEC CITY REGION

Jean-Pierre Huard, Sépaq

The Rivière Jacques-Cartier valley in Parc National de la Jacques-Cartier

Québec City Region
French regime headquarters

Parc National de la Jacques-Cartier

Jean Sylvain, Sépaq

during colonial times, Québec City was the main urban centre of New France and the centre for colonial administration. To supply produce to the city and its institutions, farms were introduced to the area in the middle of the 17th century.

The farming region on the periphery of the city was the first populated rural zone in the St. Lawrence Valley. Traces of the first seigneuries granted to settlers in New France are still visible in this historically rich rural area. The farmhouses are the oldest of New France, and the descendants of their first residents are now scattered across the American continent.

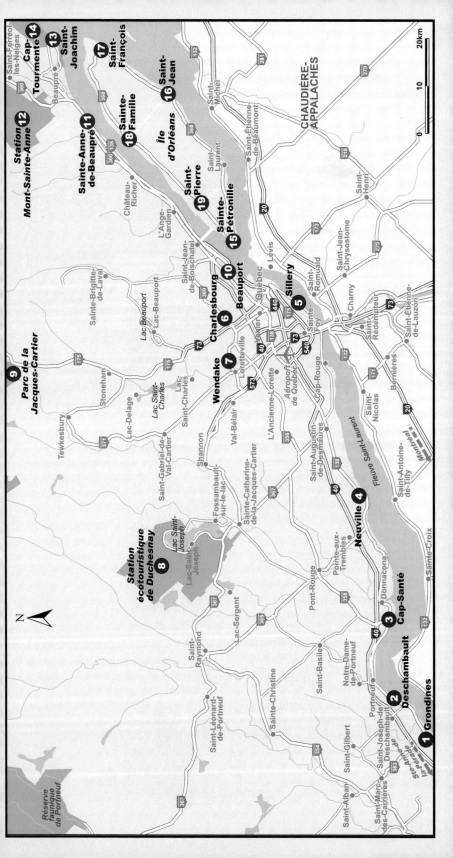

La Chevrotière mill

Jean-François Labrecque

LE CHEMIN DU ROY ★★

This road along the St. Lawrence (some parts parallel to Rte. 138) was the first road suitable for vehicles between Montréal and Québec City. It has been in use since 1734 and today is one of the most picturesque drives in Canada, with its 18th-century French-inspired houses, churches and mills.

I. Grondines ★

In the 18th century, the village of Grondines was situated on the banks of the St. Lawrence. In 1831, it was relocated inland to facilitate access and avoid flooding. Traces of the original village, found between the river and Rte. 138, show French architectural influences, whereas the core of the present village, centred around Rue Principale, displays decidedly more Victorian influences.

2. Deschambault ★★

Deschambault was founded thanks to the efforts of Seigneur Fleury de la Gorgendière, who had had a church built in nearby Cap Lauzon in 1720.

With its large facade adorned with two massive towers set back slightly from the front of the church, the **Église Saint-Joseph ★** is unique in Québec.

The **Vieux Presbytère** occupies a prime location behind the church and offers a beautiful panoramic view of the river and the south shore. The small presbytery building, set apart in the centre of a large lawn, was built in 1815 to replace the first presbytery dating from 1735.

The Chapelle Sainte-Anne de Neuville,
next to Église St-François-de-Sales
Fondation du Patrimoine Religieux du Québec

The magnificent **Moulin de La Chevrotière** ★, a former mill, now houses a facility where traditional building skills are taught. Every summer, young artisans from around Québec come to learn pre-industrial techniques of working with wood, iron and stone.

3. Cap-Santé ★

This farming village enjoys an enviable setting overlooking the St. Lawrence. Formerly part of the Portneuf seigneury, Cap-Santé came into being at the end of the 17th century and grew slowly. If there is such a thing as a typical Québécois village, Cap-Santé is probably it.

The construction of the **Église Sainte-Famille** ★ ★ went on between 1754 and 1764 under the auspices of curate Joseph Filion, but was seriously disrupted by the British conquest.

Despite this, the completed church, with its two steeples and its high nave lit by two rows of windows, is an ambitious piece of work for its time, and was possibly the largest village church built under the French regime.

Today the **Vieux Chemin** ★, the old road, is nothing more than a simple road passing in front of the church, but it was once part of the Chemin du Roy, which linked Montréal and Québec City. Numerous well-preserved 18th-century houses facing the river can still be seen along the road, making it one of the most picturesque drives in Canada.

4. Neuville ★

A vein of limestone, traversing the region from Neuville to Grondines, has been tapped for the construction of prestigious buildings across the province since the French regime. This explains the large number of field-stone houses dotting the villages in the area.

Rue des Érables ★ ★ has one of the largest concentrations of old stone houses outside Québec's large urban centres. This is explained by the abundance of the necessary raw material and the home owners' desire to make use of the talents of local builders and stonemasons.

In 1696, the villagers undertook the construction of the simple **Église Saint-François-de-Sales** ★ ★. It was added to and altered during the following centuries, to the point where the original elements of the building have all but disappeared. A newer chancel was built in 1761, the nave was expanded in 1854, and finally, a new facade was added in 1915.

Bois-de-Coulonge Park

CCNQ, Christian Sommeillier

5. Sillery ★★

This well-to-do suburb of Québec City retains many traces of its varied history, influenced by the town's dramatic topography. There are actually two sections to Sillery, one at the base and the other at the top of a steep cliff that runs from Cap Diamant to Cap-Rouge.

The **Parc du Bois-de-Coulonge** ★ to the east borders Chemin Saint-Louis. The Saint-Denys stream flows through the eastern end of the grounds at the bottom of a ravine. British troops gained access to the Plains of Abraham, where a historic battle decided the future of New France, by climbing through this ravine.

Villa Bagatelle ★ was once home to an attaché of the British governor who lived on the neighbouring property of Bois-de-Coulonge. Built in 1848, the villa is a good example of 19th-century Gothic Revival residential architecture, as interpreted by American Alexander J. Davis.

The **Maison des Jésuites de Sillery** ★★, built of stone and covered with white plaster, occupies the former site of a Jesuit mission, a few ruins of which are still visible. As European illnesses, such as smallpox and measles, devastated the indigenous population, the mission was transformed into a hospice in 1702. At the same time, work began on the present house, a building with imposing chimney stacks.

The **Domaine Cataraqui** ★ is the best-kept property of its kind still in existence in Sillery. It includes a large neoclassical residence, designed in 1851 by architect Henry Staveley, a winter garden and numerous outbuildings scattered across a beautiful, recently restored garden.

WENDAKE: THE LAND OF THE WENDAT NATION

Traditional Huron vista   <small>Nancy Picard</small>

At the time of European colonization, the Georgian Bay region in Ontario was the territory of the Wendat people, whom the French named the Huron—derived from the derogatory word *hure*, meaning "boar's head," due to their "bristly" hairstyle. These indigenous peoples and the French were then on good enough terms for the Jesuits to make their way to the region and found a mission there in 1639.

However, in 1648-49, the Iroquois attacked the village, killing Fathers Brébeuf, Daniel and Lalemant, and decimating the Hurons. In 1650, the last remaining Hurons and Jesuits sought refuge in Québec City. Most of the dispersed Hurons finally regrouped around 1674 in the village of Lorette (now L'Ancienne-Lorette), which they left in 1697 to settle in the Huron Village, a reserve officially named Wendake in 1986.

THE VALLÉE DE LA JACQUES-CARTIER ★

Here you'll enter the resort region of the Laurentians, before plunging into the wilderness of the Rivière Jacques-Cartier valley and the Réserve Faunique des Laurentides, and you'll see how surprisingly close the virgin forest is to Québec City.

6. Charlesbourg ★

In New France, seigneuries were usually laid out in a grid of rectangular strips running inland through the hills and along the coasts. Charlesbourg was the only exception to the rule, and what an exception! Indeed, it consisted of a vast square inside of which plots of land extended outward in a star pattern and around which dwellings were built.

The **Église Saint-Charles-Borromée ★★** revolutionized the art of building in rural Québec. Architect Thomas Baillairgé, influenced by the Palladian movement, showed particular innovation in the way he arranged the windows and doors of the facade, to which he added a large pediment.

7. Wendake ★

Forced off their land by the Iroquois in the 17th century, 300 Huron families moved to various places around Québec before settling in 1700 in Jeune-Lorette, today known as Wendake.

Onhoüa Chetek8e ★ is a replica of a Huron village from the time of early colonization. The traditional design includes wooden longhouses and fences. Visitors are given an introduction to the lifestyle and social organization of the Huron nation.

8. Station écotouristique Duchesnay ★

About 45km from Québec City, on the shore of the region's largest lake, Lac Saint-Joseph, the Station Écotouristique Duchesnay allows visitors to familiarize themselves with the Laurentian forest. Located on an area of 90km^2, this centre is dedicated to researching the flora and fauna of our forests and is now one of the provincial park association's tourism and recreation centres.

9. Parc National de la Jacques-Cartier ★★

Throughout the year, hordes of visitors come to Parc National de la Jacques-Cartier, a provincial park, located in the Réserve Faunique des Laurentides, 40km north of Québec City. The area is called Vallée de la Jacques-Cartier, after the river of the same name that winds through it between steep hills. The vegetation and wildlife are abundant and diverse.

THE CÔTE DE BEAUPRÉ ★

This long, narrow strip of land, nestled between the St. Lawrence and the undeveloped wilderness of the Laurentian massif, is the ancestral home of many families whose roots go back to the beginning of the colony.

10. Beauport ★

Three types of urban development have shaped Beauport over the course of its history. Originally an agricultural settlement in the 19th century, it became an important industrial town, finally evolving into one of the main suburbs of Québec City in the 1960s.

Kayaking Parc National de la Jacques-Cartier

Parc National de la Jacques-Cartier   Jean-Pierre Huard, Sépaq

Beautiful scenery in Parc National de la Jacques-Cartier
Jean-Pierre Huard, Sépaq

The large white house known as **Manoir Montmorency** ★ was built in 1780 for British governor Sir John Haldimand. At the end of the 18th century, the house became famous as the residence of the Duke of Kent, son of George III and father of Queen Victoria.

The Manoir Montmorency is nestled in the **Parc de la Chute-Montmorency** ★★. The Rivière Montmorency, which has its source in the Laurentians, flows along peacefully until it reaches a sudden 83m drop, at which point it tumbles into a void, creating one of the most impressive natural phenomena in Québec.

Parc de la Chute-Montmorency

II. Sainte-Anne-de-Beaupré ★

This long, narrow village is one of the largest pilgrimage sites in North America. Each year, Sainte-Anne-de-Beaupré welcomes more than a million pilgrims, who stay in the hotels and browse the countless gift shops, with their often kitschy offerings, along Avenue Royale.

The **Basilique Sainte-Anne-de-Beaupré ★ ★ ★**, towering over the small, metal-roofed wooden houses that line the winding road, is surprising not only for its impressive size, but also for the feverish activity it inspires all summer long. The church's granite exterior, which takes on different colours depending on the ambient light, was designed in the French Romanesque Revival style by Parisian architect Maxime Roisin, who was assisted by Quebecer Louis Napoléon Audet.

Basilique Sainte-Anne-de-Beaupré
Fondation du Patrimoine Religieux du Québec

12. Station Mont-Sainte-Anne ★

Station Mont-Sainte-Anne covers 77km^2 and includes a 800m-high peak that is one of the most beautiful downhill ski centres in Québec. Various other outdoor activities are possible, as the park has 200km of mountain bike trails, which become 200km of cross-country ski trails in winter.

13. Saint-Joachim

The first church in Saint Joachim, the **Église Saint-Joachim ★ ★** (17th century) was burned by British troops in 1759. The present church, rebuilt inland along with the rest of the village, was completed in 1779. From the outside, this church is hardly worth noting; the interior, however, remains a veritable masterpiece of religious art in Québec.

The interior decoration, undertaken between 1815 and 1825, introduced the concept of design as a whole to Québec. While decor was previously a strictly ornamental affair, that of Saint-Joachim proceeded from a precise plan wherein sculptural elements were made part and parcel of the architectural whole in the purest neoclassical spirit. The sanctuary is thus given greater coherence, exceptional harmony and rigour, as well as a richness seldom found in churches of this era.

14. Cap-Tourmente ★ ★

The pastoral and fertile land of Cap-Tourmente is the easternmost section of the St. Lawrence plain, before the mountains of the Laurentian Massif reach all the way to the shores of the St. Lawrence. The colonization of this area at the beginning of the 17th century represented one of the first attempts to populate New France.

The **Cap-Tourmente National Wildlife Area** ★★ is located on pastoral, fertile land. Each spring and autumn its sandbars are visited by countless snow geese.

ÎLE D'ORLÉANS ★★

When Jacques Cartier arrived in 1535, this island was covered in wild vines, which inspired its first name: Île Bacchus. However, it was soon renamed in homage to the Duc d'Orléans.

15. Sainte-Pétronille ★

It was not until the middle of the 19th century that Sainte-Pétronille was consolidated as a village, as its beautiful location began attracting numerous summer visitors. Anglophone merchants from Québec City built beautiful second homes here.

The Porteous family, of English origin, settled in Québec City at the end of the 18th century. In 1900, they had the **Domaine Porteous** ★ built. This vast country house surrounded by superb gardens was christened "La Groisardière." The property, which today belongs to the Foyer de Charité Notre-Dame-d'Orléans, a seniors' residence, was expanded between 1961 and 1964 when a new wing and a chapel were added.

16. Saint-Jean ★★

In the mid-19th century, Saint-Jean was the preferred home base of nautical pilots who made a living guiding ships through the difficult currents and rocks of the St. Lawrence. Some of their neo-classical or Second Empire houses remain along Chemin Royal and provide evidence of the privileged place held by these seamen, who were indispensable to the success of commercial navigation.

The most impressive manor remaining from the French regime is in Saint-Jean. The **Manoir Mauvide-Genest** ★★ was built in 1734 for Jean Mauvide, the Royal Doctor, and his wife, Marie-Anne Genest. The property officially became a seigneurial manor in the middle of the 18th century, when Mauvide, who had become rich doing business in the Caribbean, bought the southern half of the Île d'Orléans seigneury.

Canadian-style house

Wild grapes
Jeanne D'Arc Miron, Québec en images

was founded by Monseigneur de Laval in 1666 in order to establish a settlement across the river from Sainte-Anne-de-Beaupré for colonists who had previously settled around Sainte-Pétronille. Sainte-Famille has retained many buildings from the French regime. Among them is the town's famous church, one of the greatest accomplishments of religious architecture in New France, and the oldest two-towered church in Québec.

17. Saint-François ★

Saint-François, the smallest village on Île d'Orléans, retains many heritage buildings. The surrounding countryside is charming and offers several pleasant panoramic views of the river, Charlevoix and the coast. The famous wild grape vines that gave the island its first name, Île Bacchus, can also be found in Saint-François.

18. Sainte-Famille ★

The oldest parish on Île d'Orléans

The beautiful **Église Sainte-Famille ★ ★** was built between 1743 and 1747 to replace the original church built in 1669. Inspired by the Église des Jésuites in Québec City, which has since been destroyed, Father Dufrost de la Jemmerais ordered the construction of two towers with imperial roofs. This explains the single steeple sitting atop the gable. In the 19th century, new statues were installed in the alcoves, and the imperial roofs gave way to two new steeples, bringing the total number of steeples to three.

A little further along, and thanks to a citizen's group, **Maison Drouin ★ ★** opens every summer, to the delight of curious visitors. Originally built in 1675 and later expanded in 1725, it is one of the oldest homes on the island and even in all of Québec.

19. Saint-Pierre

The **Espace Félix-Leclerc ★ ★** houses an exhibit on the life and work of Félix Leclerc, a *boîte à chansons* (a music venue for singer-songwriters), a boutique and a small café. Outside trails offer views over the river.

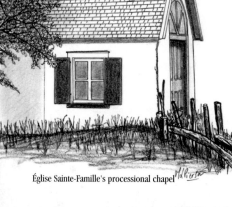

Église Sainte-Famille's processional chapel

Parc National de la Jacques-Cartier
(page 234)

Jean-Pierre Huard, Sépaq

FÉLIX LECLERC

Félix Leclerc, one of Québec's great singers and poets, was born in August 1914 in La Tuque, in the Mauricie region. However it was on Île d'Orléans, near Québec City, that he lived out his final days. He began his career in radio, and his voice was always his greatest asset. He expressed the world and humanity magically in his songs, poems and fables.

Winner of several international prizes, he spent a part of his life in Paris, where he sang his songs *Le P'tit bonheur*, *Moi mes souliers* and others on the biggest stages. Besides singing, he also wrote poetry (*Calepin d'un flâneur, Chansons pour tes yeux*), plays (*Qui est le père?, Dialogues d'hommes et de bêtes*), fables (*Adagio, Allegro, Andante*), and novels (*Le fou de l'île, Pieds nus dans l'aube*). He established theatre companies, produced radio series, recorded albums, published… Above all, this fiery individual moved and was moved.

Félix Leclerc   P404, March 9 1972, P97, P4162, 30 / Archives Nationales du Québec

It was in 1969, upon returning to Québec, that he built his house at St-Pierre on Île d'Orléans and settled there with his family. The island had cast a spell on him during his first visit in 1946, and now he explored it and drew his inspiration from it. In his song *Le Tour de l'île* he said the island was like Chartres, towering and clean, with its naves, arches, passages and cliffs.

He lived on this island for 30 years, dying here on August 8th, 1988, surrounded by his wife and children and thus leaving a heritage for them and all Quebecers to cherish.

SAGUENAY—
LAC-SAINT-JEAN

Parc National du Saguenay

Saguenay–Lac-Saint-Jean

The southernmost fjord

Village Historique de Val-Jalbert   Val Jalbert

in the northern hemisphere, the Rivière Saguenay has its source in Lac Saint-Jean, a veritable inland sea with a diameter of over 35km. In a way, these two impressive bodies of water form the backbone of this magnificent region.

Moving swiftly toward the St. Lawrence River, the Rivière Saguenay flows through a rugged landscape studded with cliffs and mountains. Further north, huge Lac Saint-Jean, feeds the Saguenay. The region's first settlers came here in the 19th century, attracted by the beautiful fertile plains and excellent farmland around the lake. The hard life of these pioneers, who were farmers in the summer and lumberjacks in the winter, was immortalized in Louis Hémon's novel Maria Chapdelaine. Residents of both the Saguenay and Lac Saint-Jean regions are renowned for their friendliness and spirit.

Most settlers came from Charlevoix and the Côte-du-Sud (the south shore of the St. Lawrence between Beaumont and Saint-André-de-Kamouraska) regions in the mid-19th century, populating the twin regions of Saguenay and Lac-Saint-Jean, which up to then had been sporadically frequented by nomadic Montagnais peoples, Jesuit missionaries and trappers. The latter were associated with small trading posts and established back in the 17th century. A few French Canadian families from the Saguenay-Lac-Saint-Jean region have actually become famous for their remarkable fertility. The Tremblays, for example, were so prolific that their surname is now closely linked with both areas.

Patrick Escudero

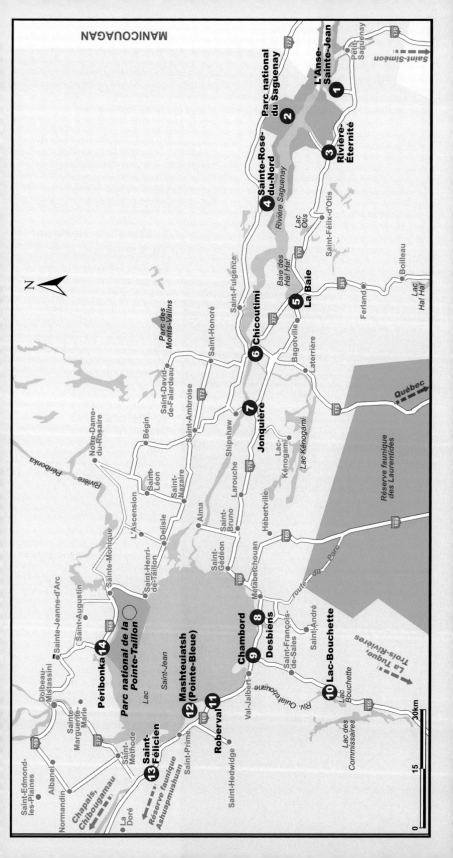

THE SAGUENAY REGION ★★

The "kingdom of the Saguenay," as its inhabitants often refer to it proudly and without an ounce of modesty, extends on both sides of the Rivière Saguenay and its gargantuan fjord. This region is characterized above all by its grandiose scenery and extraordinary flora and fauna.

Parc National du Saguenay J.F. Bergeron, Sépaq

I. L'Anse-Saint-Jean ★

In the spring of 1838, the first schooner chartered by the Société des Vingt-et-Un set off from the Charlevoix region to deposit settlers at various places along the banks of the Saguenay. The first stop was L'Anse-Saint-Jean, making this charming village with its many handcrafted bread ovens the oldest municipality in the Saguenay - Lac-Saint-Jean region.

2. The Parc National du Saguenay ★★★

The Parc National du Saguenay, a provincial park, extends across a portion of the shores of the Rivière Saguenay. It stretches from the banks of the estuary to Sainte-Rose-du-Nord. In this area, steep cliffs plunge into the river, creating a magnificent landscape.

3. Rivière-Éternité ★

With a poetic name that translates as Eternity River, how could anyone resist being carried away by the stunning beauty of the Saguenay, especially because Rivière-Éternité is the gateway to Parc National du Saguenay and the marvellous Saguenay-Saint-Laurent Marine Park, where whales can be observed in their natural habitat.

4. Sainte-Rose-du-Nord ★

Although founded just a little over 50 years ago, the charming hamlet of Sainte-Rose-du-Nord looks older than its years. It is built against the steep, rocky slopes of the Saguenay, giving it the fanciful appearance of a cardboard village set at the foot of a Christmas tree.

THE SAGUENAY FJORD

The Saguenay Fjord began taking shape 70 million years ago, when the earth's crust collapsed and produced a huge, steep-sided trough now occupied by the Rivière Saguenay. Then, about 60,000 years ago, a slight drop in the average yearly temperature was enough to cause the formation of glaciers in northern North America. As they moved southward, their huge weight hammered the earth's surface. Some of these glaciers, estimated to have been some 3,000m thick, dug deep into the bed of the Saguenay, creating its characteristic U-shaped valley. It took 2,000 years for this glacial front to carve out the area between the mouth of the Saguenay and Lac Saint-Jean as it retreated northwest.

The retreat of the continental Wisconsin ice sheet, which freed the continent from its icebound state some 10,000 years ago, then caused seawater levels to rise 150m to 250m in height. The land slowly but surely resurfaced as the sea receded.

The Rivière Saguenay

Patrick Escudero

5. La Baie ★

La Baie is an industrial town occupying a beautiful site at the far end of the Baie des Ha! Ha!, old French for impasse or dead-end. The colourful term "Ha!Ha!" was supposedly employed by the region's first explorers, who headed into the bay thinking it was a river.

At the **Palais Municipal ★**, visitors can see La Fabuleuse Histoire d'un Royaume, an elaborate historical pageant similar to those presented in some provincial French towns. Bringing this colourful extravaganza to life involves over 200 actors and 1,400 costumes, along with animals, carriages, lighting effects and sets.

The **Église Saint-Marc ★**. An emerging and relatively prosperous region, Saguenay-Lac-Saint-Jean was blessed with a host of boldly designed modern churches in the 1940s and '50s. The series of "white churches" is particularly remarkable, including the church of Saint-Marc, built in 1955 according to plans by architect Paul-Marie Côté.

The **Passe Migratoire à Saumon de la Rivière-à-Mars ★**, built on a part of the river located right in the heart of town, was designed to facilitate the migration of salmon upstream during their spawning period. From the pleasant park that has been laid out in the surrounding area, visitors can watch the salmon and occasionally fish for them.

6. Chicoutimi ★

In the language of the Montagnais, "Chicoutimi" means "there where it is deep," a reference to the waters of the Saguenay, which are navigable as far as this city, the most important urban area in the entire Saguenay-Lac-Saint-Jean region. For over 1,000 years, nomadic Aboriginal peoples used this spot for meetings, festivities and trade. Starting in 1676, Chicoutimi became one of the most important fur trading posts in New France.

The **Cathédrale Saint-François-Xavier ★** was rebuilt on two different occasions, both times due to fire. The present building, erected between 1919 and 1922, was designed by architect Alfred Lamontagne. It is remarkable above all for its high facade, the two towers of which are topped with silvered steeples that rise above the old port.

At the turn of the 20th century, several large-scale French Canadian enterprises were established in the Saguenay-Lac-Saint-Jean region, the largest being the pulp mills in Val-Jalbert and Chicoutimi. The **Pulperie de Chicoutimi ★★** was founded in 1896 by Dominique Guay and then expanded several times by the powerful North American Pulp and Paper Company, directed by Alfred Dubuc. The decline of pulp prices in 1921 and the crash of 1929 led to the closing of the pulp mill. It remained abandoned until 1980. A museum has occupied the site since 1996. The complex extends over 1ha and includes, among other things, an interpretive trail dotted with 12 stations with exhibits, as well as a thematic display. Also to be visited here is the **Maison Arthur-Villeneuve**, the foremost example of pop art in Canada.

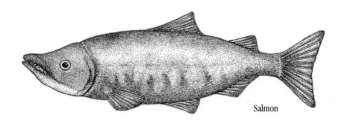

Salmon

THE KINGDOM OF THE SAGUENAY

The designation "Kingdom of the Saguenay" dates back to the beginnings of European colonization—more specifically, to Jacques Cartier's first voyage, in 1534. Two natives, whom Cartier had abducted to show off to the French Court, regaled him with tales of a wonderful kingdom filled with gold, rubies and other riches.

This kingdom was reportedly inhabited by giants who dressed as whites and lived in fortresses, or by pygmies who neither ate nor digested anything. Malevolent monsters also found refuge here... all of which did not fail to impress the then-explorers. Thus was born the great myth of the Kingdom of the Saguenay, which would fire the imagination of Europeans as much as those of El Dorado, the Fountain of Youth or the Seven Cities of Cibola.

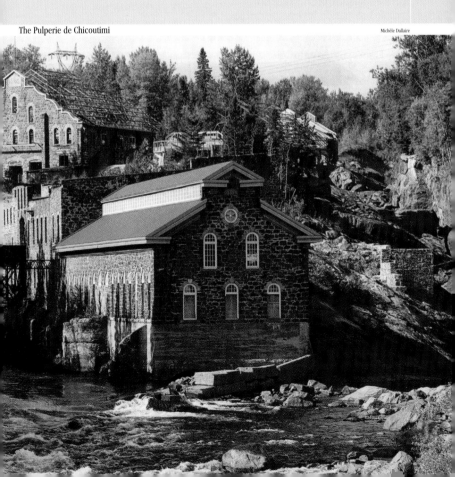

The Pulperie de Chicoutimi   Michèle Dallaire

One of the relics at the Village Historique de Val-Jalbert   Val-Jalbert

7. Jonquière

In 1847, the Société des Défricheurs (meaning land clearers) du Saguenay received authorization to set up business alongside Rivière aux Sables. The name Jonquière was chosen in memory of one of the governors of New France, the Marquis de Jonquière. Today, Jonquière is regarded as an essentially modern town, the economic mainspring of which is the Alcan aluminium smelter.

The **Centrale Hydroélectrique de Shipshaw** ★ ★, which began operating in 1931, is a striking example of Art Deco architecture. It supplies electricity to the local aluminium smelters.

The contemporary-style **Église Notre-Dame-de-Fatima** ★ is renowned as one of the most famous white churches in the Saguenay region. Designed by Paul-Marie Côté and Léonce Gagné, it was erected in 1963.

CIRCLING LAC SAINT-JEAN ★ ★

Various Montagnais nations, including the Nation du Porc-Épic (Porcupine Nation), were once attracted to the vast expanse of water known today as Lac Saint-Jean (1,350km²). Europeans were unaware of the lake's existence for many years; it was not until 1647 that a Jesuit missionary named Jean de Ouen discovered it on his way to nurse some ailing local inhabitants.

8. Desbiens

Located on either side of the Rivière Métabetchouane, this town is steeped in history. It was settled in 1652 by a Jesuit mission; a fur-trading post was added in 1676. The trading post consisted of a store, a chapel and several farm buildings. It prospered until 1880, when the buildings were dismantled and moved to Pointe-Bleue.

Many excavations have been conducted around the mouth of Rivière Métabetchouane, uncovering various archaeological traces of the Aboriginals' thousand-year-long habitation of the area, as well as remnants of the Jesuit mission and the fur trading post. A number of the objects uncovered during these digs are on display at the **Centre d'Histoire et d'Archéologie de la Métabetchouane** ★, opened in 1983.

9. Chambord

The **Village Historique de Val-Jalbert** ★ ★ began in 1901, when an industrialist by the name of Damase Jalbert built a pulp mill at the foot of the Rivière Ouiatchouane falls. The enterprise prospered quickly, becoming the most important industrial company run entirely by French Canadians. The company, closed down in 1927, however, and the town with it. Today Val-Jalbert is an important heritage site.

THE TREMBLAYS

When travelling through Saguenay-Lac-Saint-Jean, one can't help but notice that certain family names crop up more often than others, and none more so than "Tremblay," the most common last name in Québec. On August 6, 1647, at the age of 21, the clan's progenitor, Pierre Tremblay, came to New France from Randonnai, in Normandy. He then worked for merchants Robert Giffard and Noël Juchereau, before wedding Ozane Achon in 1657. The couple settled on a plot of land in L'Ange-Gardien, on the Côte-de-Beaupré, where they raised 12 children. Their descendants now number more than 80,000 in Québec, and some 160,000 in North America.

Village Historique de Val-Jalbert

10. Lac-Bouchette

The **Ermitage Saint-Antoine-de-Lac-Bouchette** ★, located between Lac-Saint-Jean and Haute-Mauricie, is a hermitage dedicated first to Saint Anthony of Padua and second to Notre Dame de Lourdes. This popular retreat and place of pilgrimage, overseen by Capuchin monks, was set up on the shores of Lac Bouchette, deep in the forest, at the instigation of Father Elzéar Delamarre, Superior of the Chicoutimi Seminary.

Surrounding the first chapel (1908) is the monastery, a hostelry, the boldly designed Marian Chapel (1950) and a Lourdes grotto, cut out of a natural crevice. The Sainte-Antoine-de-Padoue Chapel features 23 superb remounted paintings by renowned artist Charles Huot.

II. Roberval

This industrial town used to be the crossroads for the railway and the Lac Saint-Jean shipping routes. Today, it is the finishing point of the famous Traversée Internationale du Lac Saint-Jean, a swimming event held on the lake each year in July.

The **Centre Historique et Aquatique de Roberval** ★ enables visitors to familiarize themselves with the history, wildlife and plant life of the Lac-Saint-Jean region. Particularly noteworthy is the aquarium, which has collected various regional species of fish, including the famous ouananiche, a type of fresh-water salmon.

12. Mashteuiatsh (Pointe-Bleue) ★

The Montagnais lived in nomadic communities all around Lac Saint-Jean for over 1,000 years. Advancing colonization and the forest industry eventually put an end to this way of life. In 1856, a permanent reserve was established on the lake's western shore, in Pointe-Bleue, which is now home to around 1,500 of Quebec's 10,000-odd Montagnais.

The **Musée Amérindien de Mashteuiatsh** ★ focuses on the customs of the first inhabitants of the Saguenay-Lac-Saint-Jean region. Its temporary exhibitions help acquaint visitors with Canada's other Aboriginal peoples as well.

13. Saint-Félicien

Lac-Saint-Jean's southwestern lands were gradually settled between 1850 and 1870. Saint-Félicien then lay at the northernmost end of the region's settlement.

At the **Zoo Sauvage de Saint-Félicien** ★ ★ visitors can observe various species of Québec's indigenous wildlife in their natural habitat. What makes this zoo unusual is that the animals are not in cages, but roam about freely while visitors tour the zoo in small, screened buses.

The emblematic beaver played a role in the founding of New France

Steve Deschênes, Sépaq

Parc National de la Pointe-Taillon

I4. Péribonka ★

Musée Louis-Hémon - Complexe Touristique Maria-Chapdelaine ★ ★ is located in the house where Louis Hémon spent the summer of 1912 with Samuel Bédard and his wife Eva (née Bouchard). It is one of a few rare examples of colonial homes in the Lac-Saint-Jean region to have survived virtually unchanged, despite improvements in the local standard of living. The extremely modest house that inspired Hémon was built in 1903. It was converted into a museum in 1938, and its furnishings have thus remained intact, and are still laid out in their original positions in the humble rooms. A large post-modern building was erected nearby in order to house Hémon's personal belongings, as well as various souvenirs of the villagers who inspired his work, and memorabilia relating to the success of his novel *Maria Chapdelaine.*

Parc National de la Pointe-Taillon ★ lies on the strip of land formed by the Rivière Péribonka, and extends into Lac Saint-Jean. This provincial park is an excellent place to enjoy water sports, such as canoeing and sailing, and also has magnificent sandy beaches.

Parc National de la Pointe-Taillon
(next page)

MAJOR
THEMES

Seasons in Québec

SPRING

Spring is short, lasting roughly from the end of March to the end of May, and heralded by the arrival of "slush," a mixture of melted snow and mud. As the snow disappears, plants and grass, yellowed by frost and mud, come to life again. Nature's welcomed reawakening is spectacular.

Parc National de l'Île Bonaventure-et-du-Rocher-Percé
Jean-Pierre Huard, Sépaq

C-S Langlois

SUMMER

Summer in Québec blossoms from the end of May to the end of August and may surprise some who think of Québec as a land of snow and igloos. The heat can be quite extreme and often seems much hotter because of the accompanying humidity. The vegetation becomes lush, and don't be surprised to see exotic plants growing in window boxes, for example. City streets are decorated with flowers, and restaurant terraces are always full. It is also the season when many different festivals are held all across the province.

Hôtel Sacacomie in Saint-Alexis-des-Monts, Mauricie region

Turtles in Parc National de Plaisance
(*previous page*)
Pierre Pouliot - Sépaq

Windmill on Île aux Coudres
Philippe Renault

FALL

The fall colours can last from September to November, when maple trees create one of the most beautiful living pictures on the North American continent. Leaves are transformed into a kaleidoscope of colours from bright green to scarlet red to golden yellow. Temperatures will stay warm for a while, but eventually the days and especially the nights will become quite cold.

INDIAN SUMMER

This relatively short period (only a few days) during the late fall is like summer's triumphant return! Referred to as Indian Summer, it is in fact the result of warm air currents from the Gulf of Mexico. This time of the year is called Indian Summer because it represented the last hunt before winter. Aboriginals took advantage of the warm weather to stock up on provisions before the cold weather arrived.

Parc National du Mont-Saint-Bruno   M. Pitre, Sépaq

WINTER

"Mon pays ce n'est pas un pays, c'est l'hiver..."
("My country is not a country, it's winter")

– Gilles Vigneault

Mid-November to the end of March is the best time for skiing, snowmobiling, skating, snowshoeing and other winter sports. In general, there are five or six large snow storms per winter. Howling wind often makes the temperatures bitterly cold, causing "drifting snow" (very fine snow that is blown by the wind). One bright spot is that though it may be freezing, Québec gets more hours of winter sunshine than Europe.

Charlevoix   Jean-François Bergeron

Parc National du Mont-Mégantic
(next page)
M.Pitre - Sépaq

Winter Activities in Québec

DOWNHILL SKIING

There are many downhill-ski centres in Québec. Some of these have lighting systems and offer night skiing. Hotels located near the ski hills often offer package-deals including accommodations, meals and lift tickets.

Skier in the Charlevoix region

Marc Archambault

Lift tickets are generally quite expensive; in an effort to accommodate all types of skiers, most centres offer half-day, whole-day and night passes, as well as offering equipment rental and lessons for all levels. Some centres have even started offering skiing by the hour.

SNOWBOARDING

Snowboarding made its appearance in Québec in the early 1990s. Though a fringe activity at the start, it has definitely gone mainstream, to the point where some skihills find themselves with more snowboarders than skiers. The appeal is obvious: the adrenaline rush intensifies when snowboarding. Contrary to popular belief, snowboarding is for everyone, young and old. First-timers should consider taking a few lessons before hitting the slopes, and many skihills offer this service. Most centres also rent the equipment.

Snowboarder in the Charlevoix region
Marc Archambault

Parc National de la Gaspésie
(*previous page*)
M.Pitre - Sépaq

Skiers in Parc National de la Gaspésie

Jean-Pierre Huard, Sépaq

CROSS-COUNTRY SKIING

There are many parks and ski centres with well-maintained cross-country trails. In most ski centres you can rent equipment by the day. Many places have longer trails, with shelters alongside them offering accommodations for

Snowshoers in the Charlevoix region

Jean-François Bergeron

skiers. Ulysses Travel Guides publishes a French-language guide to cross-country skiing and snowshoeing in the province: *Ski de fond et raquette au Québec.*

SNOWSHOEING

Reinvented today as a leisure pastime, the snowshoe was first used by Aboriginals as a means of getting over deep snow. In Québec, this sport is mainly practised in cross-country ski-centres, parks and nature reserves.

SNOWMOBILING

Now this is a popular Québec sport! It was, after all, a Quebecer named Joseph-Armand Bombardier who invented the snowmobile, thereby giving life to one of the most important industries in Québec, now involved in the building of airplanes and railway materials. A network of more than 26,000km of cleared snowmobile trails criss-crosses Québec. Trails cross diverse regions and lead adventurers into the heart of the wilderness. Along the trails are all the necessities for snowmobiling: repair services, heated sheds, fuel, and food services. It is possible to rent a snowmobile and the necessary equipment in certain snowmobiling centres. To use the trail, you must have the registration paper for your vehicle and a membership card from the Fédération des Clubs de Motoneigistes.

Snowmobile   Jean-Pierre Huard

DOGSLEDDING

Used by the Inuit for transportation in the past, today dogsledding has become a respected sporting activity. Competitive events abound in northern countries all over the world. In recent years, tourist centres have started offering dogsledding trips lasting anywhere from a few hours to a few days. In the latter case, the tour organizer provides the necessary equipment and shelter. In general, you can expect to cover 30km to 60km per day, and this sport is more demanding than it looks, so good physical fitness is essential for long trips.

Sled dogs   Philippe Renault

Ice-fishing in Parc National d'Aiguebelle

Jean-Pierre Huard, Sépaq

SKATING

Most municipalities have public skating rinks set up in parks and on rivers or lakes. Some places have rental services and even a little hut where you and your skates can warm up.

ICE-FISHING

This sport has become more and more popular in recent years. The basic idea, as the name suggests, is to fish through the ice. A small wooden shack built on the

The Place D'Youville skating rink next to Vieux-Québec

Philippe Renault

ice keeps you warm during the long hours of waiting for the big one! The main regions for this sport are the Eastern Townships, Mauricie, Centre-du-Québec, and Saguenay–Lac-Saint-Jean regions.

Summer Activities

Hiking in Parc National de la Gaspésie

Jean-Pierre Huard, Sépaq

HIKING

Hiking is accessible to all and is practised all over Québec. Many parks have hiking trails of varying length and difficulty. A few have longer trails that head deep into the wilderness for 20 to 40km.

Respect the trail markings and always leave well prepared when you follow these trails. Maps that show the trails, campsites and shelters are available. Reservations for shelters in wildlife reserves as well as those in the parks can be made starting in May.

An excellent guide called *Hiking in Québec* (Ulysses Travel Guides) is available in bookstores and camping stores. A hiking guide with something for everyone, it suggests various trails and trips, and classifies them according to their length and level of difficulty. Ulysses also published a French-language hiking guide to Montréal: *Randonnée Pédestre Montréal et environs.*

Cycling in Parc National de la Jacques-Cartier

Jean-Pierre Huard, Sépaq

CYCLING

Exploring by bike is one of the most rewarding ways of discovering the diverse regions of Québec. There is quite a variety of publications to help organize your two-wheeled excursions. Ulysses Travel Guides publishes two French-language guides: *Le Québec Cyclable* and *Cyclotourisme au Québec*, which list short and long bikepaths in Québec.

Mountain-bike trails have been cleared in most of the parks. Check with the information desk of the particular park.

Cycling Montréal's paths is an exciting way to get to know the city in the summer. If you have time, why not tour the whole island?

Many bike shops have bikes for rent. Insurance is a good idea. Some places also include theft insurance in the rental fee, but be sure to check this when you rent.

IN-LINE SKATING

This fairly young sport is our summer version of ice-skating. It takes a bit of time to get used to it, but once you've got your skate-legs, you'll love the ease with which the kilometres roll by. In-line skating is mostly practised in urban areas, on paved paths. Several outfits rent equipment. Protective gear, including a helmet, knee-, elbow- and wrist-pads, is strongly recommended.

CANOEING

Québec's vast territory is dotted with a multitude of lakes and rivers, making it a canoe enthusiast's dream. Many of the parks and Réserves Fauniques are departure points for canoe trips of one or more days. For longer trips, backwoods campsites are available for canoeists. Maps of the canoe trips and trails, as well as canoe-rental services, are available at park information centres. River rafting is most popular in the springtime, when water levels are highest after the spring thaw.

Parc National des Hautes-Gorges-de-la-Rivière-Malbaie   M. Pitre, Sépaq

An excellent map, *Les Parcours Canotables du Québec*, (Canoe Trips of Québec) is available in travel bookstores. A series of map-guides for rivers (up to 125 different maps) is available, as is a guide for beginners called *Manuel du Canot-Camping*, available only in French. For information, contact the Fédération Québécoise du Canot et du Kayak.

KAYAKING

Parc National des Îles-de-Boucherville   Jean-Sébastien Perron, Sépaq

Kayaking is not a new sport, but it is growing in popularity in Québec. More and more people are discovering this marvelous activity that allows you to crisscross waterways in a safe and comfortable way and at a pace in keeping with the natural surroundings.

Once settled into your kayak you'll feel like you are literally sitting on water, at one with nature: a fascinating and singular experience. There are three types of kayak, the variant being the curve of the hull: lake kayak, river kayak and sea kayak. The latter, which holds one or two people depending on the model, is the easiest to manoeuver and therefore the most popular. Several outfits rent kayaks and organize guided excursions on Québec's waterways.

You'll see all manner of water craft on the St. Lawrence River near the Côte-du-Sud, in the Bas-Saint-Laurent region, near the Sorel islands, among other areas. The Saguenay is another kayaking destination, the fjord beauty is breathtaking! The Fédération Québécoise du Canot et du Kayak can provide any information you might need on kayaking in the province.

RAFTING

Rafting, or river-riding, is a sport for thrill-seekers. It consists in tackling river rapids aboard a raft or inflatable canoe. These boats usually hold about 10 people and in order to survive the rough waters are extremely resistant and flexible.

Rafting is especially popular in spring when water levels are at their peak and rivers run much faster. It goes without saying that you need to be in good physical condition to participate in such an excursion since it is the strength of a boats paddlers that steers the boat against the rapids. However, a well organized tour, lead by an experienced guide does not present a huge risk. Outfits offering such trips usually supply all the necessary safety and protective gear to participants. So come on board and let those tumultuous long-frozen waters carry you on the ride of your life!

SAILING

La Fédération de Voile du Québec (Québec Sailing Federation) is an organization of clubs, schools and associations involved in sailing and pleasure boating. The federation offers courses and a data base of important information.

WATERSKIING AND WAVERUNNING

Waterskiing and waverunning are possible on most lakes in Québec. Waverunners are also even seen on the St. Lawrence River around Montreal. Remember to exercise extreme caution when operating these vehicles, especially is there are swimmers nearby. Lifejacket use is mandatory in Québec.

Winter and summer activities can be practised here

Philippe Renault

La Fédération Québécoise de Ski Nautique (Québec Federation of Waterskiing) provides information, guidebooks and lessons.

Swimming at Parc National d'Oka's beach

Jean-Sébastien Perron, Sépaq

BEACHES

The shores of Québec's rivers and countless lakes are lined with everything from fine white sand to pebbles to boulders. You should not have any trouble finding one that suits your sport or style of sunbathing. Unfortunately, swimming in the waters around the island of Montréal is no longer possible because of the pollution in the St. Lawrence and the Rivière des Prairies.

The city does, however, run a public beach on Île-Notre-Dame, where you can splash about in filtered river water. Beware though—this place is very popular and access is limited, so get there early!

BIRDWATCHING

In addition to the national and provincial parks, there are many other interesting bird-watching spots throughout Quebec. We recommend two interesting guides:

Les Meilleurs Sites d'Observation des Oiseaux du Québec, published by Éditions Québec-Science.

Peterson's Field Guide: All the Birds of Eastern and Central North America, published by Houghton Mifflin.

The Association Québécoise des Groupes d'Ornithologues can provide more information on clubs and birdwatching activities in the province.

Black-capped chickadee
CCBB

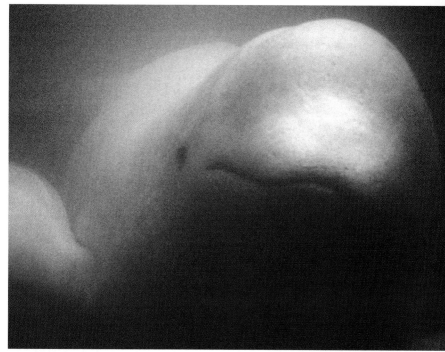

Beluga whale in the St. Lawrence   Parks Canada / D. Lefebvre

WHALE-WATCHING

The St. Lawrence is teeming with diverse marine life. A large part of it is made up of numerous marine mammals, including many species of whales (belugas, finback whales and blue whales). Whale-watching expeditions are popular in the tourist regions of Charlevoix, Saguenay–Lac-Saint-Jean, Bas-Saint-Laurent, Manicouagan, Duplessis and the Gaspésie.

When whale-watching, be sure to hire the services of a reputable company, one that respects the rules in place to protect the whales, including not chasing them or getting too close to them.

GOLF

Groomed golf courses exist in all corners of Québec and are open from May to October. The Association de Golf du Québec has more than 50,000 golfing members.

HORSEBACK RIDING

Many horse stables offer lessons or trail rides. Some even organize longer trips of more than one day. Both types of riding, English and Western, are available depending on the stable. As the two styles are very different, check which one is offered when making reservations. Some provincial parks have horseback-riding trails.

Québec à Cheval (Québec on horseback) is an organization that promotes horseback riding. Courses are also offered.

SCUBA DIVING

Most of the regions of Québec offer dive sites, and there are at least 200 diving centres, schools or clubs. For more complete information on diving in Québec, contact the Fédération Québécoise des Activités Subaquatiques (Québec Federation of Underwater Activities).

Starfish

Parks Canada / Y. Boivin and C. Harvey

CLIMBING

Climbing enthusiasts can practise their sport in summer and in winter, when there are ice walls for climbers of all levels. Adequate and reliable equipment (often rented on site) and a firm grasp of the basic techniques are crucial to this sport. Some climbing centres offer beginners' courses.

For information concerning ice and rock climbing activities, beginner courses and more advanced courses, contact the Fédération Québécoise de la Montagne.

HANG-GLIDING AND PARAGLIDING

Hang-gliding has been practised in Québec since the 1970s. The mountains and cliffs most conducive to this sport are located in the regions of Gaspésie, Charlevoix, the Appalachians and Laurentides. Paragliding is a relatively new sport in Québec.

These sports are dangerous and can only be attempted after following a course given by an accredited instructor. For more information, contact the Association Québécoise de Vol Libre (The Québec Association of Hang-gliding and Paragliding).

HUNTING AND FISHING

Hunting and fishing are both strictly regulated. As a general rule, the following applies: a Québec permit is required to hunt or fish. Permits are available in most sporting stores and from outfitters.

Hunting of migratory birds is only permitted with a federal permit, which can be purchased in any post office. A certificate to bear fire-arms or a permit by the province or country of origin is required when requesting this type of permit.

Permits are issued depending on the hunting zone, time of year, the species and the existing quotas. It is a good idea to obtain your permit well in advance, since there are numerous restrictions.

Fishing and hunting seasons are established by the province and must be respected at all times. The season depends on the type of game: white-tailed deer is usually at the beginning of November; moose from mid-September to mid-October; caribou in summer or winter, depending on the zone; bear from mid-September to mid-November; partridge from mid-September to the end of December; hare from mid-September to March.

While hunting, always wear an orange fluorescent singlet. Hunting at night is not permitted. For the purpose of conservation, the number of game is limited, and protected species cannot be hunted. All hunters must declare their kill at one of the registration centres (most of which are located on access roads to the hunting zones) within 48 hours of leaving the zone.

Hunting and fishing are permitted in the wildlife reserves and parks according to certain rules. Reservations are required for access to waterways. For more information, check directly with the park or reserve office where you plan to hunt or fish.

Moose in Parc National de la Jacques-Cartier
Steve Deschênes, Sépaq

The Evolution of Architecture in Québec

By the end of the French regime, Montréal and Québec City were both typical French provincial towns well protected within their walls. Inside, the streets were lined with churches whose steeples reached above the walls, convents, colleges, hospitals and a few aristocratic and bourgeois homes surrounded by French gardens. Added to that would be a *place d'armes* (parade ground) and a market square.

The banks of the St. Lawrence River and Rivière Richelieu were slowly cleared and farmed. The King of France, who had chosen the seigneurial system to develop Canada, conceded long rectangles of land, perpendicular to the water, to individuals and religious communities, who in exchange kept hearth and home and recruited new colonists. These new colonists in turn promised to pay the *cens* (tax) and swear *foi et hommage* (faith and homage) to their seigneur. Under the French regime, few seigneurs actually fulfilled their obligations, finding their land too isolated and exposed to Iroquois and British attacks, while others used their land as hunting grounds or for speculation. It was not until the end of the 18th century that most of the seigneuries granted between 1626 and 1758 were actually cleared and planted.

Of the enemies to do battle with, the cold was without a doubt the most dreaded. After rather difficult and often tragic beginnings, during which some colonists froze to death because their only shelter was a rickety

Traditional house in winter

Philippe Renault

wooden cabin with paper windows, French architecture slowly adapted to the long winters. It had to overcome the shortage of skilled workers, in particular stone-cutters, as well as the lack of the necessary materials on the local market, like glass for the windows and slate for the roofs, which otherwise had to be shipped in at great expense. As such, the architecture of the French regime is an architecture of colonization, pure and economic, where each element has a specific function, essential to the well-being of the inhabitants.

The architecture of the towns varied little from that of the country. The first priority remained, of course, the eternal battle with the cold. Added to this, however, was the prevention of fires, which could easily result in tragedy in the absence of an effective fire-fighting system. Two edicts written by New France Intendants in 1721 and in 1727 pertained to construction inside the town walls. Wooden houses with mansard roofs and their dangerous wooden shingles, were forbidden; all buildings had to be made of stone and be equipped with fire-break walls; attic floors had to be covered with

Basilique Notre-Dame in Montréal around 1870

terracotta tiles. Those who could not afford to obey such strict standards built up small communities outside the walls. Few examples remain of these wood houses, whose architecture was sober and functional.

The building of the Protestant orphanage in Québec City in 1823, and in particular that of the Église Notre-Dame in Montréal between 1824 and 1829, both of which are Gothic Revival style, announced the arrival of historicism in Québec architecture. Originally quite marginal, historicism would come to dominate the skyline of Québec's cities and towns in the second half of the 19th century. It is defined by the use of decorative elements taken from different architectural epochs in history, which were popularized thanks to archaeological disco-veries, the invention of photography, and the popularity of historical novels across the world.

The Victorian era might seem contradictory, since while it looked back-ward in terms of its architectural style, it looked decidedly forward when it came to comfort. As such, the technological inno-vations that made life much more agreeable are often overlooked: running water, automatic hot water heaters, more washrooms, central hea-ting, telephones and electricity.

The record birth rate in rural Québec around 1900, where families with 12 children were common, began to over-burden the land. New regions such as Abitibi were opened up for

M. Cramp Residence, Montréal, 1898   II-125201 / McCord Museum / Wm. Notman & Son

settlement by the clergy, yet the attraction of the city proved insurmounta-ble, despite the meagre wages. These uprooted workers longed for aspects of their country homes in the city: verandas and balconies, numerous well-lit rooms, a lot of storage space, which might also serve as henhouse or stables if necessary. It all had to be inexpensive to heat and relatively easy to main-tain. Thus, the Montréal-style dwelling was born! Its exterior staircases, which wound their way tightly to the second floor in the limited space between the sidewalk and balcony, avoided the need to heat an interior stairwell. The balconies were reminiscent of rural galleries, leading directly into the homes (one or two per floor), each of which had their own exterior entrance.

From 1900 to 1930, thousands of duplexes, triplexes, 4-plexes and 5-plexes were built along Montreal's grid of streets. These wooden-framed two- and three-storey buildings were built one beside the next and faced with local stone or with brick, the variety of which was endless. Though they were above all affordable, this typical Montreal-style housing was nevertheless adorned with decorative cornices or ornate parapets, balconies with Tuscan columns and Art-nouveau inspired stained glass.

At the beginning of the 1930s, some new buildings inspired by New France styling were being constructed. The Quiet Revolution during the 1960s fortunately awakened a larger portion of the population to the importance of the traditions of their French heritage. It was the beginning of an era of painstaking restoration.

However, while a part of the heritage was put on a pedestal, another part, that of the 19th century, was shoved off by the wrecking ball! The destruction went on until the 1980s. Efforts continue today to stave off the deterioration caused by the massive wave of demolition whose results have been compared to those of a military bombardment, and which left vacant lots scattered across the cities.

The favourable contacts that Québec architects and artists maintained with their colleagues in Paris, Brussels and London, did not deter them from opting out for America at the beginning of the 20th century. And so the first skyscrapers pierced the Montréal sky in 1928, following the definitive repeal of a ruling limiting the height of buildings to 10 storeys. Celebrated architects from the United States designed many of Montréal's towers, giving the downtown core its present, decidedly North-American skyline. The geometric and aerodynamic French Art-Deco style, of which there are several examples in all regions of Québec, was replaced by Modern American architecture following the Second World War. Expo '67 presented the perfect opportunity to provide Montréal and the whole province with bold, representative examples of international architecture.

The Quiet Revolution of the 1960s corresponds to a massive expansion of the suburbs and the construction of major public infrastructures. Since then, new highways crisscross Québec; huge schools, hospitals, cultural centres, and museums opened in towns where before there was only a church and a convent. Northern Québec received considerably more attention with the construction of major hydroelectric complexes. Cities underwent radical transformations in these respects: construction of the métro (subway system) in Montréal, vast modern government complexes in Québec City, etc.

At the beginning of the 1980s, the weariness resulting from the *ad nauseam* repetition of the same formulas put forward by the modernists, provoked a return to the styles of the past by way of post-modernism, which freely combines reflective glass and polished granite in compositions that echo Art Deco and neoclassicism. The 1990s for their own part present two opposing ideas: the culmination of post-modernism, in the form of a Romantic architecture, and the search for a new ultra-modern style of architecture, making use of new materials, computers and electronics.

Nature in Québec

Maple leaves

Sylvie Bouchard - CCBB

FLORA

As a result of climatic differences, the vegetation in northern Québec is sparse, while that in the south is quite lush (at least in the summer). Québec's flora can be divided into four zones from north to south: the tundra, the taiga, the boreal forest, and the deciduous forest.

The tundra occupies the northernmost reaches of Québec, principally along Hudson Bay and Ungava Bay. With a month-long growing season and severe winters when the ground is frozen several metres deep, vegetation in the tundra is limited to mosses, lichens and very small trees.

The taiga, an area of transition between the tundra and the boreal forest, covers more than a third of Québec and is characterized by sparse, very slow-growing trees such as spruce and larch.

The boreal forest covers a huge section of the province, from the edge of the taiga to the banks of the St. Lawrence in some regions. This is a very homogeneous zone made up of coniferous trees, primarily white pine, black pine, grey pine, balsam fir and larch. This forest is an important source of lumber and wood pulp.

The deciduous forest is in fact made up of coniferous and deciduous trees and covers the regions south of the St. Lawrence River to the U.S. border. Along with a variety of coniferous trees, this zone is rich in maple, birch, spruce and aspen.

FAUNA

Québec's vast and varied wilderness boasts a richly diverse fauna. A multitude of animal species populates its immense forests, plains and arctic regions, and its seas, lakes and rivers are teeming with fish and aquatic animals.

Whether you plan on bird-watching or whale-watching the opportunities are endless in every region of the province.

Black bear
Sylvie Bouchard - CCBB

Québec's Great Power Dams

THE DAMS OF MANICOUAGAN

In 1959, the strong currents of the Rivière aux Outardes and the Rivière Manicouagan were put to use with the construction of eight large generating stations. Completed in 1989, the Manic Outardes complex now produces more than 6,500 megawatts of power and has helped to make Québec a world leader in hydroelectric technology. The complex, which houses the largest arch and buttress dam in the world, is now open to visitors.

Daniel-Johnson Dam   Hydro-Québec

The Centrales Manic 2 and Manic 5 (Daniel-Johnson Dam), the generating stations and dam, are located on the Rivière Manicouagan. A 30min drive from Baie-Comeau through the beautiful Canadian Shield landscape leads to the first dam of the Manic 2 complex, the largest hollow-joint gravity dam in the world. A guided tour of the dam brings visitors inside the imposing structure. A 3hr drive farther north leads to the more impressive Manic 5 and the Daniel-Johnson dam. Built in 1968, the dam is named after the Québec premier who died on the morning the dam was officially declared completed. With a 214m central arch and measuring 1,314m in length, it is the largest multiple-arch structure in the world. The dam regulates the water supply to the generating stations of the Manic-Outardes complex. Visitors can walk to the foot of the dam as well as to the top, where there is a magnificent view of the Vallée de la Manicouagan and the reservoir, which measures 2,000km^2.

THE DAMS OF NORD-DU-QUÉBEC

Today, and for the last 30 years, the government of Québec has taken a keen interest in the resources of these lands, namely the massive potential for hydroelectric power contained in certain rivers. Huge hydroelectric dams were constructed in the James Bay region, now capable of putting out 10,282 megawatts of power.

During the 1960s, the Québec government envisioned a plan to tap the hydroelectric potential of the James Bay region by constructing dams along its rivers. It was not until the 1970s that a development project for the damming of the Rivière La Grande (the town of Chisasibi), which runs 800km from east to west before flowing into James Bay, was proposed by then Québec premier, Robert Bourassa. The project was divided into two phases, the first being the construction of three powerful damming centres along the river, namely La Grande-2, recently renamed Robert-Bourassa, La Grande-3 and La Grande-4. Construction began in 1973 and spanned several years, since damming the river was an intense and complex project. To increase the flow of the Rivière La Grande, various waterways were diverted, namely the Eastmain and the

Opinaca, as well as the Caniapiscau in the east. The source of the Rivière Caniapiscau was used to create the largest artificial lake in Québec, a reservoir covering more than 4,275km².

The town of Radisson was built in 1974 to accommodate the workers from the south who were arriving as part of the James Bay hydroelectric project. During the boom years of construction on the hydro project, around 1978, more than 6,000 people lived on the construction site. Radisson's main draw is its impressive hydroelectric complex. Visitors can tour the Centrale Robert-Bourassa, formerly known as La Grande 2 or LG-2. Visits to **La Grande-1** are also available.

The La Grande Hydroelectric complex required the construction of 215 dams and dykes. The former were used to close off the river beds and raise the water level, thereby creating falls; the latter were used to stop the rising waters from flowing out via secondary valleys. In total, the project required millions of cubic metres of gravel, rock and sand, enough to build 80 great pyramids of Cheops. All of the water is contained and swept up into the intakes, then it is directed along a series of pipes leading to the turbines, which it activates.

On October 27, 1979 the La Grande-2 (Robert-Bourassa) generating station started producing electricity. The other two, the La Grande-3 and La Grande-4 generating stations, became operational in 1982 and 1984, respectively. In

1990, these three generating stations were responsible for almost half of Hydro-Québec's total production of electricity. The second phase of the project involved the upgrading of the La Grande-2 (thereby creating the La Grande-2A generating station, which was completed in 1992), and the construction of four other generating stations, including three on the Rivière Laforge. The Laforge-1 and Brisay stations, or *centrales*, started operating in 1993; La Grande-1 was completed in 1995 and Laforge-2 in 1996.

Robert-Bourassa Facilities
Hydro-Québec

The Robert Bourassa generating station is the third-most powerful in the world (with an installed capacity of 7,326 megawatts), after Itaipu in Brazil, on the border of Paraguay (installed capacity of 12,600 megawatts), and Guri in Venezuela (installed capacity of 10,000 megawatts). Built 137m below the ground, the Robert-Bourasse station is the largest underground generating station in the world. The dam is 2.8km long and 162m-high, supplied by a 2,835km² reservoir. In years when the annual rainfall is very high, a spillway system is necessary. The engineering of such a system involves eight 12-by-20m containers, and a 1,500m-long by 110m-deep collection canal. It has been nicknamed the *escalier des géants* (giant's staircase), since it represents 10 "steps," each about 10m high and carved in the rock. When water levels are exceptionally high, the system can drain 16,280m² of water per second, the equivalent of the average flow of the St. Lawrence River. So far, the system has rarely been put to use; only between 1979 and 1981 until the turbines inside the generating station were completed, and on August 30, 1987, for a couple of hours during a visit by then French Prime Minister Jacques Chirac.

The power station consists of four levels: the first level houses the machine room, the second the alternators, the third provides access to the spiral containers (inside which are the turbines) and the last level houses the drainage gallery. To absorb the high and low pressure, which builds up when the machines are turned on and off, an equilibrium chamber was built.

The construction of this hydroelectric complex has had very serious repercussions not only for the environment but also for the Aboriginal populations living off the land in this region. To create the reservoirs, some 11,505km² of land was flooded, representing 6.5% of the hydrographic basin of the Rivière La Grande and 2.9% of Cree hunting grounds. During the whole construction of this hydroelectric mega-project, Hydro-Québec and its subsidiary SEBJ (Société d'Énergie de la Baie James), which administers all hydroelectric projects in the area, both carried out environmental-impact studies on this project, and they continue to follow up on their findings. Part of the flooded land was Aboriginal hunting ground, and the Inuit and Cree who used these lands contested the provincial government's use of their ancestral lands. The negotiations between all the parties involved continued right up to November 11, 1975, the signing day of the James Bay and Northern Québec Agreements, which established the rights and obligations of the Inuit and Cree, as well as the plan of action of the hydroelectric project. According to

Inside the Centrale Manic-5   Hydro-Québec

the agreement signed by all those concerned (the Cree, the Inuit, the Québec and Canadian governments, Hydro-Québec, the SEBJ and the SDBJ), the Cree and Inuit were guaranteed exclusive use of certain lands, as well as guarantees of exclusive hunting, fishing and trapping rights on the land, especially for certain species of animals. Those involved also received greater administrative powers over their lands, as well as monetary compensation. Since 1975, 11 supplementary agreements and eight specific accords have been signed to better define each party's rights. It should be noted that the James Bay and Northern Québec Agreement is one of the only agreements with whites since the Royal Proclamation of 1763 that the Aboriginals recognize.

The entrance to the complex is like a terrifying descent into the belly of the earth. The cathedral-sized turbine room is surreal. Megalomaniacs will thrill to the sheer size of this place.

Aboriginal Peoples

The original inhabitants of Québec, the Aboriginals now represent a small fraction of Québec's total population. The ancestors of these peoples began to cross the Bering Straight from Northern Asia more than 12,000 years ago and moved into the region which would come to be known as Québec in successive waves several thousand years later.

When Jacques Cartier "discovered" the region around the Gulf of St. Lawrence in the name of François I, the King of France, the area had already been home to a number of civilizations for thousands of years. During that period, the territory was populated by a complex mosaic of indigenous cultures, each with its own language, way of life and religious practices. With lifestyles adapted to climate and to the particularities of the landscape, northern populations survived by hunting and fishing, while the peoples of the St. Lawrence valley grew much of their food. The Aboriginal population of Québec did not have a written language. Their history comes to us through oral tradition, from explorers' journals and anthropological research.

With the arrival of the first European colonists in the 16th century, these ancient civilizations went into decline. Unlike the European conquest of certain other regions in the Americas, clashes between colonists and Aboriginals are not common in Québec history. The low population density of the vast territory allowed the first settlers to establish their small colonies without directly challenging the indigenous population, which for a long time was numerous.

However, the First Nations of Québec did suffer enormously during the first years of European colonization with the introduction of certain illnesses, such as influenza, measles and tuberculosis. In some areas, nearly half the Aboriginal population was wiped out as a result of these diseases.

Further devastation resulted as Aboriginal peoples engaged in bloody warfare against each other (using firearms provided by colonists) for control of the fur trade, a business introduced by the Europeans. Between 1645 and 1655, the Iroquois Confederacy nearly wiped out other Aboriginal peoples. The destruction of Aboriginal civilizations continued with territorial losses to the unrelenting spread of colonization. While the Aboriginals of Québec were rarely the target of European military aggression, they were nevertheless soon overpowered by the colonists.

There are roughly 74,000 Aboriginals presently living in Québec, three quarters of whom live in small communities scattered across the province. Though some of these groups live in areas where they can hunt and fish, in most cases traditional lifestyles have not survived.

Tepee
Société Touristique des Autochtones du Québec (STAQ),Michel G. Maillard

In recent years, however, Aboriginals living in Québec have managed to attract increased attention from the media, leading to a sensitization on the part of government and the rest of the population to their issues.

A young Aboriginal girl
Société Touristique des Autochtones du Québec (STAQ),Michel G. Maillard

Québec Cinema

Claude Jutra during the filming of *Mon oncle Antoine*

Mon oncle Antoine ©1971 –Office national du Canada

While some full-length films were made earlier, the birth of Québec cinema really did not occur until after World War II. Between 1947 and 1953, independent producers brought a number of literary adaptations to the screen, including *Un Homme et Son Péché* (1948), *Seraphin* (1949), *La Petite Aurore l'Enfant Martyre* (1951) and *Tit-Coq* (1952). However, the arrival of television in the early 1950s resulted in a 10-year period of stagnation for the Québec film industry.

A cinematic renaissance during the 1960s occurred largely thanks to the support of the National Film Board (NFB-ONF). With documentaries and realistic films, directors focused primarily on a critique of Québec society. Later, the full-length feature film dominated with the success of certain directors like Claude Jutra (*Mon Oncle Antoine*, 1971), Jean-Claude Lord (*Les Colombes*, 1972), Gilles Carle (*La Vraie Nature de Bernadette*, 1972), Michel Brault (*Les Ordres*, 1974), Jean Beaudin (*J.A. Martin Photographe*, 1977) and Frank Mankiewicz (*Les Bons Débarras*, 1979). The NFB-ONF and other government agencies provided most of the funding for these largely uncommercial works.

Kayak in Parc National de Frontenac
(previous pages)
Gaétan Fontaine - Sépaq

Important feature films of recent years include those of Denys Arcand (*Le déclin de l'Empire américain*, 1986, *Jésus de Montréal*, 1989, and *Stardom*, 2000, all available in English), Jean-Claude Lauzon (*Un zoo la nuit*, 1987, and *Léolo*, 1992), Léa Pool (*À corps perdu*, 1988), Jean Beaudin (*Being at Home With Claude*, 1992) and François Girard (*The Red Violon*, 1998). Director Frédérick Back won an Academy Award in 1982 for *Crac!* and another one in 1988 for his superbly animated film, *The Man who Planted Trees*. The year 2003 was a banner year for Québec cinema with *La Grande Séduction* (2003) from Serge Pouliot, *Gaz Bar Blues* (2003) from Louis Bélanger, the Oscar-winning *Barbarian Invasions* (2004) by Denys Arcarnd and *La Face Cachée de la Lune* from Robert Lepage. This renewal has been marked by the variety of films produced and their appeal to wider audiences. This new wave is thanks in part to better feature-length screenplays that speak more closely to the public, but also to the new approach to launching films the way it is done in the United States and distributing them throughout Québec and the world.

Denys Arcand in 1973

Michel Elliot, P404 1973 / Archives Nationales du Québec - M

Daniel Langlois has also made significant contributions to Québec cinema. A key player in the film industry, he has been very involved in the development of film centres and festivals. He founded Softimage, which designs special effects software that has been used in several well-known feature-length films in the past several years. One specialized publication reports that 80% of animation and special effects software programs used in the world are devised by Montréal companies like Softimage.

Music and Song

Music entered a modern era in Québec after World War II. In 1961, Québec hosted an international festival of *musique actuelle* (experimental music). Also in the 1960s, large orchestras, most notably the Orchestre Symphonique de Montréal (OSM), began to attract bigger crowds. Several important music festivals are held throughout Québec, including the festival of *musique actuelle* in Victoriaville and the summer festival in the Lanaudière region.

Félix Leclerc

Michel Elliot, P404, March 9 1972 (photos F. Leclerc)
Archives Nationales du Québec - M

The popular song, which has always been important to Québec folk culture, gained further popularity after World War I with the rise of radio and the improved quality of music recordings. The greatest success was known by La Bolduc (Marie Travers), who sang popular songs in idiomatic French. In the 1950s, the prevailing popular music trend involved adapting American songs or reinterpreting songs from France. As a result, certain talented Québec song writers working at the time, like Raymond Lévesque and Félix Leclerc, were virtually ignored until the 1960s.

With the Quiet Revolution, song writing in Québec entered a new and vital era. Singers like Claude Leveillé, Jean-Pierre Ferland, Gilles Vigneault and Claude Gauthier won over crowds with nationalist and culturally significant lyrics. In 1968, Robert Charlebois made an important contribution to the Québec music scene by producing the first French-language rock album. A string of successes in Québec music followed. Artists attract hundreds of thousands of fans for outdoor concerts during the Saint-Jean-Baptiste celebrations. Québec acts have also found audiences and much success abroad, particularly in French-speaking parts of Europe.

Currently, established performers like Plume Latraverse, Michel Rivard, Diane Dufresne, Pauline Julien, Ginette Reno, Jim Corcoran, Claude Dubois, Richard Séguin, Paul Piché and Marjo are joined by newcomers like Jean Leloup, Richard Desjardins, Daniel Bélanger, Dan Bigras, Bruno Pelletier, Kevin Parent, Lynda Lemay, Luce Dufault, Daniel Boucher, Isabelle Boulay and the band La Chicane. The most well known name these days is Céline Dion, who sings in both French and English. Her amazing voice has made her *the* pop diva around the world.

Also on the English-language scene, Montréal singer Corey Hart enjoyed considerable success in the late 1980s as did the original band Men Without Hats. English-Québec's latest golden boy of popular music is Sam Roberts

There is also the particular achievement of songwriter Luc Plamondon and his participation in the production of *Starmania* and *Notre-Dame de Paris*. In addition, certain non-francophone artists like Leonard Cohen enjoy a strong international reputation.

Visual Arts in Québec

Ice Bridge Over the St. Charles River - 1908 by James Wilson Morrice

Philippe Bérard / MBAM

Visual art in Québec through most of the 19th century displayed a rather antiquated aesthetic. With the support of major art collectors in Montréal, Québec artists began to experiment somewhat towards the end of the 19th century and the beginning of the 20th century. Landscape artists, including Lucius R. O'Brien, achieved a certain success during this period. The Barbizon school, characterized by representations of rural life, was also influential. Inspired by the La Haye school, painters like Edmund Morris began to introduce a suggestion of subjectivism into their work.

The works of Ozias Leduc, which were influenced by Symbolism, began to show a tendency towards the subjective interpretation of reality, as did the sculptures of Alfred Laliberté at the beginning of the 20th century. Some works completed around this time exhibit a certain receptiveness of European styles, among them the paintings of Suzor-Côté. It is however, in the work of James

Wilson Morrice, who was inspired by Matisse, that the influence of the European School is most explicitly detectable. Morrice, who died in 1924, is considered by most as the forerunner of modern art in Québec. It would, however, take several years, marked notably by the work of landscape and urban artist Marc-Aurèle Fortin, before the visual arts in Québec were in line with contemporary trends.

Québec modern art began to affirm itself during World War II thanks to the leaders of the movement, Alfred Pellan and Paul-Émile Borduas. In the 1950s, two major trends developed in Québec's art community. The most significant of these involved non-figurative works, of which there were two general categories: abstract expressionism, as seen in the works of Marcelle Ferron, Marcel Barbeau, Pierre Gauvreau and Jean-Paul Riopelle, and geometric abstraction, represented by artists such as Jean-Paul Jérôme, Fernand Toupin, Louis Belzile and Redolphe de Repentigny. The other major trend in art was a new wave of figurative painting by artists like Jean Dallaire and Jean-Paul Lemieux.

Post-war trends continued into the 1960s. The emergence of new painters, such as Guido Molinari, Claude Tousignant and Yves Gaucher brought increased attention to the geometric abstraction style. Engraving and print-making became more common mediums of expression, art "happenings" were frequent and artists began to be asked to provide work for public places. Styles and influences diversified greatly in the early 1970s, resulting in the eclectic art scene found in Québec today.

Québec Literature

Literary output in Québec began with the writings of early explorers, like Jacques Cartier, and members of religious communities. These manuscripts were usually intended to describe the New World to authorities back in France. The lifestyles of the Aboriginals, the geography of the region and the beginnings of colonization were the topics most often covered by authors of the period, such as Père Sagard (*Le Grand Voyage au Pays Hurons*, 1632) and *Baron de La Hontan* (*Nouveaux Voyages en Amérique Septentrionale*, 1703).

Émile Nelligan
P97, P4162 / Archives Nationales du Québec · M

The oral tradition dominated literature during the 18th century and the beginning of the 19th century. Later, the legends that had been passed down over generations, involving such things as ghosts, werewolves and pacts with the devil, were put down in writing. It was not until the end of the 19th century that Québec produced a more advanced literary movement. Most of the literary output of this period dealt with the theme of survival and reflected nationalist, religious and conservative values. The romanticization of life in the country, far from the temptations of the city, was a common element. Glorifying the past, particularly the period of French rule, was another common theme in the literature of the time. With the exception of certain works, most of the novels from this period are only of socio-historic interest.

Traditionalism continued to profoundly influence literary creation until 1930, when certain new literary movements began to emerge. The École Littéraire de Montréal (Montréal Literary School), and particularly the works of the poet Émile Nelligan, who was inspired by Baudelaire, Rimbaud, Verlaine and Rodenbach, stood in contrast to the prevailing style of the time. Nelligan, who remains a mythical figure, wrote poetry at a very young age, before lapsing into mental illness. Rural life remained an important ingredient of Québec fiction during this period, though certain authors began to put country life in a different light. Louis Hémon, in *Maria Chapdelaine* (1916), presented rural life more realistically, while Albert Laberge (*La Scouine*, 1918) presented the mediocrity of a country existence.

During the Great Depression and World War II, Québec literature began to reflect modernism. Literature with a rural setting, which continued to dominate, gradually began to incorporate themes of alienation. Another major step was taken when cities, where most of Québec's population actually lived, began to be used as settings in francophone fiction, in books such as *Bonheur d'Occasion* (*The Tin Flute* 1945), by Franco-Manitoban Gabrielle Roy.

Modernism became a particularly strong literary force with the end of the war, despite Maurice Duplessis's repressive administration. Two genres of fiction dominated during this period: the urban novel and the psychological novel. Québec poetry entered a golden era distinguished by the work of a multitude of writers such as Gaston Miron, Alain Grandbois, Anne Hébert, Rina Lasnier and Claude Gauvreau. This era essentially saw the birth of Québec theatre, as well. With regard to essay writing, the *Refus Global* (1948), signed by a group of painters, was the most incisive of many diatribes critical of the Duplessis administration.

Québec writers gained greater prominence with the political and social vitality brought about by the Quiet Revolution in the 1960s. A great number of political essays, such as *Nègres Blancs d'Amérique* (1968), by Pierre Vallières, reflected an era of reappraisal, conflict and cultural upheaval. Through the plays of Marcel Dubé and those of rising talents such as Michel Tremblay, Québec theatre truly came into its own during this period. The use by novelists, poets and dramatists of idiomatic French-Canadian speech, called *joual*, was an important literary breakthrough of the time.

Contemporary literature is rich and diversified. Writers, such as Victor-Lévy Beaulieu, Jacques Godbout, Alice Parizeau, Roch Carrier, Jacques Poulin, Louis Caron, Yves Beauchemin, Suzanne Jacob and, more recently, Louis Hamelin, Robert Lalonde, Gaetan Soucy, Christian Mistral, Dany Laferrière, Ying Chen, Sergio Kokis, Denise Bombardier, Arlette Cousture and Marie Laberge have joined the ranks of previously established authors.

Québec theatre made a name for itself in the 1980s, with the staging of numerous big productions, several of which incorporated different forms of artistic expression (dance, singing, video). As a result, many small theatres sprang up in Montréal. Among Québec's brightest stars in contemporary theatre are the troupe Carbone 14, and directors André Brassard, Robert Lepage, Lorraine Pintal, René-Richard Cyr, and the authors René-Daniel Dubois, Michel-Marc Bouchard, Jean-Pierre Ronfard and Wajdi Mouhawad.

Québec's English-language literary soul is located in Montréal and its best-known author was Mordecai Richler (1931-2001), whose sharply comic prose, as salty as smoked meat on rye, depicts life in the cold-water flats and Kosher delis of mid-town Montréal in the 1950s. Novels such as *The Apprenticeship of Duddy Krantz* (1959), *The Street* (1969) and *St. Urbain's Horseman* (1971) portray a neighbourhood whose face is now changed but still recognizable on certain corners, such as Clark and Fairmount. Richler was also a frequent contributor to the *New Yorker*, with his crusty and controversial accounts of Québec politics.

Other well-known literary voices of English-Montréal include poet Irving Layton, gravel-throated crooner/poet Leonard Cohen, novelist and essayist Hugh

Stairs in the Plateau Mont-Royal   Patrick Escudero

MacLennan and poet and novelist Mavis Gallant. On the stage, playwright David Fennario's *Balconville* (1979), which examines the lives of middle-class anglophones and francophones in Montréal, is one of the city's best-known works in English.

Montreal's latest literary star is writer Yann Martel. Born in Spain in 1963 to diplomat parents, Martel won the prestigious Booker Prize in 2002 for his novel *Life of Pi*, a fish tale of a story about a teenaged Indian boy shipwrecked on a lifeboat with a Bengal tiger.

Parc National de la Gaspésie
(next pages)
Sépaq

Index of Place Names **287**